Broadband Intern...
For Dummie...

Comparing kinds of broadband

Service	Always on?	Billing	Availability	Speed
Cable	Usually	Flat-rate	Good	28Kbps–3MB per sec
DSL	Always	Flat-rate	Limited	128Kbps–1.5MB per sec
Satellite	No	Timed	Everywhere	28Kbps–400kbps

Digital cameras vs. WebCams

Considerations	Digital camera	WebCam
Internal storage	Yes	No
Focus	Adjustable	Fixed
Video conferencing	No	Yes
Image quality	High	Low
Price	Expensive	Cheap
Portable	Yes	No

Different kinds of protective software

Software	Monitor content?	Prevent activity?
Filters	Yes	Yes
Blockers	No	Yes
Jammers	No	Yes
Snoopers	Yes	No
Recorders	Yes	No

Keeping your connections running smoothly

Possible barriers to high-quality video conferencing:

- Connections to the Internet that are too slow
- Computers that are too slow
- Improper software settings
- Too much traffic on the Internet
- Low-quality hardware (cameras, microphones, etc.)

Ways to upgrade your computer, from least to most expensive:

- Get software upgrades
- Add RAM memory chips
- Switch to a different operating system
- Increase your disk space
- Replace your video equipment
- Install a CPU upgrade
- Replace your entire motherboard

For Dummies®: Bestselling Book Series for Beginners

Broadband Internet Access For Dummies®

Cheat Sheet

Streaming video sites to check out

Site Name	Web Link (URL)
NASA	www.nasa.gov/ntv/ntvweb.html
FasTV	www.fastv.com
Yahoo!Broadcast	www.broadcast.com/television/
VH-1	www.vh1.com
MTV	www.mtv.com
ESPN	espn.go.com/broadcast/video.html
CNN/Sports Illustrated	cnnsi.com/multimedia_central/
C-SPAN U.S. Government Coverage	www.cspan.org
CNN	www.cnn.com/videoselect
MSNBC	www.msnbc.com/m/v/video_news.asp
Fox News	www.foxnews.com/video/
CBC Canada	cbc.ca/video.html
BBC United Kingdom	www.bbc.co.uk

Ways to conference over the Internet

Product	Web site
AOL Instant Messenger's talk feature	www.aol.com/aim
ClearPhone	www.clearphone.net
iVisit	www.ivisit.com
SpeakFreely	www.speakfreely.org
Microsoft NetMeeting	www.microsoft.com/windows/netmeeting/

Tips for protecting your privacy on the Internet

- ✔ Use a proxy Web site to hide your tracks
- ✔ Hide your identity in newsreaders and Web browsers
- ✔ Encrypt your messages
- ✔ Use an alias when sites don't deserve to know
- ✔ Never give accurate information about yourself unless you know *exactly* how they'll use it

Copyright © 2001 IDG Books Worldwide, Inc. All rights reserved.

Cheat Sheet $2.95 value. Item 0769-9.

For more information about IDG Books, call 1-800-762-2974.

For Dummies®: Bestselling Book Series for Beginners

References for the Rest of Us!®

BESTSELLING BOOK SERIES

Are you intimidated and confused by computers? Do you find that traditional manuals are overloaded with technical details you'll never use? Do your friends and family always call you to fix simple problems on their PCs? Then the *...For Dummies*® computer book series from IDG Books Worldwide is for you.

...For Dummies books are written for those frustrated computer users who know they aren't really dumb but find that PC hardware, software, and indeed the unique vocabulary of computing make them feel helpless. *...For Dummies* books use a lighthearted approach, a down-to-earth style, and even cartoons and humorous icons to dispel computer novices' fears and build their confidence. Lighthearted but not lightweight, these books are a perfect survival guide for anyone forced to use a computer.

> *"I like my copy so much I told friends; now they bought copies."*
>
> — Irene C., Orwell, Ohio

> *"Quick, concise, nontechnical, and humorous."*
>
> — Jay A., Elburn, Illinois

> *"Thanks, I needed this book. Now I can sleep at night."*
>
> — Robin F., British Columbia, Canada

Already, millions of satisfied readers agree. They have made *...For Dummies* books the #1 introductory level computer book series and have written asking for more. So, if you're looking for the most fun and easy way to learn about computers, look to *...For Dummies* books to give you a helping hand.

IDG
BOOKS
WORLDWIDE

Broadband Internet Access FOR DUMMIES®

by **Mike Stockman and Derek Ferguson**

IDG Books Worldwide, Inc.
An International Data Group Company

Foster City, CA ◆ Chicago, IL ◆ Indianapolis, IN ◆ New York, NY

Broadband Internet Access For Dummies®

Published by
IDG Books Worldwide, Inc.
An International Data Group Company
919 E. Hillsdale Blvd.
Suite 300
Foster City, CA 94404
www.idgbooks.com (IDG Books Worldwide Web Site)
www.dummies.com (Dummies Press Web Site)

Library of Congress Control Number: 00-107691

ISBN: 0-7645-0769-9

Printed in the United States of America

10 9 8 7 6 5 4 3 2

1B/SR/RR/QR/IN

Distributed in the United States by IDG Books Worldwide, Inc.

Distributed by CDG Books Canada Inc. for Canada; by Transworld Publishers Limited in the United Kingdom; by IDG Norge Books for Norway; by IDG Sweden Books for Sweden; by IDG Books Australia Publishing Corporation Pty. Ltd. for Australia and New Zealand; by TransQuest Publishers Pte Ltd. for Singapore, Malaysia, Thailand, Indonesia, and Hong Kong; by Gotop Information Inc. for Taiwan; by ICG Muse, Inc. for Japan; by Intersoft for South Africa; by Eyrolles for France; by International Thomson Publishing for Germany, Austria and Switzerland; by Distribuidora Cuspide for Argentina; by LR International for Brazil; by Galileo Libros for Chile; by Ediciones ZETA S.C.R. Ltda. for Peru; by WS Computer Publishing Corporation, Inc., for the Philippines; by Contemporanea de Ediciones for Venezuela; by Express Computer Distributors for the Caribbean and West Indies; by Micronesia Media Distributor, Inc. for Micronesia; by Chips Computadoras S.A. de C.V. for Mexico; by Editorial Norma de Panama S.A. for Panama; by American Bookshops for Finland.

For general information on IDG Books Worldwide's books in the U.S., please call our Consumer Customer Service department at 800-762-2974. For reseller information, including discounts and premium sales, please call our Reseller Customer Service department at 800-434-3422.

For information on where to purchase IDG Books Worldwide's books outside the U.S., please contact our International Sales department at 317-572-3993 or fax 317-572-4002.

For consumer information on foreign language translations, please contact our Customer Service department at 1-800-434-3422, fax 317-572-4002, or e-mail rights@idgbooks.com.

For information on licensing foreign or domestic rights, please phone +1-650-653-7098.

For sales inquiries and special prices for bulk quantities, please contact our Order Services department at 800-434-3422 or write to the address above.

For information on using IDG Books Worldwide's books in the classroom or for ordering examination copies, please contact our Educational Sales department at 800-434-2086 or fax 317-572-4005.

For press review copies, author interviews, or other publicity information, please contact our Public Relations department at 650-653-7000 or fax 650-653-7500.

For authorization to photocopy items for corporate, personal, or educational use, please contact Copyright Clearance Center, 222 Rosewood Drive, Danvers, MA 01923, or fax 978-750-4470.

About the Authors

Mike Stockman: Mike works as a freelance technical writer and lives in the Boston area. Mike has been writing computer hardware and software documentation in the U.S. and Europe for over 12 years, and recently co-authored *Peter Norton's Guide to Network Security Fundamentals*. He is fluent in Windows, Mac OS, UNIX, and other fun operating systems. His constant search for speed has led him from analog modems to ISDN to cable modems, and now to DSL, and it's still not fast enough.

Derek Ferguson: Derek Ferguson is Head of Development for InterAccess, an Allegiance Telecom subsidiary and the first company in the world to offer commercial Internet access via DSL. You may visit him on the World Wide Web at www.eviloscar.com (Oscar is his cat).

ABOUT IDG BOOKS WORLDWIDE

Welcome to the world of IDG Books Worldwide.

IDG Books Worldwide, Inc., is a subsidiary of International Data Group, the world's largest publisher of computer-related information and the leading global provider of information services on information technology. IDG was founded more than 30 years ago by Patrick J. McGovern and now employs more than 9,000 people worldwide. IDG publishes more than 290 computer publications in over 75 countries. More than 90 million people read one or more IDG publications each month.

Launched in 1990, IDG Books Worldwide is today the #1 publisher of best-selling computer books in the United States. We are proud to have received eight awards from the Computer Press Association in recognition of editorial excellence and three from Computer Currents' First Annual Readers' Choice Awards. Our best-selling ...*For Dummies*® series has more than 50 million copies in print with translations in 31 languages. IDG Books Worldwide, through a joint venture with IDG's Hi-Tech Beijing, became the first U.S. publisher to publish a computer book in the People's Republic of China. In record time, IDG Books Worldwide has become the first choice for millions of readers around the world who want to learn how to better manage their businesses.

Our mission is simple: Every one of our books is designed to bring extra value and skill-building instructions to the reader. Our books are written by experts who understand and care about our readers. The knowledge base of our editorial staff comes from years of experience in publishing, education, and journalism — experience we use to produce books to carry us into the new millennium. In short, we care about books, so we attract the best people. We devote special attention to details such as audience, interior design, use of icons, and illustrations. And because we use an efficient process of authoring, editing, and desktop publishing our books electronically, we can spend more time ensuring superior content and less time on the technicalities of making books.

You can count on our commitment to deliver high-quality books at competitive prices on topics you want to read about. At IDG Books Worldwide, we continue in the IDG tradition of delivering quality for more than 30 years. You'll find no better book on a subject than one from IDG Books Worldwide.

John J. Kilcullen
John Kilcullen
Chairman and CEO
IDG Books Worldwide, Inc.

Eighth Annual
Computer Press
Awards ≥ 1992

Ninth Annual
Computer Press
Awards ≥ 1993

Tenth Annual
Computer Press
Awards ≥ 1994

Eleventh Annual
Computer Press
Awards ≥ 1995

IDG is the world's leading IT media, research and exposition company. Founded in 1964, IDG had 1997 revenues of $2.05 billion and has more than 9,000 employees worldwide. IDG offers the widest range of media options that reach IT buyers in 75 countries representing 95% of worldwide IT spending. IDG's diverse product and services portfolio spans six key areas including print publishing, online publishing, expositions and conferences, market research, education and training, and global marketing services. More than 90 million people read one or more of IDG's 290 magazines and newspapers, including IDG's leading global brands — Computerworld, PC World, Network World, Macworld and the Channel World family of publications. IDG Books Worldwide is one of the fastest-growing computer book publishers in the world, with more than 700 titles in 36 languages. The "...For Dummies®" series alone has more than 50 million copies in print. IDG offers online users the largest network of technology-specific Web sites around the world through IDG.net (http://www.idg.net), which comprises more than 225 targeted Web sites in 55 countries worldwide. International Data Corporation (IDC) is the world's largest provider of information technology data, analysis and consulting, with research centers in over 41 countries and more than 400 research analysts worldwide. IDG World Expo is a leading producer of more than 168 globally branded conferences and expositions in 35 countries including E3 (Electronic Entertainment Expo), Macworld Expo, ComNet, Windows World Expo, ICE (Internet Commerce Expo), Agenda, DEMO, and Spotlight. IDG's training subsidiary, ExecuTrain, is the world's largest computer training company, with more than 230 locations worldwide and 785 training courses. IDG Marketing Services helps industry-leading IT companies build international brand recognition by developing global integrated marketing programs via IDG's print, online and exposition products worldwide. Further information about the company can be found at www.idg.com. 1/26/00

Dedication

To my parents, for their constant love and support.

— Derek

For my wife Chris and son Adam, both of whom were outrageously patient during this project. May we have loads of free time together in the foreseeable future.

— Mike

Authors' Acknowledgments

Derek would like to thank . . .

Cate Perko and John Lam at DevelopMentor for giving me the opportunity to show everything I know about Microsoft Web development, and for reminding me that I still don't know it all! Rob Howard, John Montgomery, and David Kurlander at Microsoft receive mega-kudos for taking time away from their busy release schedules to help me understand the mysteries of wireless development using the .NET platform. Dr. Alexander Nakhimovsky and Dr. Tom Myers are both hereby acknowledged for inviting me to speak at Wireless DevCon 2000. And, as always, my part of this book was written entirely to the music of Spirit, Procol Harum, and Marillion . . . lots and lots of Marillion!

Mike would like to thank . . .

My agent, Chris Van Buren; Ed Adams, who gradually approached me with this project; and my excellent project editor, Marla Reece-Hall, who oddly enough still doesn't have broadband. I'd also like to thank the other folks at IDG, especially our illustrator, for thorough and valuable support. Finally, I'd like to thank the creators of wonderful Internet search tools such as Sherlock 2 (on the Mac OS), Yahoo!, and Google, without which I'd probably still be wondering what "IP" stands for.

Publisher's Acknowledgments

We're proud of this book; please register your comments through our IDG Books Worldwide Online Registration Form located at `http://my2cents.dummies.com`.

Some of the people who helped bring this book to market include the following:

Acquisitions, Editorial, and Media Development

Project Editor: Marla Reece-Hall

Acquisitions Editor: Ed Adams

Proof Editor: Teresa Artman

Technical Editor: Jeff Wiedenfeld

Editorial Manager: Constance Carlisle

Editorial Assistants: Candace Nicholson, Sarah Shupert

Production

Project Coordinator: Maridee V. Ennis

Layout and Graphics: Brian Torwelle, Julie Trippetti

Proofreaders: David Faust, York Production Services, Inc.

Indexer: York Production Services, Inc.

General and Administrative

IDG Books Worldwide, Inc.: John Kilcullen, CEO; Bill Barry, President and COO; John Ball, Executive VP, Operations & Administration; John Harris, CFO

IDG Books Technology Publishing Group: Richard Swadley, Senior Vice President and Publisher; Mary Bednarek, Vice President and Publisher; Walter R. Bruce III, Vice President and Publisher; Joseph Wikert, Vice President and Publisher; Mary C. Corder, Editorial Director; Andy Cummings, Publishing Director, General User Group; Barry Pruett, Publishing Director

IDG Books Manufacturing: Ivor Parker, Vice President, Manufacturing

IDG Books Marketing: John Helmus, Assistant Vice President, Director of Marketing

IDG Books Online Management: Brenda McLaughlin, Executive Vice President, Chief Internet Officer; Gary Millrood, Executive Vice President of Business Development, Sales and Marketing

IDG Books Packaging: Marc J. Mikulich, Vice President, Brand Strategy and Research

IDG Books Production for Branded Press: Debbie Stailey, Production Director

IDG Books Sales: Roland Elgey, Senior Vice President, Sales and Marketing; Michael Violano, Vice President, International Sales and Sub Rights

◆

The publisher would like to give special thanks to Patrick J. McGovern, without whom this book would not have been possible.

◆

Contents at a Glance

Cartoons at a Glance

By Rich Tennant

"FOR US, IT WAS TOTAL INTEGRATION OR NOTHING. FOR INSTANCE- AT THIS TERMINAL ALONE I CAN GET DEPARTMENTAL DATA, PRINTER AND STORAGE RESOURCES, ESPN, HOME SHOPPING NETWORK *AND* THE MOVIE CHANNEL."

page 9

"I don't mean to hinder your quest for knowledge, however it's not generally a good idea to try and download the entire Internet."

page 331

"YOU'D BETTER GET OUT HERE- ONE OF THE LINKS IN THE NETWORK IS ACTING UP."

page 175

Arthur inadvertently replaces his mouse pad with a Ouija board. For the rest of the day, he receives messages from the spectral world.

YOU WILL FORGET YOUR PASSWORD YOUR HARD DISK WILL CRASH AAAHAHAHAHA

page 357

"THIS IS YOUR GROUPWARE?! THIS IS WHAT YOU'RE RUNNING?! WELL HECK- I THINK *THIS* COULD BE YOUR PROBLEM!"

page 257

"What do you mean you're updating our Webpage?"

page 73

Fax: 978-546-7747
E-mail: richtennant@the5thwave.com
World Wide Web: www.the5thwave.com

Table of Contents

Introduction

● ●

*I*f you're still using your modem to surf the Internet, you haven't really surfed the Internet yet. The World Wide Wait isn't the way it's supposed to be; Web pages should appear on your screen quickly, before the information is out of date. That's where broadband, your high-speed Internet connection, comes into the game.

Broadband replaces the kitchen faucet that your modem provides with a fire hose of data. Using a broadband connection, you can get sound, music, video, and above all fast connections to anywhere in the world, even your workplace. Best of all, it's always on when your computer's on, so you don't have to wait for your modem to dial up every time you need some information from the Web.

With a broadband connection, you can communicate instantly with anyone, host a Web site, stay home from work (while you keep working), and have a video conference, all without slowing down to take a breath. This book will show you how.

About This Book

Broadband Internet Access For Dummies is an introduction to the faster world of high-speed connections to the Internet. With a connection that's fast and always on, new options become available that simply weren't practical with a slower modem connection.

Using this book, we hope you'll get new ideas about what you can do with your computer and the Internet, including some of the following topics:

- Knowing what to look for in a broadband connection, and especially how to get connected in the first place
- Communicating with people anywhere in the world, either by voice, video, or chat/e-mail
- Using your connection to *telecommute*, letting you stay home while continuing to work as if you were in the office
- Setting up a network at home, and sharing the broadband connection as needed

✔ Protecting each computer in your home, your network if necessary, and especially your family from people who would invade your privacy and threaten your computers

✔ Using the Internet to achieve your dreams, from publishing your own Web site of information to having a face-to-face conversation with a loved one thousands of miles away

System Requirements

Except as noted, this book doesn't have much in the way of system requirements. Broadband connections can work with any computer that is network-capable, no matter what some broadband providers may tell you. That includes computers running Mac OS, Windows, OS/2, BeOS, Linux, UNIX, and even some handheld computers. Because of this, most of the information in this book applies to any computer and operating system.

That's not to say it's all universal; some of the software included in the chapters may be available only for Mac, or only for Windows, but if you like the descriptions we include of some software, odds are there's a version somewhere that applies to your computer. Fortunately, you can perform an Internet search to find exactly what you need.

That said, there are a few recommendations we'll make:

✔ **Mac OS Computers** should be running the latest version of the Macintosh System possible, anywhere from version 8.6 on up. That's because Apple improved the networking in 8.6 and has kept improving it since then, so more recent versions will work best with your broadband connection.

✔ **Windows** users can run any operating system from Windows 95 on up. Sure, Windows 3.x will work, but why would you want to use that? All of the best Internet software works with Windows 95 or higher, so upgrade at least that far.

✔ **UNIX-like operating systems** users don't need any advice from us. If you've gone to the trouble of setting up your own Linux computer, or NetBSD, or something equally complex, you're already equipped to take advantage of your broadband connection. The programs and services described in this book still apply to you, so keep reading for some great ideas.

Other than these general tips, follow the guidelines provided by your broadband company and be sure you're using the minimum configurations they recommend. This varies widely among the companies, so check their literature or Web site if you're unsure.

Conventions Used in This Book

Naturally, we had to make some choices about how to present information in this book. Our style may be different from other books you've read, so skim this list of conventions we've followed to be sure you don't miss anything important:

- New words or phrases usually appear in *italics* to make sure you don't overlook them, but if you stumble over one of the many acronyms associated with broadband, check the glossary in Appendix B.

- Internet addresses (such as Web sites) usually appear in monospaced font like this:

  ```
  http://www.idgbooks.com/
  ```

- In the broadband discussion, we use a lot of terms related to speed and size. Follow these abbreviations to get the lowdown on bits, bytes, and so forth:

  8 bits = 1 byte

  28.8 Kbps = 28.8 kilobits per second (a rate of data transfer)

  256K = 256 kilobytes (a file size)

  32MB = 32 megabytes (as in the bare minimum of RAM you should have for most programs nowadays)

  100MB per second = A fast connection! (or 100 megabytes per second)

  10 Mbps = 10 megabits per second

  We talk more about what these speeds and sizes mean in terms of files you can send and receive and how various types of broadband access compare to standard connections.

What You're Not to Read

Here and there in this book, you'll see sections marked with Technical Stuff icons. Read them if you want to, but you'll get everything you need to use your broadband connection without the Technical Stuff. The Technical Stuff icons talk about the details behind the stuff you really want to accomplish, answering questions like "how" and "why." We hope you'll find these sections interesting, but you can still master your broadband connection without them.

Foolish Assumptions

Everybody's got to start somewhere, right? Although assumptions can get you into trouble, we're making the following assumptions about you, the reader. Our material's right for you if:

- ✔ You're tired of modems, because they're slow, slow, and slow.

- ✔ You've heard about broadband (a.k.a. high-speed) Internet access and you think it's right for you.

- ✔ You're using a Mac OS, Windows (any flavor), although most of this material applies to any operating system, even UNIX-like operating systems such as Linux.

- ✔ Surfing the Web and using e-mail are old news to you, and you're ready for more.

- ✔ You're using your computer at home or in a home office, or possibly on a small office network.

- ✔ Instructions like "launch this program" or "open this Web page" are comfortable for you to follow.

- ✔ Working with broadband customer service departments that give "bureaucracy" a bad name doesn't scare you

- ✔ You're willing to spend a little more for higher-speed Internet access than you're using now.

How This Book Is Organized

This book contains six major parts that are designed to move you along the road to broadband, from ordering it to connecting it to taking advantage of your newfound Internet speed. You can read any part or chapter by itself, but they're all interconnected as well to provide the information you need to get going.

Part I: Getting Ready to Race Along the Internet

This part explains how to choose from among the various broadband options, and how to navigate the obstacles life may place in the path between you and the service you want. We'll show you three of the most popular broadband options available today: cable modems, DSL, and satellite access. We'll tell you what they have in common, and what makes each of them a little different. By the time you're done reading this section, you should be able to choose the right option for yourself with confidence. (Or, maybe you'll just wish you lived some place where the option you like is available!)

Part II: Surfing at Warp Speed

By the time you finish Part II, you'll be able to impress your friends and colleagues with all of the cool things you can do with your broadband connection. Even better, you'll be doing the things you want, efficiently and quickly. You'll learn about using broadband to talk to others through video and audio, to entertain yourself with music and video, and other uses of broadband that simply weren't possible with modems.

Part III: Getting Down to Business

In Part III, you'll find out how to extend your broadband connection to handle multiple computers and users in your home or small office. Instead of connecting only your computer to the Internet, you'll learn about connecting all of the computers in your home, making your family even happier than they already are that high-speed Internet has entered your lives. You'll also see how to keep your connection humming and find new reasons to become a mouse potato . . . er, work out of your home!

Part IV: Protecting the Wealth of Broadband

In Part IV, you'll learn about caution. There are some pitfalls to a broadband connection that can make you a target as you surf the Internet. Computer crackers are a big part of the danger, but you also have to watch out for corporate villains as well who would invade your private life and learn more about you than you may know yourself. This part of the book teaches you how to take some easy precautions to save yourself, and your children, from the problems that may arise because of your fast, always-on connection to the Internet.

Part V: The Part of Tens

This part covers all the stuff that we couldn't fit anywhere else in the book! In a lot of ways, it is the most fun part of the book because we finally get to point out all of the great stuff that you can actually do with your new broadband Internet connection. We'll also tell you all of the tools you can get for free, and all of the best places to visit on the World Wide Web.

Part VI: Appendixes

What would a computer book be without appendixes and a glossary of useful terms and definitions? We don't know either, but you're not going to find out from this book. Appendix A tells you how to keep your old e-mail account so your friends don't have to learn a whole new address for you. The Glossary is the place to turn when you run into a new term or just need to be reminded of the meaning of a word you already know.

Icons Used in This Book

If you're like most people, you'll skip around this book looking for the information you need or the cool stuff you want, while ignoring the rest. That's why we've organized the book into complete, self-contained pieces that are easy to find. On top of that, we've used a bunch of icons to draw your attention to special information as your eye scans down the page.

Here's a list of the icons we use and what they mean.

Hey, this book is about using the Internet, right? So, we've got tons of links for you to explore. You'll find fun and cool sites as well as serious resources for getting the tools you need for broadband access.

This icon lets you know that some really geeky stuff is coming your way that you can safely skip without losing the flow of the material; of course, if you decide to read it you'll be way ahead of the game.

Next to the tip icon you'll find handy little tricks and techniques for getting some additional *oomph* out of your broadband connection.

If we used this one, you should pay close attention to the information provided.

Before you jump in and start applying the information in any given section, read these sections to make sure you've got everything covered.

Where to Go from Here

You're getting ready to dive in to a new kind of Internet that you haven't encountered before using a slow modem, and Chapter 1 is the place to start diving. If you already have broadband hooked up and running, read Chapter 1 and the chapter about your kind of broadband connection anyway, then skip ahead to Chapter 5 to start getting the most out of your newfound speed. This book can help you take advantage of the speed in ways you never thought possible, while keeping your computers and family safe and sound. Above all, have fun.

Part I
Getting Ready to Race Along the Internet

The 5th Wave   By Rich Tennant

"FOR US, IT WAS TOTAL INTEGRATION OR NOTHING. FOR INSTANCE—AT THIS TERMINAL ALONE I CAN GET DEPARTMENTAL DATA, PRINTER AND STORAGE RESOURCES, ESPN, HOME SHOPPING NETWORK AND THE MOVIE CHANNEL."

In this part . . .

*I*n this part, you will begin to understand the many different options for broadband Internet access that are available to you. It is important to understand all of the kinds of broadband Internet access because some of the options discussed may not be available in the area where you live. Others may be too expensive or not fast enough for your needs.

We begin, however, with a brief overview of broadband Internet access as a whole. Specifically, what is it? And, how does it differ from the other kinds of Internet access that are out there?

Chapter 1

Why Broadband Access Rocks

In This Chapter

▶ Finding out what broadband is and why you need it

▶ Exploring just what you can do with broadband

▶ Checking out the fun stuff that broadband makes possible, or at least much more convenient

▶ Ways to justify broadband to yourself and other skeptics

*I*f you're not already convinced that you need a faster connection to the Internet than the one provided by your current modem, read this chapter to learn one important piece of information: you *need* broadband. Anything you can do with a modem, you can do faster with broadband — *much* faster. Not only that, you can do things with broadband that you'd grow old waiting to do with a modem.

There are a lot of fun things you can do with a really fast Internet connection. We'll provide descriptions of many of those things in this book. There are also a lot of practical, business-like things you can do with a really fast Internet connection. If you need to justify broadband to a spouse, colleague, or boss (or someone who's more than one of those things), we'll provide that information as well.

You'll find a lot of options, possibilities, and three-letter acronyms out there in BPL (Broadband-Purchasing Land) — we'll help you understand them so you can choose the ones you want and that suit your needs best. Read on to see in summary what this book provides in detail.

Buying into Broadband — And That's Not a Bigger Belt

Before we get too far into this, let's define a few terms. *Broadband* is a generic term that describes fast connections to the Internet. That's all — nothing fancy or esoteric — just a faster connection to the Internet.

The *kinds* of broadband connection require a few more definitions:

- **DSL:** DSL stands for *Digital Subscriber Line*, not that it's any clearer spelled out. What it really means is that the pair of copper wires that the phone company has been connecting to your house all these years can now be used in a different way than modems work to provide a really fast connection, if all of the conditions are right. DSL is provided through your telephone company's offices and over the same kinds of lines as your telephone connection.

  Not everyone can get a DSL line because of their distance from the telephone company's central switching office, but it's worth looking into just in case you're close enough. See Chapter 3 for details.

- **Cable modems:** The cable companies were connecting huge wires (by comparison to telephone lines) to people's houses for years before someone thought of sending computer data over the same connections. The result is that, in many communities, anyone with cable television service can also have cable *modem* service, which is a fast connection similar in speeds and capability to DSL.

  Instead of attaching a box to the cable and hooking it up to your television, they attach a different box to the cable and hook it up to your computer. Sure, it's available through the same cable monopoly that cut off your pay-per-view boxing match in the middle of a round, but they're being very, very careful with data connections. Really. See Chapter 2 for details.

- **Satellite connections:** The third option in the broadband arena involves using the satellites that are in orbit around the earth many miles over your head. Some companies decided that, if the satellites were up there anyway, why not drop some Internet data on people's heads instead of that surveillance-nonsense they had been dumping. The great thing about satellite Internet service is that it doesn't require any new wires connected to your house; you simply attach a dish to an exposed place, and away you go. There are some drawbacks, too, but if you want to read Web pages and download files like lightning, or if you just got electricity and aren't likely to get cable or DSL for several years, satellite service may be for you. See Chapter 4 for details.

Most broadband providers have a number of packages available that vary in cost, speed of the connection, and even the tasks you're "allowed" to use the connection for. If you're a typical home user with a single computer, you'll probably want a different connection package that fits a smaller budget from, say, someone connecting a small office or home office to the Internet, who will likely have huge bags of money to throw around. Perhaps that's a stretch, but the first few chapters will help you decide which packages to look for when considering broadband access.

Some other useful terms have an important distinction because of how we discuss broadband speeds.

> ✔ **Upload:** The process of sending information from your computer to someplace else, usually the Internet.
>
> ✔ **Download:** The process of grabbing information from someplace else (usually the Internet) and storing or displaying it on your computer.

These terms come into the broadband discussion because, unlike modems, broadband speeds have two parts. Where a modem's speed is given as a single number (28.8 Kbps, 33.6 Kbps, 56 Kbps, and so on), broadband usually appears as two numbers: the download speed, and the upload speed (as in 416/208, 640/90, and so on). These numbers may be the same, but not always, and those differences are discussed in each chapter on signing up for service. Other related terms that you'll see are uplink, upstream, downstream . . . you get the idea.

Upgrading the 2400 Baud Dataflow Drip

For years, people have been connecting with modems to transfer files, visit bulletin board systems, use e-mail services, and (in more recent years) the Internet for all of those things. Modems have been getting faster and faster. But with the 56 Kbps models, they have reached an apparent upper limit in what they can manage to squeeze out of standard phone lines. Some companies are now marketing technologies to connect several modems in parallel in the hopes of getting a faster connection that way.

The goal here is *bandwidth*, as much of it as possible. If you think of your connection to the Internet as a flow of water, a standard modem is a bathroom faucet, an ISDN line is a garden hose, and any of the broadband connections is a fire hose. Higher bandwidth is like a larger pipe to the Internet.

That's why people are abandoning modems altogether nowadays. They're switching instead to one of several faster connections that are available for computers: DSL, cable modems, and satellite connections.

Faster than a speeding bullet

Each one of the available broadband connections has its pluses and minuses, but they all have one thing in common: They let you get information into your computer *fast*. Much faster — as much as 5, 10, or 15 times faster than a modem, depending on the kind of connection. Figure 1-1 shows the relative speeds of the recent generations of modems and the current offerings of broadband.

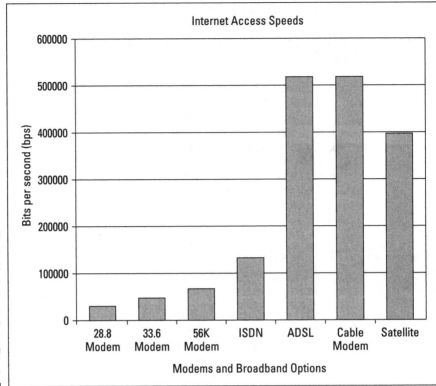

Put another way, if you try to load a Web page containing, say, 256 Kb worth of text and graphics (a small page in this day and age), it takes over a minute to load on a 28.8 Kbps modem, 38 seconds on a 56 Kbps modem, and only four seconds on a decent broadband connection.

Given how slow many of the popular Web sites are, any speed advantage can help eliminate the "World Wide Wait" from your life. Broadband can give you that speed advantage.

Quieter than a squealing modem

One of the best things about a cable modem or DSL connection can be summed up in two words: *always on*. The cable or DSL hookup is connected to the Internet 24 hours a day, seven days a week. If your computer is turned on, you're on the Internet, even if you're not using it. While you're word-processing, the Internet is there, quietly waiting for you to use it.

With a modem, the first time you try to read your mail or load a Web page, you have to wait while the connection is opened. You may have to listen to the tones while the modem dials your ISP, then enjoy the squealing sounds as the modem negotiates the connection. All of this can take upwards of 30 seconds. What fun.

With DSL or cable modem, the *always on* part means there's no waiting at all. When you open your Web browser, you can enter an address and open a page, instantly.

Always On has some drawbacks, too. The obvious one (Internet Addiction Syndrome, a malady as-yet unrecognized by the medical establishment) is a subject for a different book, but security and privacy are both subjects covered in *this* book. When your computer is always on the Internet, it becomes more of a target unless it's protected in some way. Those ways are discussed in Chapters 15 and 16.

Bigger pipes than the Hoover Dam

The faster a connection is, the more data that can pass through the connection in a given amount of time. As we describe at the beginning of this chapter, it helps to think of the connection as a flow of water — the faster the connection, the bigger the pipe. If your modem were a faucet giving you a gallon of data each minute, the DSL, cable, or satellite connection would be giving you 20 or 30 gallons each minute.

This is important because the larger *amount* of data you're receiving means you can do new and different things with your Internet connection. E-mail and Web browsing use very little bandwidth, really. Text takes up very little space in an Internet connection. Audio, video, and graphics take up much more space because they consist of so much more data than plain text.

If you try to grab some music through a slow modem connection, you'll grow old waiting for each song to finish, much less start playing so you can listen to it. With a broadband connection, large, complex downloads become possible. You can hear a song play within seconds of clicking it. You can see a high-resolution photo almost as soon as you decide you *want* to see it.

Suddenly, all of those features you never used (like listening to speeches on C-SPAN, hearing a radio station from the other side of the world over the Internet, or taking a virtual walk through a house) because your modem just couldn't handle them are not only possible, they're easy to do, with little or no waiting at all. Think of it as drinking from a fire hose.

How Can I Possibly Use All of That Speed?

Before you order your broadband connection, you'll need to justify it to yourself, which means identifying things you'll do with the extra bandwidth. This section describes, briefly, many of the cool reasons you want high-speed Internet access to begin with. Many of these concepts are described later in this book, but they're provided here in case you haven't decided to take the plunge into broadband yet.

If you've already decided to get broadband, or it's already hooked up and you're wondering what to do with it, this section can give you ideas of how to saturate your new connection completely, leaving you with a desire for even faster connections which are available, but, unfortunately, at a higher price.

Video and audio conferencing

Suddenly, with your broadband connection, you understand why the computer superstores carry all of those inexpensive cameras that connect to your PC. Sending your image over a modem is too slow to be worth trying, but sending your moving image combined with sound is child's play for your broadband connection.

This power opens up a whole new world: making free voice calls around the world; attending meetings at work by videophone instead of driving two hours through traffic; or finding out *before* it's too late that your e-mail darling on the far side of the continent is actually the wrong gender and an age that you barely remember.

On a more positive note, imagine showing your parents live images of their grandchild on their computer, or seeing your sister's new boyfriend without taking a three-hour plane ride?

All of this is possible with video and audio conferencing over the Internet, if your connection is fast enough. See Chapters 5, 7, and 9 . . . heck, a whole bunch of odd-numbered chapters for more details.

Speaking of audio . . .

You've read about it in the newspapers, but couldn't imagine yourself waiting for hours while your modem downloaded a three-minute Top 40 music hit. Now that you have your broadband connection, however, you can download an entire music CD in MP3 format while you're eating dinner. Not only that, but you can (copyright laws permitting, of course) send the latest song that you absolutely *loooove* to your best friend in Alaska by e-mail, knowing that it will take you only minutes to convert, package, and mail over your broadband connection. Chapter 6 provides the necessary links.

Chat, weather, news and info 24 x 7

With a broadband connection, you're always on the Internet, as long as your computer is on. That means people *always* know how to reach you, if you keep any of the numerous text-chat programs running, such as AOL Instant Messenger, MSN Messenger, Yahoo! Messenger, and others, described in Chapter 14. Even if you stay up until 3:00 am meeting that project deadline, your friend who's in a far-off time zone can still reach you for a quick conversation about something that probably doesn't really matter.

It also means you can track your stocks, catch the news, and follow the path of a hurricane in real time, just by keeping a connection open to whichever site carries the information you need.

Serious Ways to Justify the Upgrade

Of course, having a broadband connection isn't all beer and skittles. Using broadband has a serious side as well, and it's that serious side that will get you approval from your spouse, parents, boss, roommates, or others who need convincing that broadband is a Good Thing to get, install, and pay for.

Finding work-related information in a snap

Oh, sure, you can surf the Web for frivolous reasons all day, but when that project deadline approaches, you'll find that no tool can help your research better than the fast Internet connection you're already using.

Internet search sites (such as Yahoo.com, Google.com, Lycos, and many, many others) can find just about any word, sentence, paragraph, or chart ever produced, at least as long as that information has been published on a Web site somewhere. And remember: the faster your connection is, the faster you can scroll through the thousands of search results that almost, but not quite, bear no resemblance to what you wanted. Newsgroups and Web-based discussions can provide you with hundreds of experts who have nothing better to do than answer your questions, some of them even correctly.

The faster your connection to the Internet, the faster you can get someplace, find the answers you're looking for, and move on to the next site for a better answer. When time is of the essence, your broadband connection can save you time, and that's worth paying an installation and monthly fee.

Staying home from work more

No, we're not suggesting staying home from work just to surf the Web undisturbed. In reality, your broadband Internet connection can connect your home computer to the network at your workplace, just as if you were sitting at a computer in the office. That lets you use the office e-mail system, file servers, printers, and other computer resources that are usually available only in the office.

After you make the connection between your computer and the office (using something called VPN, or *Virtual Private Networking*), you're in the office in all of the important electronic ways. We'll help you stay home more in Chapter 11. You can even use video and audio conferencing to stay in contact with your co-workers as if you were down the hall or even attend meetings remotely.

The best part is that with the two hours of driving time you save every day, you can either knock off work early, or work that much more productively, depending on your work ethic and level of dedication. If *that* doesn't convince your boss to help pay for the broadband connection, you may need to explore that "knock off work early" option more closely.

Becoming a publisher without buying a printing press

Thanks to the wide availability of Web servers and Web publishing software, you can create your own Web site with little difficulty, and (your broadband agreement permitting) you can host the Web site from your own home.

That means you can finally publish your ongoing review of local restaurants, your novel-in-progress, or your data on continental drift, all without depending on anyone else's computers or servers to be there when you need them. You'll also have more control over how your information appears and who gets to see it than you would at almost any other provider's Web server. To get the word out, see Chapter 10.

Knowing the Stuff to Watch Out For

Along with new ways to use your computer, life with an always-on, high-speed connection to the Internet brings with it new challenges. For one thing, you can fall victim to the almost-discovered Internet Addiction Syndrome. Here's a hint: if you fail to notice that your spouse, children, and pet have left you, you're spending too much time on the Internet.

Seriously, however, having a connection that's always on can make your computer more of a target, either for direct attacks (people trying to steal or damage your data) or for indirect attacks (people using your computer to attack others, or silently monitoring your system to collect passwords, credit card information, and other sensitive data).

In a similar vein, the more you surf the Web and connect to other Internet services, the more opportunity others have to breach your privacy, collecting information about your name, age, income, purchasing habits, hobbies, and so on that you might rather keep to yourself. Even worse, your children may encounter people more unscrupulous than direct marketers (if you can imagine that) who want to find out information about your kids that you would *definitely* rather keep to yourself.

Fortunately, none of these things have to happen. *Firewalls* are devices that stand between you and the Internet, monitoring the connection and blocking anything malicious. By installing a firewall (as software, or as a separate piece of hardware you can buy), you can do most of the work protecting your computer or network from attacks.

Education, both for you and for your family, is the best solution to privacy invasions. You can avoid letting the direct marketers and retailers of the world know who you are or what your habits might be by using some common sense and a number of different software packages. You can educate your children to keep their personal information to themselves while installing software that will help protect them from accidental disclosures.

Once you set up a few basic precautions described in Part IV, your broadband connection will be nothing but a source of joy and productivity to you and your entire household. Unless, that is, you surf the Web so much that your body needs a sunlamp just to produce enough vitamin D. Once that happens, you're on your own.

Looking at the Bottom High-Speed Line

Ultimately, your broadband connection is simply that — a connection. Broadband won't change your life, heal the sick, feed the hungry (well, unless you visit www.hungersite.com, seriously) or bring on world peace. What it will do, however, is provide you with a view of the Internet that you always thought was possible, but could never prove while using a modem.

Just as buying a fast computer can suddenly make it clear why people rave about resource-hungry software and how cool it is, buying a broadband connection can open your eyes to why people go on and on about how much fun the Internet is, how they can get so much done, and how they have the world at their fingertips. Now that you've decided to get a broadband connection, read on to find out how to take the most advantage of it.

Chapter 2

Setting Up Cable Modem Service

●●

In This Chapter

▶ Discovering the potential of cable Internet access

▶ Understanding the upgrade cable dilemma

▶ Choosing the necessary equipment

▶ Obtaining service

●●

*O*ne of the best ways to connect to the Internet is via the wires that have already been run into your home or office. Most of us already have telephone wires in place. These wires form the basis of dialup Internet connections using regular modems.

In residential areas, many houses now also have cable television connections, whether they use them or not. New technology allows people in some areas to use these same cables to connect to the Internet at amazing speeds.

In this chapter, we show you how to go about getting broadband Internet access from your cable company. We tell you the positives and negatives of this kind of broadband. Finally, we try to give you a rough idea of how much it's all going to cost!

Finding Something Good on Cable — Finally!

Internet access via cable is becoming a reality in many areas. The availability of this service varies from one location to another because not all cable companies have elected to upgrade their networks in the way necessary to offer cable Internet service. In areas where this has been done, however, cable Internet access offers a number of advantages, including:

✔ Faster connectivity

✔ Always-on connectivity

✔ Cheaper access

✔ Easier setup

A key part of the upgrades that cable companies must perform in order to offer Internet access is the switch from analog to digital signals. Analog signals may be thought of as constant currents of electricity along your cable wires. Digital signals, on the other hand, are more like pulses of high and low energy with very specific starting and ending times. Most modern computer technologies rely upon digital signals to operate — the Internet is no exception!

Faster connectivity

You can think of your connection to the Internet rather like the plumbing in your house. The small pipes underneath your sink would carry much smaller amounts of water than the big pipes under your toilets over the same amount of time. In this analogy, the small pipes are like your telephone lines and the big pipes are like your cable television wires.

You may hear Internet experts among your friends, colleagues, or people you see on television actually referring to various network connections as pipes. These pipes are the same, regular wire connections with which you are already familiar — nothing to do with water or sewage!

The idea behind accessing the Internet via your cable connection is to swap a bigger pipe in for a smaller one, thereby increasing your maximum amount of data flow. In comparison to a regular telephone line, a cable connection can deliver speeds of hundreds of times faster! Of course, this increase happens only under ideal circumstances! We'll show you those "not-so-ideal" circumstances in this chapter, too.

Always-on connectivity

Suppose you are about to go outside for a walk and would like to find out whether or not it is going to rain before you leave. If you are used to connecting to the Internet via a standard telephone modem, then you probably know all of the steps that you would need to go through to download this simple piece of information:

1. **Turn on the modem.**

2. **Dial your Internet Service Provider (ISP).**

3. **Log in to your ISP account.**

4. **Navigate to your local weather report.**

5. **Disconnect from your ISP.**

6. **Turn off your modem.**

With a cable modem, this procedure would be greatly simplified.

1. **Navigate to your local weather report.**

The reason for this simplification is that, with a cable modem, your Internet connection is always on. You don't ever need to dial your ISP or log in to any account just to get access to the Internet. If you elect to also leave your cable modem on all the time, you can make sure your computer is a constant part of the Internet.

Cheaper access

The average monthly cost for Internet access via cable modem is about $40–$50 in the United States at the time of this writing. The average cost of Internet access via dialup telephone connection is approximately $20. How is it, then, that we consider this to be a cheaper form of access?

To begin with, it is unfair to compare cable modem access to Internet access via a regular telephone modem because cable modems, like DSL and Satellite Internet access, all constitute implementations of broadband. Broadband Internet access provides so many more benefits than regular telephone connections to the Internet that they can really only be fairly compared among each other in terms of price.

Judged this way, cable modems generally provide the absolute cheapest path to broadband Internet access. DSL lines can cost up to hundreds of dollars per month for connections capable of achieving comparable speeds. Satellite access methods generally have similar monthly fees as cable connections, but they require the considerable upfront expenses involved in purchasing a satellite dish and having it installed.

Everything is an upgrade! The price quoted to you for cable modem Internet access will typically not include television programming. If you want to receive both, you should let your cable provider know in advance so the installer can be prepared to install TV as well during the same visit to your home or office.

Finally, you should consider the value of time when pricing any new technology purchases. How much is it worth to you not to have to deal with having your own satellite dish installed and maintained — or to avoid dealing with your local telephone company? Both of these factors weigh heavily in favor of cable modem Internet access.

Easier setup

You are typically responsible for only two pieces of equipment with a cable modem connection to the Internet: your computer and your cable modem!

Better yet, in some areas the cable company will rent cable modems to people who purchase cable Internet access from them. This reduces the pieces of equipment that you've got to keep running to just one: the computer itself.

The obvious benefit to this is that, in general, the fewer pieces involved in an information system (and you already have six things per PC, right?), the fewer things that can possibly go wrong!

Breathing New Life into Old Wires

So, just how does this whole cable Internet system work? Well, it begins when local cable companies first decide that they want to begin providing Internet access over their network. This decision is usually completely dependent, as is the case with *all* business decisions, upon money.

If your cable company believes that folks in your area produce a great demand for Internet access in your area, they are much more likely to offer Internet service. On the other hand, if they think that the people in your neighborhood could care less about the Internet, they probably haven't and won't spend the money required to bring you this extra service. This means, among other things, that you stand a much better chance of getting cable Internet service in a high-income or urban area than in a low-income or rural area.

Remember that there is strength in numbers. Have you ever seen an advertisement for a new cable TV station and wished that your cable company would offer it? Usually, these ads end with the suggestion that you "contact your cable operator" and ask them to start carrying the new channel. Internet access via cable modem is much like a new channel in this respect — if enough people in your neighborhood ask for it, you stand a much better chance of getting it.

The only problem is that the cost associated with adding Internet access to a cable system is much, much greater than the cost of adding new channels. It probably won't be good enough simply to call your operator on your own if you don't already have Internet access in your area. Be prepared to organize your neighbors, and demand broadband!

To get started in the Internet business, you need connections

If cable carriers decide to offer Internet access, they must first secure a connection to the Internet for their own offices. To continue our plumbing analogy from earlier, the connection that cable companies purchase for themselves must be a very big pipe, indeed. This pipe is the connection that they ultimately use to carry all of their customers' traffic to and from the Internet. An illustration of this pipe system is shown in Figure 2-1.

Figure 2-1:
Even your cable company has to get Internet access from somewhere.

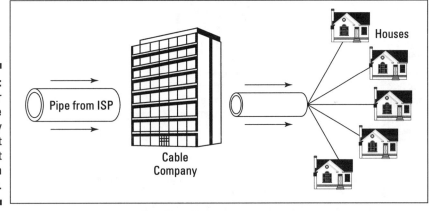

Cable companies buy these big connections, which are known as dedicated lines, from telephone companies and even, in some cases, from other ISPs. Ideally, your cable company should have more than one of these connections — each one from a different source. This way, if one source loses its ability to talk to the Internet, your cable company can simply redirect all of their customer traffic to the other source, as illustrated in Figure 2-2.

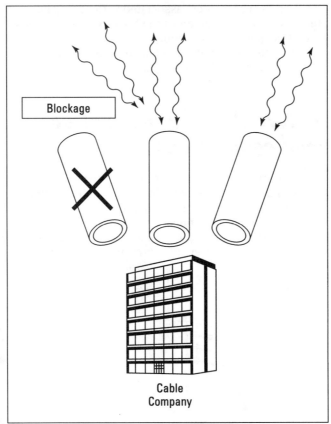

Figure 2-2:
Ensuring
reliable
Internet
access
through
redundancy.

Blockage

Cable Company

Maybe burying those cables wasn't such a good idea

When your cable company brings Internet connectivity to their own offices, they then must extend this access onto their own networks of cable. They face are two main obstacles in this pursuit:

- ✔ Cable networks were originally designed for strictly one-way communication, that is, television.
- ✔ Those cable networks are (usually) buried under the ground.

So, if cable companies really want to shell out the money to make true Internet access available (or extend it to new areas), then they have to buy a lot of new equipment and dig up miles of old cable. This expense forces these businesses to be pretty well convinced that you and your neighbors are Internet hounds before they will commit the funds.

All that glistens is not good Internet access! In a bid to reduce expenses, some cable operators have opted for a mediocre, hybrid approach to offering Internet access to their customers. This usually extends to purchasing the specialized equipment, which is the cheaper of the two costs. It does not, however, include digging up their existing cables and replacing them with systems capable of 2-way communications. We describe the implications of this middle-of-the road effort in the section on cable's darker side.

One fortunate trend in the industry that is working in favor of true two-way Internet communications via cable networks is the advent of interactive television and so-called "smart cable boxes." If you haven't yet used one of these devices to pull up instant information about whatever program you were currently watching or to participate in a live game show — you soon will! More on these devices appears in the section on the different kinds of cable modems.

Watching Out for the Dark Side of Cable Access

As we mention in the first section of this chapter, the original construction of most cable networks leads to a number of challenges when it comes to providing Internet access over them. Among these challenges are

- ✔ Poor scalability
- ✔ Non-broadband upstreams
- ✔ Low reliability

Poor scalability

Cable networks were originally designed and installed strictly for the purpose of carrying television signals. Used this way, TV signals first go to satellite dishes at your local cable company's headquarters. Then, they are pumped out to every house with a cable connection Houses with a cable subscriber have a special box that allows them to decode these signals into something that you can see on your television.

As you can see in Figure 2-3, the network itself looks kind of like an upside-down tree. The trunk of this tree is the bit that connects to the cable company's headquarters. The trunk then branches out so that each leaf represents a different house with cable access.

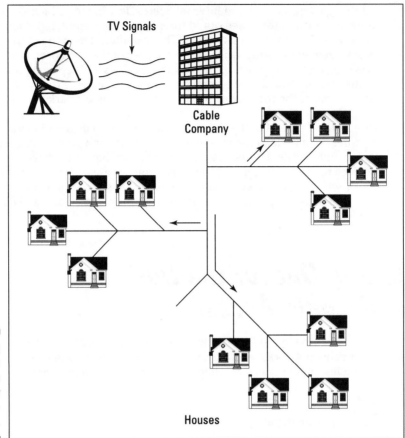

Figure 2-3:
Television
signals
always flow
down-
stream.

TV Signals

Cable
Company

Houses

When the technicians first designed and installed these networks, they *thought* they had a very clear picture of the kind of data that would be traveling over these wires and figured they knew exactly how much data we'd all need, so they let the "trunk" be limited to carrying exactly this amount. Of course, they knew which direction data would travel, and made the system in a way that prevents the "leaves" from ever talking back to the "trunk."

Obviously, the development of cable Internet access turns both of these assumptions on their heads, not to mention turning upside-down trees into pipes overflowing with data. As you read in the previous section, cable companies can undo their assumptions about one-way communication by digging up their old cables and installing new ones that allow data to travel in both directions. Their assumptions about how *much* data needs to be carried, however, are far more difficult to overcome.

One of the main differences between 1-way and 2-way cable networks is that 2-way communication always happens over digital networks, whereas 1-way networks tend to be analog. This is best thought of as the difference between audiocassettes and CDs. Audiocassettes are analog media, which puts a definite limit on their overall sound quality. CDs are digital, which allows for very precise controls over their sound and recording.

Any gardener could have told them upside-down trees don't grow very well

The problem with how much data cable networks can handle involves their unique upside-down tree structure. The trunks of these trees are charged with ultimately carrying all of the data from a given neighborhood to and from the cable company's main offices. The trunks are typically capable of carrying anywhere from about 30 to 50 megabits per second.

An Mbit is not an Mbyte. Cable companies tend to measure their networks' capacities in megabits rather than in megabytes (MB). Because you get 8 bits in 1 byte, you should divide any megabit measurement by 8 to get the equivalent speed in megabytes. When we're talking about these bits and bytes in terms of speed, keep in mind that because bps means *bits* per second, we abbreviate them as so: 1MB per second, which is equal to 8 Mbps (megabits per second). And you thought calculus was hard!

If you have the only cable modem in your neighborhood, then you will represent the only "leaf" on this trunk. This means that you will get the full benefits of the trunk's data transfer capabilities — a full 30–50 Mbps for your enjoyment. This works out to approximately 4–6MB per second!

Unfortunately, these networks are designed to support up to 2,000 modems on a single trunk! In these instances, you are forced to share your data transfer with all of the other modems in your neighborhood. In a worst-case scenario, this would mean sharing a 4MB per second connection potential with 2,000 other users, leaving you with a measly 2 Kbps transfer rate — you'd be better off going with a regular 28.8 Kbps telephone modem!

Figure 2-4 compares the layout of a typical DSL network to that of a typical cable network. Notice that, with DSL connections, each user has an individual path from home all the way to the Internet connection. This direct path allows DSL users to avoid the kind of bandwidth sharing that cable users must tolerate.

The upside to being a hermit

Of course, it is important to realize that "sharing the tree" only arises when everyone is actually trying to use cable modems at the same time. If you live in a neighborhood where you can be pretty sure that none of your neighbors give a hoot about getting cable modems, then you don't have to worry about sharing your speed as much. On the other hand, cable companies are much less likely to make access available in such areas for reasons described in the section on converting old wires.

You can also avoid the worst of these Internet traffic jams by restricting your use to periods when other people are typically gone or asleep. In a residential area, business hours and the middle of the night tend to be times when cable networks are relatively clear of traffic. Of course, these tend to be highly inconvenient times for most people to surf the Internet — unless, of course, you're telecommuting or staying up for that video conference with the office on the other side of the globe!

Non-broadband uploads

In this chapter, we describe two big obstacles that all cable companies must confront when they decide to offer Internet access. The most difficult of these obstacles to overcome is the inherent one-way design for bringing TV to your tube.

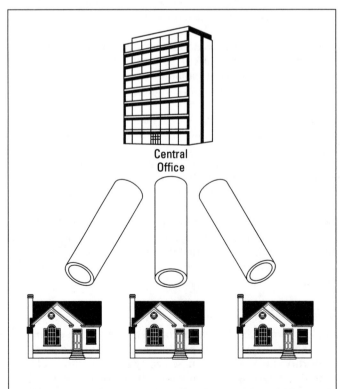

Figure 2-4:
One
advantage
of DSL
over cable
access.

Central
Office

To overcome this obstacle, cable companies must usually dig up some or all of their existing cable lines and replace them with new, improved versions. And again, because of the extreme expense, many cable companies suggest a different approach. In some areas, cable companies still require Internet users to utilize regular modems and telephone lines for the upload portion of their connections.

As you can imagine, you'll encounter a few problems with this approach:

- ✔ Increased costs
- ✔ Less convenience
- ✔ Slower access
- ✔ Keeping your current ISP
- ✔ Less reliability

Increased costs

Because you still have to use a dialup ISP, you need to consider your phone costs as well as your cable bill. Under most calling plans, every telephone call you make costs you some amount of money. If your ISP happens to have a number that is considered "local" to your calling area, then this may only be a single, flat-fee charge. On the other hand, how can you ever really be sure whether or not a number is local until you have called it and seen it on your telephone bill? If you've ever really tried to get this information from your local telephone company, you will know that this is rarely a simple answer!

Many telephone companies now have tools on their Web sites that will tell you whether or not a given telephone number represents a local telephone call from your location. When using these, it is important to note whether they are intended for consumer or business use, as telephone charges work quite differently for either of these. Also, you should look carefully for any fine print that denies responsibility for the inaccuracy of such information. If your phone company won't stand behind the results delivered by their Web tool, then you shouldn't finalize your calling plans until you have spoken to one of their representatives directly!

Less convenience

It is much less convenient to access the Internet if you must always turn on your modem, dial the telephone, and log in to your ISP account every single time. Unfortunately, this process is exactly what cable companies that refuse to upgrade require of their Internet customers.

Slower access

Current telephone modems are capable of reaching speeds approaching only 56 Kbps. Cable modems, on the other hand, can reach speeds of up to 6 Mbps. This represents a reduction in the possible speed of your upstream by as much as 90%!

Even with cable systems that do support two-way communications without the use of telephone modems, upstreams currently tend to be significantly slower than downstreams. The uneven flow is a result of cable companies mindset that most consumers are more interested in receiving items (such as pictures and music) than giving.

Maybe they've made an accurate assessment in the case of most casual Internet users. But if you're very interested in running your own Web server, playing online games, or doing other activities that require a substantial upstream, you should seriously investigate the two other kinds of broadband discussed in this book: DSL and satellite. See Chapters 3 and 4 for more details.

Keeping your current ISP

Some cable Internet connections only provide broadband for downloads. For uploads, these services require you to continue using your existing, dialup Internet connection. If your cable company works like this, you will have to consider the expense of retaining your existing ISP account.

Less reliability

A dialup Internet connection is always less reliable than an always-on connection. A few of the reasons why this is true include

- ✔ Higher incidence of service interruption (for example, call waiting)
- ✔ Potential for busy signals
- ✔ Increased likelihood of system failures
- ✔ Greater chance of forgetting required account information (like your password or your ISP's telephone number)
- ✔ Greater risk of having your account broken into

If you are forced to use an Internet connection that requires you to enter a password as part of your routine, then you should at least take a few basic steps to ensure your account's security.

- ✔ Never write down your password.
- ✔ Never choose a password that can be found in any dictionary.
- ✔ Never choose a password that is of any personal significance to you (such as a birthday, person's name, or social security number).

> ✔ Always include at least 1 letter and 1 number in your password.
>
> ✔ Never give your password to anyone on the Internet, no matter who they claim to be or for what reason.

Low reliability

In many areas, the cable goes out whenever there is a storm. If this describes the situation where you live, then you should understand that this will affect your cable modem as well. Similarly, many people believe that their cable company could use a little improvement in the area of customer service.

You should also remember that cable companies are fairly new to the realm of two-way communications. They do not have anywhere near the level of expertise in fixing broken Internet connections that established telecommunications companies have.

Choosing Your Weapons

Cable modems come in a variety of shapes and sizes. Furthermore, the features and functionalities provided by these devices differ widely from one unit to another.

Describing the exact capabilities of every cable modem currently being manufactured is beyond the scope of this book. Instead, we divide all of the available modems into three main groups:

> ✔ **First generation:** The original recipe, dating from about the early 1990s.
>
> ✔ **Second generation:** New and improved, produced about the mid 1990s.
>
> ✔ **Tomorrow and Beyond:** The stealth cable modem, a state-of-the-art proposition.

First generation: The original recipe

The very first cable modems were largely experimental affairs. A number of manufacturers in North America and Europe were working simultaneously — desperately competing to be the first to get their ideas to market. As a result of this intense competition between competitors, the first cable modems were marked by an almost complete lack of standards or interoperability.

The old saying, "Buy in haste, repent at leisure," applies to this group. Cable companies that were early adopters of Internet access technologies generally require you to use modems specifically designed to work with their own systems. If you bring a modem with you from a previous service or purchase a new one in a store, the chances are good that it will not work with such a hookup.

Many of the first-generation cable modems were also strictly one-way communicators. These devices force you to continue using your telephone line and modem for the upstream portion of your connections. For more information about this problem, see the previous section in this chapter.

Second generation: New and improved

The second generation of cable modems has seen an increased emphasis on industry standards and two-way communication.

If you really want to outwit the cable guy, you should know the two current, major standards for cable modems. One of these, DOCSIS, is the major force in North America; it stands for *Data Over Cable Service Interface Specification* — basically just a fancy way of saying "a set of rules stipulating how information should be formatted before being sent over your cable wires." In Europe, a competing standard is DVB (which stands for Digital Video Broadcasting). At the time of writing, it is quickly losing ground to the older, more established DOCSIS standard. To support two-way communications, the new breed of cable modems assume a connection to the kind of upgraded cable network we describe in this chapter. If you attempt to use such a second-generation modem with a network that has not been upgraded fully to two-way flow, you will be quite out of luck!

Tomorrow and beyond: The smart cable modem

Eventually, it seems probable that every person with a cable television connection will also have a cable modem. In fact, many people in the United States today have cable modems without even realizing it! You may not have guessed that the latest, *smart* cable boxes, growing more popular now, are really just cable modems in disguise!

If you're able to pull up information on your screen about whatever program you are currently watching, then you probably have one of these new devices connected to your television. Other common features you can access include

> ✔ Private radio stations
>
> ✔ Ability to order pay-per-view programming just by clicking a button
>
> ✔ Programming schedules
>
> ✔ Limited ability to interact with game shows and other programs

Creating Your Cable Shopping List

If you're ready to get the (digital) show on the road, you may be wondering to yourself, "Self, what am I going to need to get hooked up with all of this fancy new cable Internet gear?"

Well, self, you are in luck. The minimum system requirements for obtaining cable Internet access are arguably the lightest of all forms of broadband access. In general, you can get by with the following:

> ✔ Pentium-level or better processor
>
> ✔ 32MB RAM
>
> ✔ 100MB free disk space
>
> ✔ SVGA or better video card
>
> ✔ One of the network connectors discussed in the next section

Selecting a network connector

Your computer's network connector is the portion of your system into which your cable modem attaches.

The wiring shown in Figure 2-5 illustrates how the configuration for either an Ethernet or USB connection to your cable modem. If you are using an internal cable modem that fits into one of your computer's PCA slots, then this extra link is not needed.

Ethernet card

An Ethernet card is the traditional means for connecting a PC to a network. We tell you all about Ethernet connections in Chapter 13. For now, you should know that you can usually identify these cards by two distinguishing marks on the portion that remains visible even after they're installed in your computer:

> ✔ A plug-in that looks like an over-sized telephone jack
>
> ✔ One or more lights

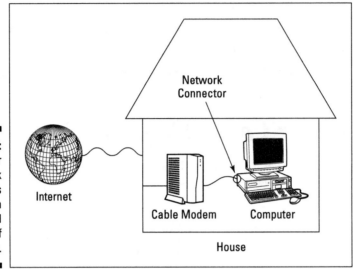

Figure 2-5:
Your
network
connector's
place in
the grand
scheme of
things.

To use an Ethernet card, you must connect an Ethernet cable from the plug-in on your card to the plug-in on your cable modem. One light on the back of your card should come on as soon as you have both your computer and cable modem turned on. Another light may flash every time that data comes in or goes out over your Internet connection.

The lights on your Ethernet card provide a great deal of information about the source of any problems you may eventually experience with your Internet connection. If you ever need to call your provider's technical support service, they are almost certain to ask about the status of these lights. For this reason, don't put the modem-side of your computer anywhere you can't get a good look at these lights.

Universal Serial Bus port

Universal Serial Bus (USB) ports represent a more modern and sophisticated technology than Ethernet cards. So, most of the newer cable modems particularly target this standard. If you have a newer computer, you should be all ready to go. The iMac is just one example of a modern computer that comes with out-of-the-box support for USB connections.

If you have an older computer, you may first need to buy a special USB card for your computer. These cards often redirect the internal portions of your computer that would ordinarily operate one of the other ports on the back of your computer. This means that, when you install such a card, you gain one or more USB ports, but you may lose the use of at least one of your other pre-existing ports.

Another disadvantage to USB cable modems is that it's much harder to share access to such Internet connections among multiple computers. Whereas a simple Ethernet hub would suffice for this task with an Ethernet modem, for a USB modem you would need something more sophisticated. See Chapter 13 for more information on sharing access.

Internal slots

Some cable modems come in the form of a card that fits in a slot inside your computer. The primary advantages offered by this approach are

- Less clutter
- Less expense
- Ability to access the Internet via cable regardless of what kind of network connector your computer supports

Unfortunately, cable modems are not available for all kinds of computers.

No, You Can't Avoid Dealing with Your Cable Company

At this point, you should understand exactly what cable Internet access is. We also hope you have a good sense for what you need in order to get connected. The one question that we haven't answered yet is, "How do I go about actually getting a cable Internet connection?" Use these sections to help form a checklist:

Buying your modem

You can check out a number of places to buy a cable modem: You can expect to pay approximately $100 for a state-of-the-art unit.

Your cable provider

Most cable providers are more than willing to sell cable modems to people when they sign up for Internet service. Sometimes, you can even get a cable modem "for free" when you sign an extended service contract with your provider. This obligates you to continue your Internet service for a period of (typically) a year or more, but saves you the expense of the cable modem.

Before you buy any modem from your cable provider, you should try to find out in advance exactly what kind of modem it is. In particular, you should try to obtain the name of the manufacturer and its model number. You can then use this information to research the modem and find out whether or not it is generally accepted as a quality piece of hardware or largely unheard of, or worse.

A retail outlet

Some large retail outlets sell cable modems, especially computer or business supply stores. Often, you can sign up for service at the same time as you purchase your modem. This is much like buying your modem directly from your cable company, because it is often your cable company ultimately fulfilling the orders taken by these establishments.

Keep location in mind when you're shopping if you decide to sign up in the store some distance from your house. If your area has regional cable companies, you need to make sure the company covering the sale at the store is also the company that provides service to your local area back home.

On the other hand, buying your modem from a large retail outlet will often give you a greater selection than you might have otherwise. As always, if price is a significant factor in your buying decisions, remember to comparison shop before making your final purchase.

The Internet

People are buying more and more stuff on the Internet nowadays. If this is your cup of tea, there are plenty of places out there on the Net for you to find a cable modem that suits your needs.

A few sites to check out include

- http://www.3com.com/products/broadband.hml
- http://www.cisco.com
- http://www.mot.com/MIMS/Multimedia
- http://www.nortelnetworks.com/link/cable_modem_100
- http://www2.be.philips.com/pbn/products/pd10d.html
- http://www.thomson-broadband.com
- http://www.zenith.com/network_systems/ntwks.html

Getting your connection

Typically, the journey toward your own cable Internet hookup begins with a telephone call to your local cable company. Follow this guideline to get connected:

1. **Start with the primary information.**

   If you are already a cable television subscriber, then they will probably already have most of your information on file. If not, then you should be prepared to provide them with:

   - Your name

   - Your address

   - Your credit card information (possibly)

   - How many connections you would like

   - Whether or not you also want TV service

   - Whether or not your house is already "cable ready"

2. **Ask about options and select the billing plans you want.**

   Timed charges, meaning youre charged so much per hours of usage, are almost unheard of with cable Internet access. A current typical fee is likely to be $40–$50 US per month, flat rate, but that's subject to change.

3. **After you give all of the necessary information, they will schedule a time for an installer to come to your house.**

   In most areas, the wait for this installation should be much less than it would be if you were to order a DSL circuit because most cable companies retain their own staff of experienced installers. DSL companies, on the other hand, usually rely on the availability of independent subcontractors.

4. **At the installation itself, the installer will probably work a great deal outside of your home or office first to upgrade the exterior lines.**

   The portion of the cable network immediately outside your house is normally only upgraded for two-way access on an as-needed basis. And until you ask for Internet access — it isn't needed!

5. **After setting everything up outside of your house, the installer will come inside and prepare whatever cable jacks inside of your house are in the rooms where you would like cable access.**

6. **Next, the technician will probably hook up your cable modem for you and may even help configure your computer initially to access the Internet.**

Of course, it always breaks right after they leave! If you can get them to stay for just a couple of extra minutes, it will be worth your while to restart your computer once or twice while they are still there. If you are able to successfully access the Internet after each restart of your computer, then you are probably good to go.

Now, your Internet connection is ready. Provided that your neighborhood doesn't have too many other ardent Internet users in it sharing your cable network, you should be in a good position now to enjoy some of the best access speeds available.

If, on the other hand, you find that the speed you are getting for your money is less than acceptable, you might wish to investigate other alternatives. In the next two chapters, we tell you all about two of the most popular alternatives: DSL and satellite access.

Chapter 3

Switching to a DSL Service

A few years can seem like several centuries where computer technologies are concerned. New technologies are often now obsolete before they are even installed! CIO's and other sorts of managers that are fond of talking in collections of buzzwords and catch phrases sometimes refer to this phenomenon as Internet Time. For example:

Mr. Employee: "Gee, Mr. Boss, sleeping in my office and working every weekend for the past year finally seems to have paid off. Our entire office is all ready to go with that new dedicated T1 line you ordered!"

Mr. Boss: "Darn it, Employee! We're on *Internet Time* at this company. I cancelled that dedicated line project back when ISDN was all the rage — six months ago."

Mr. Employee: "So now you want me to start working on getting ISDN hooked up?"

Mr. Boss: "Of course not! I cancelled the ISDN project last month. Its all about DSL now — DSL!"

Mr. Employee: "And what, may I ask, is DSL?"

Mr. Boss (suddenly looking like a deer in the spotlights): "Uhhhh . . ."

Mr. Employee (rolling eyes): "I'll see if there's a Dummies book about it."

Deciphering DSL: Not Just Another TLA

Chances are, you've already heard something about DSL from one source or another.

DSL stands for digital subscriber line. Using DSL, you can connect to the Internet from your home or business at speeds of anywhere up to 1.5MB per second. Most importantly, DSL can provide these speeds at a fraction of the cost of competing technologies.

What makes DSL so revolutionary is its ability to function over the existing telephone lines already installed in most buildings. Before the development of DSL, many people thought that the fastest speed they could ever achieve over these lines was a mere 56 kbps.

The unique cost/benefit ratio offered by DSL makes it a very strong contender in the burgeoning bandwidth (try saying "burgeoning bandwidth" 10 times fast) market. DSL may not be the final word in high-speed Internet access, but it is definitely the hottest word at the moment.

From boring to broadband

DSL was initially developed in the late 1980s as a possible means for transmitting video-on-demand to televisions. The idea was fairly simple:

1. Joe Teenager and Sally Adolescent decide that they'd like to stay home on their next date and watch a horror movie.

2. Rather than hopping in the car and going to their local video store, they call up a video-on-demand service.

3. After requesting the movie that they would like to watch, the full video and audio for the film is electronically transmitted to their home via DSL.

4. The credit cards of Joe Teenager and millions of other video-on-demand customers are automatically charged and the entire proceeds are given to Bob Programmer, the developer of the video-on-demand system.

5. Bob Programmer becomes fabulously wealthy as the facilitator for millions of stay-at-home dates, but still finds it impossible to get a date himself.

6. The irony of his situation causes Bob Programmer to renounce technology and move to a log cabin in Montana.

What DSL looks like under the hood

The telephone lines in most houses were originally designed to carry all kinds of sounds (even unsolicited sales calls in the middle of the Superbowl) from one point to another. Sounds occur as *analog signals* in nature. In other words, it is impossible to divide any particular sound, such as a tree falling in a forest (when people are around to hear it) into smaller pieces; sounds, as heard by humans, seem to be single, continuous events. For example, into how many pieces would you divide the sound of a babbling river? Even if you devised some answer to this question, you can be sure that a different person would have a completely different answer.

Personal computers, on the other hand, deal strictly with non-continuous events that occur in several, distinct pieces. The word digital, as in digital computer (which is what all personal computers are), derives from the bits on/off.

Standard modems help computers communicate over telephone lines by converting their digital signals into analog signals for transport out over the telephone lines or to bring data off the telephone and into your computer.

Unfortunately, an analog signal can carry a relatively limited amount of data — about 56 kbps. DSL circumvents this limitation by using existing telephone wires in a way that is 100% digital.

Perhaps it is just as well for all of us that none of the above ever actually happened. It turned out that receiving and displaying full-screen video and audio for feature-length movies was quite beyond the technical abilities of most late-1980s home computers. As you see in Chapter 5, however, this idea's time may finally have come!

Without the goal of enabling video-on-demand, DSL remained a technology without a purpose for the next few years. And then came the Internet!

By 1996, millions of computer users had already been exposed to the seemingly limitless possibilities of the Internet. However, they all seemed to share the same questions: Why is it so horribly slow and how could it be made better? Many large telephone companies were experimenting with DSL at this point, but the mountains of red tape and procedures followed by such organizations made it seem likely that any consumer offerings would be years in the future.

Fortunately, many smaller, quicker, and (quite frankly) smarter Internet Service Providers have popped up in the few short years since the Internet's rise to fame. When DSL was ready for a comeback in the mid-1990s, the ISPs were ready and waiting! In the summer of 1996, InterAccess Company in Chicago became the first company in the world to commercially offer DSL service. Many other ISPs followed suit, and eventually even the telephone companies have been forced to market DSL or face permanently losing control of their own technology!

Telco alphabet soup

You may have noticed that the name of this section asked whether or not DSL was just another TLA. What is a TLA? TLA stands for three-letter acronym. There are many, many acronyms associated with DSL and getting it hooked up in your home or office.

Use acronyms proudly and fear no one. Don't be intimidated by how many strange acronyms are associated with getting a faster Internet connection. Many of these were invented a long time ago by phone technicians who just wanted to seem impressive. After all, who else would refer to a plain old telephone as a POT?

Table 3-1 lists some of the more common acronyms used in discussing DSL. For more information about terms like these, refer to Appendix B.

Table 3-1	Common DSL-Related Acronyms
Acronym	*Meaning*
ADSL	Asymmetric Digital Subscriber Line
CLEC	Competitive Local Exchange Carrier
CO	Central office
DSLAM	DSL multiplexer
ILEC	Incumbent Local Exchange Carrier
LAN	Local Area Network
LERG	Local Exchange Routing Guide
MB per second	Megabytes per second
Mbps	Megabits per second
SAG	Street Address Guide
SDSL	Symmetric Digital Subscriber Line

Acronym	Meaning
SOHO	Small Office / Home Office
TCP/IP	Terminal Control Protocol / Internet Protocol
TLA	Three-Letter Acronym
VDSL	Very high bit-rate Digital Subscriber Line

The Protocol of a Thousand Faces

Probably the single biggest issue facing DSL today is a complete lack of standards within the industry. Several different flavors of DSL have emerged, all of which use completely different (and largely incompatible) hardware. It is important that you understand how the various flavors differ so that you don't wind up ordering the wrong thing for your needs!

xDSL

The first variety of DSL isn't really a variety at all. xDSL is the name that the industry has come up with to represent DSL in *any* of its forms: ADSL and SDSL are included beneath the umbrella term *xDSL*. Like Billy Joel sings, "It's still rock'n'roll to me."

ADSL

ADSL was the first kind of DSL developed and is probably the implementation most widely available today. Under ADSL, the speed of your downstream can be quite different (usually higher) from the speed of your upstream. This means that you may be able to download content off the Internet quite quickly, but you may experience long delays whenever you try to send large files.

I feel quite intelligent, but everyone says I'm slow. Most Internet users are primarily data consumers, rather than providers. Some prime examples of consuming data would be browsing the World Wide Web and reading your e-mail. If this is the only thing you ever plan on doing with your Internet connection, then ADSL may be just the thing for you. On the other hand, some people don't just want to surf the World Wide Web — they want to be a part of it.

If running a Web site or any other kind of server on the Internet is of great interest to you, then ADSL may not be a very good choice for your applications. If your upstream is very slow (as it typically is with ADSL), then visitors to your server may experience substantial delays.

SDSL

SDSL stands for symmetric digital subscriber line. This name is intended to suggest that, unlike ADSL, whatever upstream and downstream speeds are achieved while using this product will always be equal. This makes SDSL an optimal choice for the following kinds of people:

Telecommuters / Home Office Users

Telecommuters and people with home offices often use their connections in ways that are hard on both their up- and downstreams. One moment they are dragging enormous files from their computers at work to their PCs over the Internet. The very next second, they are e-mailing copies of their new database to everyone at their company's overseas branches.

Hard-core gamers

Many of the games that you buy in stores come with trial subscriptions to gaming services that allow you to compete head-to-head against other players. When a professional gaming service is providing the servers for game play, ADSL is just fine.

In contrast, many of the games that can be freely downloaded off the Internet require that at least one of the players in any given game volunteer their computer as a server for the duration of the game. If you plan on doing this frequently, you will definitely want SDSL.

People who don't know whether they're coming or going

If you can't be sure exactly what your future needs will be, then you might consider going with SDSL just so you can have both sides covered.

G.Lite

G.Lite is a proposed standard with the backing of several big-name corporations, Microsoft and Intel among them. The idea driving this standard is that it is simply too difficult and tedious to get set up with DSL as things now stand. In this chapter, you will find out all about some of the things that make this the case.

G.Lite addresses the installation difficulty issues of DSL by completely removing the need for an installation visit to your house. You simply buy a G.Lite
modem and plug it into a regular telephone jack.

Of course, nothing this good ever comes without a price. In the case of G.Lite,
that price is speed. Currently, G.Lite modems are only capable of hitting
speeds 25 times faster than regular 56 Kbps version 90 modems. What a
shame!

The more you get, the more you want. Connecting to the Internet 25 times
faster probably seems like a dream come true right now. Of course, it is a
tremendous improvement if all you are used to is a standard, analog modem
connection. You should bear in mind, however, that the more bandwidth you
get, the more you are likely to want.

IDSL

Using IDSL, your computer can connect to the Internet at the same speed as
an ISDN line. IDSL is just ISDN masquerading under a fancier name. Many
regard this as the final proof that marketing people truly are the bane of
modern man's existence.

In all fairness, by paying extra for IDSL rather than ISDN, you get an always-on
connection. Many systems can be cheaply configured to automatically redial
your ISP if your connection should ever drop, however. So, to be diplomatic
(too late!), let's just say that the benefits of IDSL are not completely clear at
this point.

VDSL

In a moment of unprecedented kindness, the folks developing this DSL standard have opted to spare the world from a potentially tongue-twisting
acronym. VDSL stands for *very high bit-rate digital subscriber line*, which is a
lot shorter than the VHBRDSL acronym that it could have been!

Using VDSL, you can achieve speeds of up to 10MB per second on your
Internet connection. This is the maximum speed allowed by the Ethernet
cards in many home computers! So, using VDSL can make accessing the
Internet just as fast as accessing a LAN.

LAN (local area network), like the Internet, is essentially just a bunch of computers connected together. Unlike the Internet, however, a single individual or organization typically owns all of the computers in a given LAN. Also, all of the computers in a LAN are usually located at the same place, thus the name Local Area Network rather than a Scattered All Over The Place Without Any Rhyme Or Reason Network: SAOTPWARORN (don't show that acronym to anyone from the phone company or they may actually start using it!). Chapter 13 has more detail about LAN.

Currently, VDSL is available for purchase by consumers only in the land of your wildest dreams. It will likely take a while longer to become available, and even then it will remain too pricey for most consumers for quite some time. Even so, you can feel pretty safe betting on this as the next big thing for DSL.

Prerequisites Aren't Just for College Kids

If you think back to your days in school, you may remember carefully planning out the sequence of classes you would take until graduation. You have to fulfill certain prerequisites before you can get where you really want to go. The only difference between then and now is that you can't bribe your way through the DSL prerequisites.

Getting the necessary hardware

The hardware requirements for DSL service are surprisingly light. You need a computer (duh!) and a DSL modem.

Computer

The main requirement for a computer to use DSL is the ability to talk to whatever DSL modem you will be attaching to it. DSL modems vary from one model to the next, but they all expect to ultimately attach to an Ethernet card in your computer. The real determinant of whether or not a computer can use DSL, then, is whether or not an Ethernet card is made for it.

Ethernet cards are made for all modern computers and have been around long enough that you shouldn't have too hard a time with any computer less than 10 years old. It is important that the Ethernet card in your computer support 10BASE-T, as this is the speed at which most DSL modems wish to communicate internally.

If you aren't sure whether or not your computer contains an Ethernet card, there are a couple of rules of thumb you can use to try finding out. To begin with, all Ethernet cards have to expose a port to the outside world in order for your DSL modem to have some place to connect. So, begin by examining the back of your computer for a port that looks like an oversized telephone jack. If you discover such an animal, chances are good that you have found your Ethernet card. For more positive identification, look for little electronic lights above, below, or to the side of this port. They don't need to be lit up, but if you see these you can be even more certain that you are looking at your computer's Ethernet cable.

Modem

The modem that you use with your DSL line is quite different from whatever modem you may have been using with your current telephone line. Many DSL providers have arranged partnerships with manufacturers of DSL modems. You can purchase the device as a package included in the cost of your monthly service.

If you are the sort that insists on buying your modem separately (or if your provider won't sell you one because they're afraid that might make it too easy on you), then you may want to check out the following DSL modem manufacturers' Web sites:

- ✔ http://www.coppermountain.com
- ✔ http://www.efficient.com
- ✔ http://www.westell.com

Once you get your new DSL line up and running, you are bound to ask yourself, "Who do I know that would be gullible enough to buy my analog modem from me?" Well, we can't help you find suckers, but we can suggest that you hang on to that modem for a while. You never know when that new DSL line is going to break and a good backup connection to the Internet for emergencies never hurts!

Finding compatible software

In general, any software that works with a dialup Internet connection should also work with a DSL line.

Operating system

All of the latest versions of the most popular operating systems include built-in support for the Internet. Specifically, they all speak a language (which computer geeks like myself prefer to call a *protocol*) known as TCP/IP (the official networking language of the Internet). Any of these systems work with DSL:

- ✔ All versions of Microsoft Windows since 3.1 includ support for TCP/IP, including 95, 98, NT, and 2000.

- ✔ All versions of MacOS since 7.5 have featured similar support.

- ✔ All versions of Linux since its first public release support TCP/IP (it's a Unix thing).

Applications

Standard Internet applications work equally well whether you are using a dialup connection or a DSL line because the TCP/IP portion of your operating system sits between your applications and your connection to the Internet. So, from your applications' standpoint, they never have to deal directly with whatever kind of connection you have to the Internet — your operating system handles that for them! This mediation is illustrated in Figure 3-1.

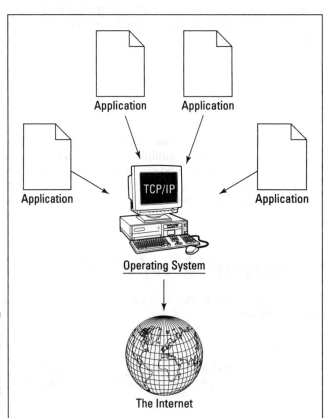

Figure 3-1:
Your operating system, the great mediator.

You may experience problems if you are used to connecting to the Internet via a specialized service, such as AOL. The software supplied by companies such as AOL is designed specifically for use with their own systems. These systems do not speak TCP/IP natively and are, therefore, not an instant match for DSL lines. Fortunately, most DSL providers are happy to provide you with free copies of software that you can use to connect to the Internet. This typically includes both the Internet Explorer or Netscape browser software and the e-mail software that comes as a part of these packages.

Being in the right place

Yes, it is important that you have a location in order to get DSL service. Ghosts and other disembodied spirits wandering freely about the ethereal plane are exceedingly difficult to bill and are, therefore, ineligible to receive most telecommunications services.

Those of us still in possession of our physical bodies are in only slightly better circumstances. To use DSL, you must

- Live in a location where DSL is offered
- Be less than three miles from your phone company's central office (CO)

Making the Dream Become a Reality

Many people think long and hard about whether they want to order DSL service. The higher-than-usual costs ($50–$500) associated with this kind of connectivity are often a major deterrent to many people who would otherwise gladly jump through flames for a faster Internet experience. Other people find the prospect of an always-on connection to the Internet a little scary and resist the lure of DSL until they can be assured that the files on their computer are *not* going to wind up all over the Internet (provided they take the few simple precautions that we show you in Part IV).

The one thing that all of these "speed resisters" have in common is that, when they do decide to order DSL, they usually want it *yesterday!* Unfortunately, the process of turning the dream of faster Internet access into the reality of DSL in your home or office usually involves at least these three steps:

1. **The local telephone company connects a DSL line from their CO to your home or office.**

2. **An inside wiring specialist connects the DSL line to whatever rooms in your home or office will require DSL service.**

3. **Your DSL service provider will turn on your line and begin giving you access to the Internet.**

The first piece of bad news in all of this is that all three steps are very likely to occur on different dates. Both of the first two steps involve *truck rolls* that must occur in sequence. To make sure that everything happens in the appropriate order, these visits are likely to be scheduled far enough apart to allow for missed appointments and other errors.

A truck roll is what telecommunication companies call any service for which they must dispatch people to a given location in order to provide service. In the list above, the first two steps both involve truck rolls because, in both cases, your DSL provider must arrange to have people actually come to your home or office.

The other piece of bad news is that, depending on the kind of DSL provider you choose, there may be completely different people and organizations performing any and all of these steps. Your exact situation here may vary depending largely upon the provider that you choose.

Finding a good provider

The company from which you purchase your DSL line is one of the key determining factors in the future usefulness of your Internet connection. So, choose wisely! A substandard DSL company can make your life miserable in a number of ways:

- ✔ Poor reliability, so your connection goes down more often

- ✔ Poor technicians, so problems go unresolved for long periods of time

- ✔ Poor technical support, so you are never able to fully understand your new purchase

- ✔ Poor customer service, so billing and related issues are impossible (or, at least, highly unpleasant) to resolve

Fortunately, with all the competition for Internet-subscriber dollars nowadays, the chances are good that you live in an area where you can pick from several different providers. These options came available when the US government broke up the telephone monopoly. Several other companies formed, but many of them still use the larger companies physical networks. This section lists the options you may choose from.

Weighing provider options

We use a few general categories to classify most DSL providers. Perhaps the most established of these are the Incumbent Local Exchange Providers

(ILECs). Competing directly against these are the, appropriately named, Competing Local Exchange Carriers (CLECs). ISPs and other resellers currently have the largest number of DSL subscribers.

ILECs

An Incumbent Local Exchange Provider, or ILEC as those in the know refer to them, is just the traditional local telephone company. Examples of some well-known ILECs in the United States include

✔ Ameritech

✔ Southwestern Bell

✔ Bell Atlantic

✔ Pacific Bell

One of the main advantages to choosing an ILEC for your DSL service is that you shouldn't have too much difficulty in figuring out how to contact them. The chances are good that they are still providing your regular telephone service and would be only too happy to discuss extending their service at your home or office to include DSL.

Another advantage to going with an ILEC DSL provider is that they are usually able to do everything for you themselves. This means that, besides providing the initial DSL line from their CO to your house, they will also do the inside wiring and, ultimately, give you your connection to the Internet. If you value simplicity above all else, this may very well be the choice for you!

Of course, some people seem to have pretty strong feelings about their local telephone companies — and they aren't always positive ones! If you are among the many who wouldn't trust your telephone company to find their own office without a map, then you may want to think twice about hiring them as your DSL provider. This kind of thinking has, in many areas, led to the formation of competing local exchange providers, or CLECs.

CLECs

A Competitive Local Exchange Carrier, as its name would suggest, is a company that competes with the ILEC in a given area to provide various telecommunications services. The only service that people had in mind when these companies were first being formed was regular telephone service. With the dawning of the Internet, however, CLECs are selling a whole range of connections, DSL foremost among them! A few of the well-known CLECs in the United States include

✔ Allegiance Telecom

✔ Focal

InterAccess

McLeod

The great thing about going with a CLEC is that they are generally much younger and more flexible companies than your local telephone service. This is great from a consumer's standpoint because it typically results in a wider choice of products at better prices with superior customer service. Such are the benefits of increased competition!

One disadvantage to buying your DSL service from a CLEC is that it introduces one more link in the chain between you and the ultimate source of your connection to the Internet. Because the ILEC actually owns the broader telephone network, your local telephone company, the ILEC, still has to run the DSL line from their CO to your house. The CLEC merely rents space in the ILECs CO in which to set up shop.

Another disadvantage is that CLECs are not available in all locations. If you live in anything less than a major metropolis, the chances are good that your only options for DSL service are an ILEC or an ISP/reseller.

ISPs and other resellers

It seems at the present time as if the single biggest trend among DSL providers is ISPs that purchase their service from large wholesalers and then resell it. By following this model, small, local ISPs that would otherwise be unable to afford the cost of providing DSL service directly are still able to bring their special skills to the marketplace.

Ideally, the special skills offered by these smaller ISPs would include an increased focus on customer service and value for the cost. Under the best circumstances, this is exactly what happens, making a local ISP your best choice for DSL service. Unfortunately, the very nature of this model makes the ideal difficult, if not impossible, to attain.

What has my reseller done for me lately?

When people first begin to learn about the wholesaler/reseller model of DSL connectivity, one of their first questions is often, "So what exactly does the reseller/ISP do, besides take my money?" The reseller provides several valuable services to the wholesaler — finding customers for their product not the least among them! But they also assist you, the end-user, in many (mostly technical) ways.

For example, most people would rather be spared the complexity of maintaining their own mail, news, and DNS servers. Your ISP can maintain machines like this for you. Also, a good ISP can act like an advocate for your interests in dealing with the wholesaler — a level of clout that you will desperately need, should you ever require their assistance.

The problem is that, by purchasing DSL service from a reseller, you are forced to deal with (at least) two other organizations on a regular basis: the local telephone company and the reseller. We discussed your local telephone company in previous sections, so who are these wholesalers and what do they do?

DSL wholesalers can provide every portion of your DSL connection except for the actual physical line running from the CO to your house. If you buy your DSL service from a small ISP, the chances are good that you will need to deal with their wholesaler for much of your installation and anytime that anything goes wrong thereafter.

Unfortunately, you aren't usually allowed to talk directly to the wholesalers; you must always go through your ISP first. This adds several additional layers of people and processes through which all communications must pass before you can get what you need, often resulting in circular blame, as illustrated in Figure 3-2.

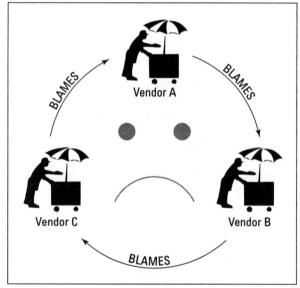

Figure 3-2:
Vendor A + vendor B + vendor C = zero account-ability.

Some of the larger DSL wholesalers in the United States include

- ✔ Covad
- ✔ NorthPoint
- ✔ Rhythms

Deciding what you need

After you find your dream DSL provider, you need to choose from their various product offerings to find the package that is just right for your needs. Obviously, product names and details vary widely from one company to another. However, a few general kinds of offerings seem common enough to warrant mention here.

Consumer-only offerings

Many DSL providers view consumers as far less burdensome users of their systems than businesses. The reasons cited for this view vary, but they commonly include

✔ Connecting to the Internet during non-peak hours (meaning, outside of 9 a.m.–5 p.m.)

✔ Placing fewer calls to Technical Support (because outages aren't as likely to cause a loss of revenue)

✔ Consuming less bandwidth

Many providers with this view are willing to sell DSL to consumers at a much lower rate than they would typically offer their business customers. If you use your connection from home for strictly non-business purposes, check first into any non-business product offerings that your DSL provider may have.

You may be thinking to yourself, "Self, why not order a consumer DSL product even though you'll be using it for work?" If you happen to work out of your house, this tactic just might work (whether or not it is moral is a question left entirely up to your conscience, or lack thereof). But remember, big brother is watching. If you try this at a business address, however, be prepared to have your order cancelled on you or automatically upgraded with or without warning!

So what? SOHO!

In Chapter 11, you find out all about the wonders of telecommuting using your fancy new Internet connection. DSL providers have already given this topic a great deal of thought and many have come up with products made especially for you and other small office/home office users. These are typically known as SOHO (Small Office/Home Office) DSL products.

SOHO products typically come bundled with SDSL lines, rather than the ADSL lines generally associated with simple consumer lines. Many small businesses want to run web servers and other applications requiring more uplink capacity than that typically available with ADSL connections. For more information on the differences between ADSL and SDSL, see the section earlier in this chapter, "The Protocol of a Thousand Faces."

SOHO products often also offer support for multiple computers attached to the same DSL line. Unlike purely business products, however, the number of computers supported is usually fairly low.

Strictly business

If you are purchasing your DSL line for a business address, then you may have no choice but to go with the business products offered by your DSL provider. On one hand, you can expect to pay a premium for the service that you receive. On the other hand, many providers truly offer additional value in exchange for the extra cost associated with these products.

For example, many ISPs offer special technical support numbers for business customers with critical emergencies — such as a complete loss of service. The number of computers that can be (legally) connected to such a connection is usually also much higher than that of the other product types.

Helping the provider find you

When you place your order for DSL service, the address you give plays a vital role in determining whether or not your application is accepted or rejected. Are we suggesting that DSL providers are snobs that only sell to you if you live in the fashionable part of town? Not at all, it's just that the mechanics of DSL and the high costs associated with offering it in each new city combine to greatly limit most providers' service areas.

Often, a provider will accept an order for DSL, only to reject it at a later date. Common reasons for this change include:

- Old, nasty wiring (either in your house or under your street)
- Strange, twisting wiring (which makes the distance from your house to the CO much longer than the provider originally thought)
- Maladjusted wiring that kidnaps the installer and holds him for ransom (I just made this one up, but it is fun to imagine)
- An address that doesn't match the phone company's records

If your order is rejected because your address doesn't match the phone company's records, you will generally be notified that your provider can't find your address. This may come as a shock to you, because they will often send a letter *to* your address specifically to tell you that they can't find it. No, this isn't a joke.

This confusion occurs because immediately after you place an order for DSL, your provider will place an order themselves with your local telephone company. (If your DSL provider *is* your local telephone company, this will save a step.) If the address you give your provider deviates greatly from the way your address is listed by your telephone company, then your order is likely to get lost.

It is absolutely essential when giving your address to a DSL provider that you state your address exactly as it appears on your telephone bill!

Chapter 4

Hooking Up to a Satellite Service

· ·

In This Chapter

▶ Looking at the benefits and limitations of DSS

▶ Understanding the satellite data path

▶ Making preparations

▶ Getting information on available providers

· ·

*F*ifty years ago, many Americans were horrified when the Soviet Union became the first country to place a satellite into permanent Earth orbit. Beyond the obvious potential for nuclear annihilation, many Americans felt that it simply wasn't cool to be beaten by any country where indoor toilets were still considered a luxury item.

Today, satellites are most widely used to facilitate the broadcast of television signals from one point on the Earth to another. Like the atomic weapons we feared they'd deliver, modern satellites can now bring bad 1980's situation comedies, such as "Momma's Family," to virtually any spot of the globe at any hour of the day or night.

Fortunately, every cloud has its silver lining. In the case of satellites, high speed Internet access may yet prove to be that silver lining.

Twinkle, Twinkle, Little DSS

Direct Satellite Service (DSS) allows you to interact with satellites orbiting the Earth straight from your own roof or backyard. One of the kinds of interactions that is now being offered by many satellite systems is access to the Internet. Accessing the Internet via satellite is different from using a regular dialup Internet account in many ways.

What's so good about DSS?

The principle advantages to direct satellite Internet access are

- ✔ Faster access speeds
- ✔ Wider availability
- ✔ Extra features

Faster access

The average speed at which a satellite connection can download data from the Internet is approximately 400 Kbps. The typical dialup Internet user is accustomed to speeds anywhere from 28 to 56 Kbps. This, therefore, represents an improvement of anywhere from 7 to 14 times most people's current connection performance.

Even though you may have been previously using a 56 kbps modem to connect to the Internet, the chances are good that you have not been getting your full 56 kbps' worth out of your telephone connection. Most of these modems are rated with the assumption of an absolutely perfect telephone line, completely free of all noise and interference. Reaching full speed is a potential that few, if any, people ever experience. The good news is that by upgrading to satellite service, you may notice increases in speed of anywhere up to 20 times your current connection speeds!

Unlike regular modems, the quality of the telephone lines in your house and under your street tends not to affect the speed of downloads from your satellite service. To put it simply: There are no telephone lines involved in downloading data from a satellite, only air and space!

The situation is quite different in terms of sending data back to the Internet, however. We show you more about this in the section on how satellite Internet access works.

Wider availability

To get cable Internet access, you have to live in an area where the local cable company provides Internet service. For DSL Internet access, you need a local telephone company (or one of their competitors) that offers Internet access. But to get satellite Internet access, you only need to live on a continent with access to satellite receivers. (Check out Chapters 2 and 3 to review cable and DSL provider limitations.)

The good news is that this currently constitutes all of North America and Europe. If you live elsewhere, however, chances are excellent that you will be seeing opportunities to purchase satellite Internet access within the next few years. At any rate, you will probably see satellite availability before either DSL or cable access.

The reason that satellite Internet access is so much more widely available than either cable or DSL access is that it's much cheaper for companies to provide this service to extremely large areas. The exact reasons for this will be dealt with in the next section on how satellite Internet access works. For now, we will just tease you with the fact that the world looks much smaller from space . . . and satellites use this fact to their advantage!

Extra features

To paraphrase a not-so-ancient television commercial, satellite Internet access " . . . slices, dices, and chops — but wait — that's not all!" Many of the companies currently involved in providing Internet access by satellite are the same companies that have been providing television programming this way for several years now. Some of them are using this fact to their advantage, and yours, by throwing in several optional extras when you purchase your Internet connection from them.

Many of the extra features being offered by satellite providers as a part of their Internet service offerings would be equally available to you if you only purchased your television programming from them. If you have the availability of another kind of broadband Internet access in your area, then this may be a better choice for you. To find out why, read about the disadvantages of satellite Internet access in the next section.

What's wrong with getting Internet from a satellite?

You didn't really believe that Internet-via-satellite was going to be completely without its disadvantages, did you? Nothing in this world is totally devoid of problems, and satellite Internet access has its fair share of them. Some of the bigger ones include

- Expense
- Difficulty of setup
- Slow uploads
- Vulnerability

Expense

Satellite Internet access is much more expensive than regular dialup Internet access. This is true for most kinds of broadband Internet access, as you are probably already aware if you have read the earlier portions of this book. (If you haven't read the earlier portions of this book, then you should really feel quite guilty about your lack of patience!)

Even in comparison to other forms of broadband Internet access, however, satellite access is more expensive. There are three points on which satellite access tends to be more expensive than other broadband kinds of Internet service.

✔ **Equipment:** The initial charge for equipment can range anywhere from a couple hundred to a thousand dollars, depending on how elaborate you want to get. In general, if you just want standard Internet access, you can get by with the cheapest equipment. If you also want to be able to watch the latest TV broadcasts from Outer Mongolia, however, get your checkbook out and ready!

✔ **Installation:** Installation fees are included in the setup charge for most other kinds of Internet service. For example, very few cable companies will charge you an hourly rate for the time that their installers spend getting your house ready for Internet access via cable modem. If you want to have your satellite provider install and configure your new satellite dish, however, you can expect an hourly fee of anywhere up to $100 per hour!

How many trips to the Emergency Room have begun with the words, "Oh come on, how dangerous could it possibly be?" At first, the work involved in setting up a satellite dish on your own roof may seem short, simple, and perfectly safe. It's none of the above. Unless you have extensive experience walking around on your own roof, this can be an exceedingly dangerous undertaking and should not be attempted without serious consideration beforehand. Having a satellite dish mounted on the ground in your yard may not be as attractive, but it's much safer. It's also easier to perform maintenance in the (likely) event that something eventually interferes with your reception.

Surprisingly, you probably won't encounter much resistance from your satellite sales representative if you tell them that you intend to setup your new dish yourself. If you are technically inclined, this is certainly one option for saving some cash upfront. On the other hand, if you are technically challenged, you should carefully consider the value of your time before committing to such a project.

✔ **Recurring charges:** Most Internet Service Providers (ISPs) nowadays charge a single, flat-rate fee on a monthly, quarterly, or annual basis for Internet access. For example, you might expect to pay $19.95 per month for unlimited use of a service such as AOL or InterAccess. If you are willing to commit to a longer period of service, such as a year, you can often get a considerable reduction in your monthly rate. For example, you might pay $200 per year (which would work out to about $16.50 per month). This opportunity for savings is illustrated in Figure 4-1.

In our Internet travels, we haven't found any satellite ISP's following this model. To begin with, the only plans that are available are the monthly-billing plans. This means that the opportunity to reduce your expenditures by committing to longer periods of service simply is not there!

This isn't so horrible, because the monthly charges levied by most satellite providers seem more-or-less comparable with the fees being charged by most cable and DSL companies — between $30 and $50 per month. On the other hand, satellite providers have brought back one of the most dreaded billing schemes of the olden days — hourly charges!

Typically, each plan comes with a certain number of "free hours" and any use beyond this gets billed at anywhere from $1–$2 per hour. If you hardly ever use the Internet, this may not be much of a problem. But hey, if you hardly ever use the Internet, then why are you even reading this book? Shouldn't you have bought a book about gardening or sports instead?

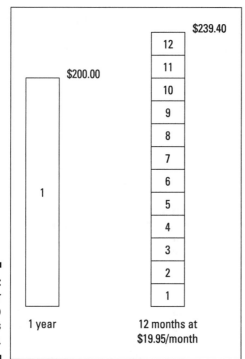

Figure 4-1: The longer you sign-up for, the less you pay.

For the rest of us, hourly charges can be a tremendous financial burden. Unless you are independently wealthy, this will almost certainly make maintaining any kind of constant Internet connection completely out of the question. This will, in turn, make it impossible for you to run a Web server or any of the other neat things that require a dedicated Internet connection that we show you later on in the book.

Difficult setup

As you see in our preceding description, one of the first costs associated with getting satellite Internet service is the purchase and installation of your own satellite dish. If you elect to install your satellite dish yourself, you are in for one of the more difficult jobs in obtaining a broadband Internet connection.

You have to work through a number of issues (put on your hard hat!) to set up your computer for direct satellite Internet service, but the usual steps follow this pattern:

1. **Position and mount your satellite dish.**

   To begin with, your dish will need to be positioned somewhere where its line-of-sight won't be blocked. If you live in a heavily urbanized area, tall buildings will be difficult to avoid. If you live in the suburbs, trees will probably get in your way. If you live in the country, exceptionally large cattle might be a problem, but you will still probably have to worry most about trees.

2. **Align your satellite dish.**

   When you find a location that is relatively obstruction-free, you have to align your satellite dish properly, but Where do you point the thing? In the Northern hemisphere, you generally need to direct your dish to face South. In the Southern hemisphere, turn it to face North. You will see why this is the case in the next section on how satellite Internet access works.

3. **Connect your dish to your satellite modem.**

   This connection means that, somehow or another, you need to run a wire from the dish to the modem, almost certainly through the walls and/or roof of your house. If you aren't comfortable working with drills and similar power tools, this will be the hardest part of the job.

4. **Connect your satellite modem to your computer and install your Internet software.**

   Connecting your satellite modem to your computer and installing the special software that allows your computer to talk to the modem are probably the easiest tasks involved in the entire installation. Your modem will simply connect to a port on the back of your computer. The software comes with an installation program that will guide you through all of its required procedures in a step-by-step fashion.

Slow uploads

It's true that satellite Internet access will almost always prove to be a faster mechanism for downloading data than connecting over a standard telephone line. Transmitting data back to the Internet is generally not faster, however. Unfortunately, current direct satellite Internet access schemes all use a standard modem and telephone for the uplink portion of their data connection.

On the other hand, if you intend to run any kind of multimedia applications, like real-time video or audio conferencing, over the Internet, you may very well find that satellite access is not sufficient for your purposes. Graphics and sound tend to consume a lot of bandwidth, and real-time conferencing uses a lot of both graphics (in the form of video) and sound.

Less than a decade ago, local telephone companies were ballyhooing ISDN as the last word in high-speed data connections. Since the advent of cable modems, DSL, and satellite access, ISDN has fallen into a state of relative disuse. If you require a better uplink than satellite access can provide, but are unable to purchase cable or DSL access in your area, then you might consider using an ISDN line with your existing ISP for the uplink portion of your connection. For exact details on how to do this, you will want to consult your satellite provider. If this sounds like something you would like to do, make sure to ask your provider if they support this approach before purchasing your service from them!

Vulnerability

In the previous section on satellite access benefits, we mention that your ability to get satellite service is not dependent on the condition of the cables lying under your street or inside the walls of your building. In contrast, at least the state of those buried cables is usually constant — the condition of your wires is unlikely to improve or degrade dramatically within the course of just a few hours. Your ability to receive satellite transmissions, though, can experience exactly such ups-and-downs.

To begin with, the fact that you are ultimately responsible for the main piece of equipment providing your Internet access is a major factor contributing to the unreliability of this medium. With DSL, the central piece of equipment providing your Internet connection is sitting in your telephone company's central office (probably) providing similar service simultaneously to several other customers. You can rest assured that if something goes wrong with it, the providers will have someone there trying to fix it in a relatively short amount of time. The last thing these companies want are many angry customers clogging their telephone lines with complaints!

Contrast this with the situation when you have your own satellite dish. If a tornado blows your dish off the roof, who's problem is it? It isn't your satellite service provider's. And it certainly is not your telephone company's problem. It's yours and yours alone!

The other major reason why satellite access is inherently less reliable than other forms of Internet access is that the signals involved in the downlinks for these connections must travel through air and space. While the signals are still in the Earth's atmosphere, they can be susceptible to interference by severe weather. Once the signals make it into space, they can be disturbed by sources as distant as solar flares and sunspot activity!

"Dishing" up an ounce of prevention

If you live in an area that is prone to severe weather, you might consider taking steps to protect your satellite dish in advance. Here are a few suggestions:

✔ Mount your dish in a place where it is somewhat sheltered from the elements — nestled in an outside corner of your building, for example.

✔ Purchase or construct a covering for your dish that will allow you to shelter it in whatever location you choose to mount it.

✔ Secure the cables connecting your dish to the inside of your house so that, if anything happens to pull your dish away dramatically (such as strong winds), the contents of your house will not be damaged by the cables.

Hooking Your Cyber-Wagon to a Star

The basic principles behind satellite Internet access are not much different from the other kinds of Internet access that you see throughout this book. At one end of the circuit is your computer or set of computers, connected to your satellite dish via a special modem. At the other end is your choice of provider, connected to the Internet via one or more high-capacity dedicated lines, such as T3s.

The glue that connects you to your provider is the satellite itself. The satellite orbits the Earth in a *geosynchronous orbit*, approximately even with the Earth's equator.

A geosynchronous orbit is just one of many ways that a satellite can travel around the world. What sets this way apart from all others is that it allows a satellite to remain constantly above the same point on the Earth at all times because the speed and direction attained by the satellite are exactly the same as that of the point on the Earth below it.

Fresh off the Internet and into your computer!

Whenever you request information from the Internet, a page on the World Wide Web, for example, this data is sent by your provider up to the satellite, where it's then reflected back down to your satellite dish. This happens even if you elect to retain your previous Internet Service Provider for your uplink data service. You may wonder, then, how can your provider possibly know what data you are requesting?

When your computer requests information from the Internet, the special software that you've installed on your PC first intercepts the request and sends it to your satellite provider. Your satellite provider then requests the data you need directly from its source out on the Internet and passes it back to your computer via the satellite. This process is illustrated in Figure 4-2.

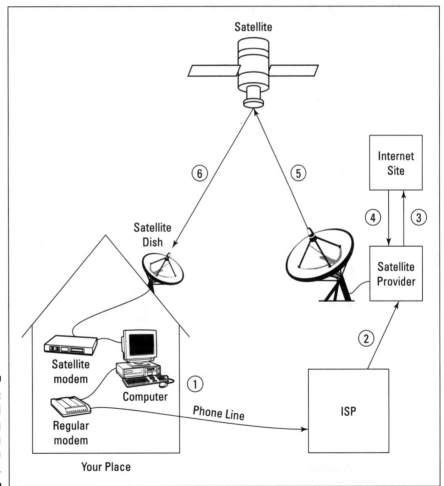

Figure 4-2:
Sending and
receiving
data using
satellite
access.

The short trip home

Data that you merely wish to send from your computer back to the Internet travels in an even simpler path. Since your satellite dish is only used for the downlink portion of your Internet connection, your modem is able to handle everything here by itself. The data simply flows out through your telephone or ISDN line just as it always has and proceeds directly to whatever site on the Internet you desire.

Preparing Your Machine

Almost everything you might want to do with your computer has some minimum requirements associated with it. It would be unrealistic, for example, to hope that you could run the latest and greatest Doom-style shoot 'em-up game on an old 286 computer with 640K of RAM. Similarly, there are certain basic hardware requirements for your new broadband Internet connection.

- ✔ An IBM-compatible computer
- ✔ A minimum 200 Mhz Pentium-compatible CPU
- ✔ At least 32MB RAM
- ✔ 28 Kbps or faster modem
- ✔ Windows 98 or NT

Notice that these requirements are heavily focused on the so-called Wintel platform. This is because the software required by the major satellite Internet providers is highly specialized. In order to capture the largest possible market, they have currently decided to go strictly after the Windows platform. You can be sure that if satellite Internet access really takes off (no pun intended), they will be making Mac and Linux versions of their products available shortly.

Getting the Necessary Equipment

We haven't yet discussed exactly what hardware components are typically required for purchase as a part of your actual satellite Internet connection. These components, shown in Figure 4-3, are

- ✔ **A satellite dish:** Your dish is the piece that sits outside your home or office and talks directly to the satellite. You may either elect to setup your satellite dish yourself, or pay your provider to do it for you. Unlike in the movie *ET*, you cannot make one of these for yourself out of an umbrella!

- ✔ **A satellite modem:** The satellite modem is responsible for converting the signals received by your satellite dish into a format that your computer can understand. Note that it's not responsible for converting any of the signals from your computer into a form that your satellite dish can understand. The communication here is strictly one-way: from your dish to your computer.

All data sent by your computer to the Internet will still travel over your regular, low-speed Internet connection via your modem or ISDN adapter. So you may want to upgrade your upload equipment to even things out.

✔ **An optional TV receiver:** If you are only going to be using your satellite dish for Internet access, then you can get by with just the two pieces of equipment described above. If, on the other hand, you would also like to receive television broadcasts via your dish, then you are going to need a special receiver.

The function of the receiver, much like the satellite modem, is to act as a translator. Your television would never be able to understand the language spoken by your satellite dish without a receiver to act as a translator for it.

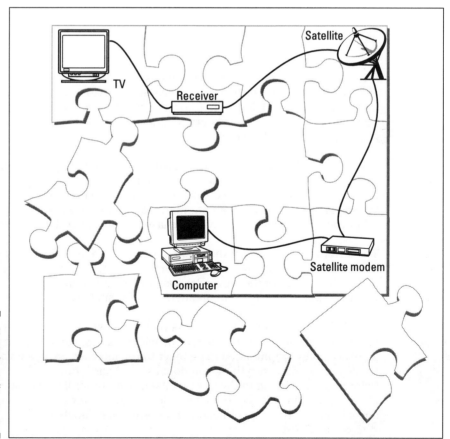

Figure 4-3:
Fitting together all the pieces of your home DSS puzzle.

Just because you're getting hooked-up with satellite TV is no reason to abandon the regular television antenna that you've used up to this point. In many communities, local television stations are not yet available for satellite reception. If you get rid of your standard TV antenna, you may find yourself able to watch TV programs from a different continent with greater ease than those from your own city!

Choosing a Provider

You'll be astounded by the number of DSS providers . . . *not!* Currently, you get to choose from only two satellite Internet providers in North America:

- ✔ **DirecPC:** DirecPC is an offering from the same company that sells DirecTV, and focuses mainly on standard Internet connectivity.
- ✔ **WebTV:** WebTV, on the other hand, is focused on offering a whole host of value-added content in addition to your regular connection.

DirecPC

DirecPC is the latest offering from Hughes Network Systems. Hughes Network Systems is an enormous telecommunications provider that maintains their own satellite network in addition to cable and a variety of other products. If you are looking to buy your Internet connection from the most established source possible, look no further!

Because DirecPC focuses on offering what might be called standard Internet service, unlike services such as AOL, you don't get access to any special content included with the price of your subscription. When you connect to the Internet, all you have are your standard Web browser, e-mail, and whatever other tools and games you have purchased for use over the Internet.

The advantage here is that the connection you have to the Internet is a true connection — you will never have your choices of tools and accessories limited by the design of the particular system you are connecting to. You run into this limitation with content-laden services such as AOL.

The difference between the networks built by most regular ISPs like DirecPC and those of AOL and other content providers is that most content providers were originally not intended to connect to the Internet. So, when you connect to their networks, everything you do must first pass through their systems before it ever gets out to the Internet itself. With other ISPs, you are given a direct connection. This both makes your service faster and allows you to use any software with your connection that is Internet-capable.

Here are a couple of places on the Internet that you can visit to find out more about DirecPC and the rest of Hughes Network Systems' offerings:

- ✔ http://www.direcpc.com (the main homepage for their Internet service)

- ✔ http://www.hns.com (the main homepage for the entire company)

- ✔ http://www.directv.com (the main homepage for their Television service)

WebTV

As a content provider, WebTV is more like AOL. Besides the Internet content that WebTV provides for you, the service works through your television rather than your PC! To work with this service, then, you must first purchase a WebTV console and connect it to your television.

You may, in fact, elect to do this even before you own a satellite dish. WebTV allows you to sign up with many ISPs for access via your regular telephone line. WebTV supplies its own Web browser and e-mail software, but it doesn't feature a disk drive — so you don't have any way to load your own software if you don't like theirs!

After you have your WebTV console installed and functional, the next step is to buy one of the satellite packages from Echostar that supports Internet access. You can find the latest list of these packages on the WebTV website.

One advantage to buying your Internet access via WebTV and Echostar is that you get many extra features for your money. For example, most of Echostar's dishes feature hard disks that allow you to record up to 12 hours of video without even using a VCR or videocassette! Or, you can put the dish into a mode where you can pause live television shows for up to half-an-hour.

The extra features of the WebTV service itself are also very attractive: six e-mails, chatting, parent-designated controls, call-waiting support, and so on, and so on. You find out more about parent-defined controls in Chapter. Suffice it for now to say that it's very important when dealing with the Internet!

Here are the three most important spots on the Internet for getting more information about WebTV satellite access:

- ✔ http://www.webtv.net (the main page for WebTV Internet access)

- ✔ http://www.echostar.com (the main page for the Echostar satellite company)

- ✔ http://www.dishnetwork.com (the main page for Echostar's consumer satellite services)

Part II
Surfing at Warp Speed

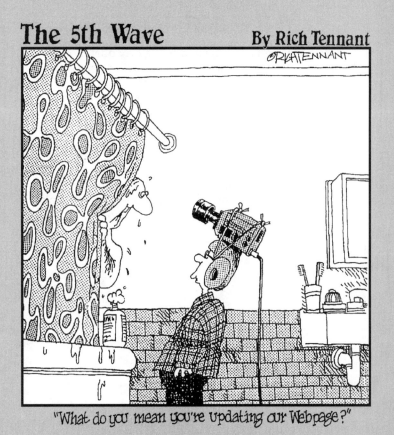

The 5th Wave   By Rich Tennant

"What do you mean you're updating our Webpage?"

In this part . . .

*N*ow that you're connected to the broadband option
of your choice, what can you do with it that you
couldn't do, or that wasn't practical, with your old, slow
modem? More than you expected, we're pretty sure.

This part leads you through the cool stuff you can do now
that you have a fast enough, wide enough connection to
the Internet. You'll find out how to see streaming video,
hear streaming audio, and transmit a little audio and
video of your own to communicate with others. We also
show you how to use your always-on connection to make
immediate contact through instant messaging.

Chapter 5

Screaming Video and Audio

In This Chapter

▶ Deciding what you want to hear and see using your high-speed connection

▶ Listening to radio, music, conferences, and speeches live on your computer

▶ Watching television, movie trailers, and politics using streaming video

▶ Finding and installing the tools you need for streaming audio and video

. . . .

*I*f you live in an area with poor radio reception, or you can't attend a trade show but would like to, or you want to see movie previews without paying big bucks to see a movie first, streaming audio and video is for you.

Using free or inexpensive tools, you can download streams of video and audio, including live radio and television broadcasts, and play them on your computer while you do other tasks. You no longer have to be limited to the radio stations that broadcast in your area or television stations your cable company decides to offer you. You no longer have to fly to the nation's Capitol to sit in the halls of Congress to hear laws being made. Once you install the necessary software, such as QuickTime, RealAudio, or Windows Media Player, a whole new world of broadcasting is at your fingertips.

Gently Down the Stream

Before you get into watching and listening online, you should know about *streaming* audio and video. You've always been able to download audio and video, as we describe in other chapters in this part, as self-contained files. When you download a sound from your favorite Web site, you're copying a file from that site and saving it on your local computer, where you can play it as many times as you want after that. The same goes for self-contained movie files — you have to download the whole movie file to watch it, for the most part.

Streaming is different. With streaming audio or video, the signal is played as it arrives, bit-by-bit. Instead of downloading a large file and playing it back, you download a small file that tells your video or audio player where to find the signal on the Internet. Your player then connects to that signal and plays it for you as it arrives.

To use a real-world analogy, regular video is like renting a movie from your local video store, while streaming video is like catching it live off of the airwaves.

One word you'll encounter a lot while exploring the world of streaming audio and video is *content*. Content encompasses the material you can listen to or watch, as in "Whoa, that music video site has some awesome content!"

Streaming good, downloading bad

Streaming is an improvement over downloading for listening to audio or video mainly because transmitting audio and video over the Internet takes a lot of bandwidth. It can also be very slow, even over a high-speed connection. For example, one minute of high-quality audio can be over 6MB in size and would take several minutes to download over most high-speed connections. (At an average download speed of 48Kbps, the 6MB sound would take over two minutes to download.)

By downloading the files, to listen to even a one-minute sound you'd have to wait several minutes just to begin listening. If the sound is streamed over the Internet, you can begin listening within seconds of deciding you'd like to hear it. Your computer downloads just as much data, but because you're listening to streaming audio, you don't have to wait.

That example was for a one-minute sound. Imagine listening to a one-hour speech if you had to download the entire sound file first, and *that* assumes you'd even have enough disk space to store it on your computer.

Spotting the free-loaders

So why is streaming content free? Organizations broadcast their information on the Internet for two main reasons: to expand their listener base (in the case of radio stations) and to get their message out. However, since you're not paying anything for the signal, and since it costs them money to set up the servers to stream their audio, most of the broadcasters decide they have to recoup their money somehow. As with most services on the Internet, that *somehow* is advertising.

Most of the streaming players can display advertising while you're listening to the audio. That's not so bad, because you can always minimize or otherwise hide the audio application while you're listening. Many broadcasters also include a short commercial before the actual streaming content starts. You're usually stuck with that, although if you click the Forward button in your player you may be able to skip the ads.

On top of that, you're exposed to any advertising embedded in the stream you're hearing or seeing. If a food chain advertises on the radio station you're listening to, you hear the ad even if you're thousands of miles from their nearest restaurant. Technically, that expands the advertising base for the TV or radio station, although their advertisers may not be impressed by that.

Given that the advertising, in whatever form, is supporting the broadcast on the Internet, you may as well relax and chalk it up to the cost of listening to the content you want to hear.

Streaming Audio Feeds

I called up a friend in Calgary, Alberta (Canada) the other day and asked him about some minor current events in his city. He was amazed that it had been important enough for the international news media to pick it up, until I explained to him that I'd been listening to his local radio stations from 2,691.5 miles away. I hadn't been on my roof with a huge antenna; instead, I had been listening to his local station over the Internet, in this case using a multimedia program called Real Player, which is shown in Figure 5-1.

There are thousands of radio stations re-broadcasting their signals from a server instead of a tower, as well as an ever-growing number of Internet-only stations broadcasting music, news, computer information, and other useful content.

Information available through streaming audio includes, but is definitely not limited to, the following:

✔ AM and FM radio stations from all over the world

✔ Governmental proceedings (for the United States, this is available mainly through C-SPAN, at www.cspan.org)

✔ Speeches and keynote addresses (most notably at computer conferences, but elsewhere as well)

✔ Religious teachings, including those at Islaam.com (`www.islaam.com/audio/lectures/`) and ThinkJewish International (`www.thinkjewish.com`)

✔ Classroom lectures, such as those available at Harvard University's Extension School (distanceEd.dce.harvard.edu) and the University of Illinois College of Law (`www.law.uiuc.edu/i-auditorium/`)

Figure 5-1:
The RealPlayer application playing a radio station over the Internet.

Web sites can serve streaming audio live, as in the case of the radio stations or keynote addresses, or recorded for later streaming, as in the case of virtually any audio source. Often, a computer conference such as Macworld may broadcast its keynote addresses live but then leave the recordings on their server for anyone who may have missed the speeches to hear, using streaming audio for both live and recorded content.

For very popular events, such as major corporate announcements or space shuttle launches, the computers serving up the streaming audio may be overwhelmed, or their capacity may be used up within minutes of the event. If you must listen to an event live, try to connect just prior to the scheduled start time, and keep trying to connect until a minute or two after it has begun. For all but the most exciting events, however, I recommend waiting until after the event is over, and listening to the streaming recordings, when fewer people are competing with you for time.

Where to tune your ears

If you listen to the radio while you work on or near the computer, you can expand your listening options immensely by listening to streaming audio instead. Because your connection to the Internet is always on, you can leave the computer playing streaming audio the same way you'd leave the radio playing, and continue working in other programs on your computer or anywhere else in your home of office within earshot.

One excellent use of streaming audio is to listen to exactly the radio station you want, whenever you want it. That could be a local radio station that broadcasts on the Internet if your radio reception is poor, or it could be the one radio station in the world that plays the combination of music and news you want, that just happens to be in Utica, New York.

Destination, please

If you already know of a radio station, conference, university, or other organization that is providing streaming audio content, the easiest thing to do is go to their Web site and look for the links.

For example, to hear your favorite shows on National Public Radio, you could open www.npr.org and click the appropriate audio link for the audio player you're using. (NPR is unusual in that they support all three of the major streaming audio players.)

Most radio stations that have Web sites use their call letters as part of their names, so you might have success opening the site for station WOUR by entering www.wour.com into your browser. Note that public radio stations are non-profit organizations, so their Web sites are likely to be at a .org instead of a .com. For example, you can find public radio station WHYY in Philadelphia at www.whyy.org.

Radio stations whose call letters spell common words may have to get more complex Web addresses, because the chances are good that someone else already had their "word" as a Web address. If you can't find the station under its call letters, try adding the word radio to the call letters. For example, to find WOOD-AM in Michigan, you would have to enter www.woodradio.com, because www.wood.com belongs to someone else.

Once you connect to a site, watch for links that will lead you to the streaming audio. Key words to look for are "Listen Live," "Hear It Now," and so on. See Figure 5-2 for an example.

Remember that you can always request content by contacting the Web master or the management of the site. If a radio station gets enough requests to stream their broadcast on the Internet, they may do it.

Spinning the digital tuner

Don't worry if you don't have any radio station or other Internet broadcaster in mind. There are plenty of ways to search for the sites you're interested in. Remember that the whole point of streaming audio onto the Internet is to get listeners, and providers can't get listeners if they make the content hard to find.

Figure 5-2:
A sample
radio
station's
Web page
with a Listen
Live button
that links
us to the
streaming
audio.

The first place to start is, of course, your trusty search engine of choice, such as Yahoo!, Lycos, or others. Enter enough search words to narrow the choices, such as `streaming audio live country music radio stations` or similar words that describe your interests.

Another way to find content is to open the home page for the audio player you're using. Real Networks is very happy to provide an audio search site, as are Apple Computer's QuickTime and Microsoft's Media Player groups:

- Real Network's site at `realguide.real.com`
- Apple's QuickTime site at `www.apple.com/quicktime/qtv/`
- Microsoft's list of sites at `windowsmedia.com`

There are also organizations that consolidate online audio and video content. They team up with the radio stations and other broadcasters to offer the streaming content plus advertising provided by the central site. This provides a way for broadcasters who might not otherwise be available on the Internet to provide a connection.

Examples of streaming audio sites include

- Yahoo! Broadcast, at `www.broadcast.com`
- Internet Radio Index, at `www.internetradioindex.com`
- WebRadio, at `www.webradio.com`
- Lycos's radio network search site, at `music.lycos.com/radio/`

Most of these sites let you search based on broadcast type, such as music type, talk radio, sports, and so on, as well as region, such as searching by state, country, or even broadcast language.

Once you find a broadcaster's site, be sure to bookmark it (or add it to your Favorites) so you can find it again. Most of the streaming audio players let you bookmark the audio signal, too, so you can start or resume playing streaming audio just by choosing a menu command or clicking an icon.

Streaming Video

If you're using a cable modem for your high-speed Internet access, you may appreciate the process by which you're using the cable television lines to connect to the Internet so you can download television content to your computer, but the fact is that anyone with a high-speed connection has a world of video available.

Video available on the Internet includes, but is certainly not limited to, the following:

- ✔ Movie and television previews

- ✔ Music videos

- ✔ Webcam broadcasts, where people and organizations set up small cameras to pick up anything from beach conditions to fish tank activity

- ✔ Speeches and keynote addresses (most notably at computer conferences, but elsewhere as well)

- ✔ Government-sponsored proceedings, especially NASA space missions (www.nasa.gov) and U.S. Government activities available from C-SPAN (www.cspan.org)

- ✔ News, such as that available from CNN (www.cnn.com) or the BBC (www.bbc.co.uk)

- ✔ Television broadcasts outside of news shows, such as the Public Broadcasting System channel WGBH-Boston (www.wgbh.org)

- ✔ Internet-focused broadcasts, such as Ziff-Davis's ZDTV (www.zdtv.com) or iTV.net

Don't expect streaming video to be as high quality as your television. Streaming video may appear blocky or low-resolution at times, and the action may be choppy or jumpy. Even with a high-speed connection, video takes a lot of bandwidth to carry a full-motion, full-color motion picture, not to mention the sound track. However, streaming video is certainly good enough to watch your favorite news show, music video, or fun-filled governmental hearing. A sample video broadcast is shown in Figure 5-3.

Figure 5-3:
A sample
RealPlayer
window
showing
some
proceedings
in the U.S.
House of
Represent-
atives
broadcast
on C-SPAN.

On most operating systems and with most streaming video players, you can leave the video playing in the background while you continue to work in your word processor, spreadsheet, or other applications. Just be aware that any operation that really ties up your computer (modifying a large graphic in Photoshop, for example, or launching several programs at once) may interrupt the video playback temporarily. Once your computer has completed the operation, however, the video resumes automatically.

Where to tune your eyes

Due to complex licensing restrictions, there aren't very many television stations that re-broadcast their continuous video signals over the Internet. Instead, they post excerpts, individual broadcasts or shows, and other pieces of their regular broadcasts. However, that doesn't mean that good video content is scarce. In fact, there are all kinds of fascinating sites you can visit to watch streaming video on the Internet.

Here are my video site suggestions:

✔ **National Aeronautics and Space Administration (NASA,** `www.nasa.gov/ntv/ntvweb.html`**).** NASA provides some very cool video (as well as audio) of their space missions, live as the action is happening. Be aware that during a shuttle mission or other high-profile mission, especially right at the beginning, the video sites may be very busy, and you may not be able to load the image right away. If that happens, wait a while for the excitement to level off, then try again.

✔ **FasTV (**`www.fastv.com`**), Yahoo!Broadcast (**`www.broadcast.com/television/`**), and other video search sites.** These sites provide links to streaming video all over the Internet, one after the other after the other after the other... You can spend hours watching the news from almost every area of the world, and still not tap into the full potential of streaming video.

✔ **VH-1 and other music video sites (**`www.vh1.com`, `www.mtv.com`, **others).** If you like music videos and the extra dimension they add over just listening to the music, visit the Web site for your favorite music channel. They all include entire videos or clips from popular videos, usually in full stereo sound as well. Unfortunately, you have to pick each video you want to watch; none of these sites offers continuous streaming video without manual intervention to mimic watching them on television. Still, they're fun to watch, and they sound great with a high-speed connection.

✔ **ESPN, CNN/Sports Illustrated, and other sports flavor of the season sites (**`espn.go.com/broadcast/video.html`, `cnnsi.com/multimedia_central/`**, and others).** As with the music video sites, the sports sites don't just broadcast continuous content, such as games in progress. However, they do offer clips from games, interviews, commentators, and other individual streaming video clips that you may not be able to find anywhere else.

✔ **C-SPAN U.S. Government Coverage (**`www.cspan.org`**).** As they do on cable television networks, C-SPAN on the Internet provides live and archived coverage of just about everything that the U.S. Government is doing, including congressional votes, hearings, speeches, and conferences. If you want to stay informed about your elected officials, this is the site to visit.

✔ **CNN (**`www.cnn.com/videoselect/`**), MSNBC (**`www.msnbc.com/m/v/video_news.asp`**), Fox News (**`www.foxnews.com/video/`**) and other news sites.** If you have to know what's going on in the world, and hearing it on the radio or streaming audio isn't enough, tune in to any of the news Web sites for the latest footage.

✔ **International news video broadcasts, including CBC Canada at** `cbc.ca/video.html`**, BBC United Kingdom at** `www.bbc.co.uk`**, and others.** To break out of the bounds of the United States, visit some of the news sites from other countries. CBC posts many of its shows for viewing, while the BBC has a continuous live video feed 24-hours-a-day. Visit your favorite search page to find video news from other countries as well.

If this list doesn't satisfy your appetite for video content, you can always visit an Internet search site for more. For example, Yahoo! has a video search page with hundreds of streaming video sites and links at

```
digital.broadcast.com/digital/broadcast_video_tree.
```

Installing and Configuring Available Players

The three main standards currently fighting it out for the free audio and video streaming markets are

✔ **RealPlayer, from Real Networks** (`www.real.com`). This is the leader in the streaming audio and video market, and you'll find the most content in RealPlayer format. Real provides a free player as well as a commercial version with more features. RealPlayer is available for Mac OS, Windows 95 and higher, Solaris, several flavors of Linux, and some other UNIX-based operating systems.

✔ **QuickTime, from Apple Computer, Inc.** (`quicktime.apple.com`). With version 4.0, Apple added streaming video and audio support to their QuickTime multimedia software. The player is free and is included with all Mac OS releases in recent years, with an optional commercial upgrade that lets you create your own content in QuickTime format. QuickTime is available for Mac OS and Windows computers.

✔ **Windows Media Player, from Microsoft Corporation** (`www.microsoft.com/windows/mediaplayer/`). A version of Windows Media Player is included with recent releases of Microsoft Windows (98 and 2000), but newer versions may be available on Microsoft's Web site. The player is free for any Windows user to download. You can also find a Mac OS–compatible version that is free, although it currently lacks many of the features of the Windows version.

✔ **Streaming MP3 (many players).** As you can read in Chapter 6, MP3 is a popular format for downloading and listening to audio on the Internet. However, MP3 can also be streamed to your computer instead of downloaded, with all of the same benefits for streaming audio using other formats. Each of the three players mentioned here (RealPlayer, QuickTime, and Windows Media Player) can play streaming MP3s, and there are many other freeware and shareware players available (including WinAmp for Windows users, at `www.winamp.com` and AppleSource MP3 for Mac OS users at `applesource.hypermart.net/software/amp3`). For sources of streaming MP3s, see `www.radiomoi.com`, among others.

So which player should you use? The answer depends on what you want to watch and listen to. Although the majority of streaming audio and video sites support RealPlayer, many sites provide their content only in QuickTime or Windows Media Player format. Some sites even provide their content in several of the different formats, so users can choose which player they want.

I recommend installing all of the Big Three players (RealPlayer, QuickTime, and Windows Media Player), plus the MP3 player of your choice if you like it better. If you have all of these players installed, then when you click a link on a Web site to listen to some audio or watch some video, the appropriate player launches automatically, and you don't need to worry about which format the sound or video is in.

The following sections contain tips about downloading and installing each player.

RealPlayer

Real Networks makes their free RealPlayer Basic only after you're first "encouraged" to purchase and download their commercial RealPlayer Plus. Don't give up, though, and keep hunting for the links to the Basic version.

After you provide some information about yourself and download the RealPlayer Basic installer, follow the instructions they provide to install the player on your computer. Real Networks is by far the most inquisitive company of the three, and will ask for information about you plus your permission to send you alerts, news flashes, updates, offers, and other important information. You can accept or decline this process, but remember that none of it is required to use the RealPlayer. See Chapter 17 for useful tips on protecting your privacy on the Internet if the questions get too overwhelming.

Once the RealPlayer is installed, check out the Channels menu for a predefined collection of "special" broadcasters (that is, broadcasters who have come to some arrangement with Real Networks to appear on the Channels menu) that you can link to with a single menu command.

The Radio menu contains a list of broadcast categories you can use to narrow your choices for the streaming content you want to hear, such as Classical, Country, Rock, and so on. Many of the stations you'll find also include a video component as well.

Finally, the Favorites menu contains a tutorial for using the RealPlayer, and it's also where you can save links to streaming audio or video for future use. When you find something you like to hear or see, choose Add to Favorites from the Favorites menu to name it and save it in any category you'd like. You can also import and export folders or items on the Favorites menu, so you can share the Favorites among multiple computers or with friends and colleagues.

QuickTime

QuickTime is available from `quicktime.apple.com` for Windows or Mac OS, and you can download it easily after you provide a name and e-mail address. Beyond that, Apple doesn't request any information about you before you can start using the QuickTime player.

Once QuickTime is installed and you launch the QuickTime Player, you'll see an "encouragement" to upgrade to QuickTime Pro, which allows authoring of audio and video content and lets you modify existing QuickTime files. You can click the Later button, but expect to see this offer occasionally as you use QuickTime.

When the QuickTime Player is done launching, you'll see a new window appear with a list of preset audio and video stations, as shown in Figure 5-4.

Figure 5-4:
The default QuickTime Player window after launching.

Each of the icons represents a saved streaming audio or video site, identical to the list on QuickTime's Favorites menu.

When you find streaming audio or video you like, choose Add Favorite from the Favorites menu to save it for future use. Your favorite content is then added to the Favorites menu and appears as an icon in the lower panel of the QuickTime window.

Windows Media Player

To Microsoft's credit, the Windows Media Player is the least intrusive and requires the least pressure to upgrade anything of the three major players. You can download the Windows Media Player from www.microsoft.com/windows/mediaplayer without even providing your name, and there is no pro version to upgrade to. It's simply a free player.

Remember that the Windows Media Player is available for Windows and Mac OS, although the Mac OS version currently lacks features compared to the Windows version and is updated less frequently.

For Windows users, the Windows Media Player may already be installed, and you can make sure you're using the latest version by visiting the download site mentioned earlier or by using the Windows Update feature to let Microsoft's Web site determine if a new version is available for you. Launching the player opens the window shown in Figure 5-5.

Figure 5-5:
Default
Windows
Media
Player
window
after first
launching
the program.

Once you launch the player, you can click the Radio button to open windows-media.com to a radio station search site. Then click the Music button to open windowsmedia.com to a location where you can search for music by genre, and click the Media Guide button to see a collection of links and search sites that let you find any kind of streaming media that is available for the Windows Media Player.

Chapter 6

The Chips Are Alive with the Sound of Music

*O*ne of the great new developments made practical by the spread of high-speed connections is that people can trade recordings of music in minutes that are 3, 4, 5, even 10MB in size, a single one of which would have taken hours to download over a modem. You can build your own collection of high-quality, digital music on your computer without ever using your CD player.

The music files most often posted on the Internet are in a format called MP3, which allows the creators to compress music to much smaller sizes — such as taking a high-quality recording weighing in at 50MB and packing it into a more portable 4MB — without losing very much in the process.

Most of the music published anywhere in the world is protected by international copyright laws. Copying music from one medium (such as a CD) to another for your own listening is often allowed under the law, but copying music to give or sell to others is usually illegal. If the musical artists give permission to distribute their music, you're fine to make and trade copies, but you need to make sure of the rules before you start copying and trading songs. Check with the artists, the music publisher, and the laws in your area before getting into the music trading scene.

What the Heck Is an MP3?

By far the most popular format in which you'll find music on the Internet is called *MP3*, pronounced "emm-pee-three." MP3 (short for *MPEG-1 Audio Layer-3*) is a clever way to take huge quantities of sound, and convert it to much smaller sizes that people with broadband Internet access won't mind downloading.

A single three-minute song from a music CD would take up around 240MB of hard disk space, and would take even a broadband Internet user over an hour to download. The same song in MP3 format would take anywhere from 3–5MB, and take only a few minutes to download. The MP3 format accomplishes this magic by compressing the data, and discarding the parts of the sound that the human ear won't notice anyway. Turns out music's got a lot of that, so the files can get much smaller.

The MP3 files are created by capturing the digital sound from an audio CD, referred to as *ripping* it, and converting it using a special utility into the MP3 format. That file can then be copied, transmitted over the Internet, or uploaded to a portable MP3 player for listening on-the-go.

The great thing about MP3s is that you can avoid the tedious, impatient downloading process using modems. Because you have a high-speed Internet connection, you can have any song you want within minutes, not hours.

To play an MP3, you need the following:

- ✔ **An MP3 file with the music you want.** You can download these from MP3 Web sites, or using any of the multitude of music-sharing software packages available, such as Napster or Gnutella.

- ✔ **An MP3 player.** Software for playing MP3s is included with most major operating systems these days, including QuickTime for Mac OS computers and Windows Media Player for Windows, but we know some better players out there you can download for almost any computer.

- ✔ **Good speakers or headphones.** Heck, as far as your ears go, this stuff is CD-quality, so make sure you have the speakers or headphones to take advantage of it. A subwoofer wouldn't hurt, either.

That's it. The rest of this chapter talks about how to get or make your own MP3s and where to find players.

MP3? Is that all there is?

MP3 is definitely not the only way to listen to music on the Internet. Many radio stations that have always broadcast their signal over the airwaves have begun sending out their broadcast live over the Internet as *streaming audio*. There are even Internet-only stations that you can't even pick up on a radio.

Many of the music players mentioned in this chapter, including QuickTime, RealPlayer, and Windows Media Player, can play both MP3 files and play Internet broadcasts. That may be a factor when you decide which to install and use.

(As a side note, don't feel restricted to just one, either — they can all co-exist on the same computer without any conflicts.) See Chapter 5 for complete information on listening to and viewing streaming Internet broadcasts.

A Plethora of Music Players

As we mention in the introduction, most operating systems include an MP3 player (that can usually handle multiple other audio formats as well), but you can download better players from sites around the Internet.

What makes a better player? For one thing, *playlists*. A playlist is a list you can build in some players that lists the MP3 files you want to play, in the order you want to play them. Programs that let you create and save playlists give you your own customizable jukebox, or (to use another analogy), a way to create custom virtual CDs using the files on your hard drive. You could even think of playlists as the ability to create a virtual radio station on your computer, without commercials and where you're the DJ.

To show you what I mean, Figure 6-1 shows a sample playlist in a popular MP3 player:

Figure 6-1:
Assembling
a playlist in
WinAmp,
one of the
leading MP3
players
for the
Windows
operating
system.

Given the sheer number of players that support MP3 files, this section mainly deals with players that are included with your operating system or are included with other products and therefore appear on most people's computers. Other MP3 players are available, and I'll provide a list of some of them later in this chapter.

QuickTime

QuickTime from Apple Computer (www.apple.com/quicktime) has a number of features, one of which is the ability to play most common sound files, including MP3 files.

Yo, slip me some skin

One of the expressions you'll encounter a lot in dealing with MP3 players is the concept of skins. A skin is a customized user interface for a product that completely defines the look and feel of the software. For example, when you run an MP3 player, you'll see a certain arrangement of buttons, tools, menus, and window elements. However, with many MP3 players, you can download and install custom skins that change *everything* about the player's appearance.

Why would you want to change the appearance, when it doesn't change how you use the software or how well it performs? Just for superficial reasons, really: it just looks cool.

Taking a perfectly normal looking piece of software and adding a skin that makes everything look as though it's made of metal and chrome, or another skin that looks like everything's under water, can make the program a lot more interesting, and your computer's appearance much less boring.

You don't have to worry about any requirement to use skins. You're free to use the software in its default skin, exactly as it appears when you first install it. If you ever get bored, however, and the player supports skins, go to the software's Web site and start downloading some new looks for your MP3 player.

If you have a Macintosh computer purchased in the last couple of years, QuickTime is probably already installed on your computer. Look for a folder called Quicktime(tm) Folder in your main hard disk window, or in the Applications folder on your hard disk.

If you have a computer running Microsoft Windows, you can download the latest version of QuickTime at www.apple.com/quicktime/download. Once you have QuickTime installed, you'll see a QuickTime group in the Programs group on your Start menu.

For either operating system, follow these instructions to play an MP3 file:

1. **Open the QuickTime Player application (in the QuickTime Folder, on your desktop, or on the Windows Start menu).**

2. **Choose FileÍOpen, and locate the MP3 file you downloaded.**

3. **When QuickTime opens the MP3, as shown in Figure 6-2, press the spacebar once or click the Play button to begin playing the file.**

Although QuickTime 4 doesn't currently support playlists, choose Add Favorite from the Favorites menu to save a bookmark to the MP3 file for future use. Once you've added a file to the Favorites, you can just choose it from the Favorites menu to play the song.

Figure 6-2:
Loading an
MP3 file
plays it
immediately
— they
don't call it
QuickTime
for nothing.

RealPlayer and RealJukebox

Real Networks software, called RealPlayer, began its life as a streaming audio and video player (described in detail in Chapter 5). In recent versions, and most particularly in version 8, Real Networks has provided features to make RealPlayer, along with its companion product RealJukebox, an all-around multimedia machine. Of most interest to this chapter, of course, is the ability to play MP3 and other sound files.

RealPlayer is available for Mac OS, Windows, Linux, UNIX, and other operating systems and platforms. Although RealPlayer is included with numerous other software packages you may already have installed (Netscape Communicator, for example), you can find the latest version on Real Networks' Web site at www.real.com.

Real Player comes in two flavors: free, and not-so-free. All of the features discussed in this book are available in both versions, so you don't have to shell out money just to listen to songs on your computer. If you visit Real Networks' Web site, you'll find tons of links to their commercial version, and not-so-many links to the free version (also called the Basic version) of RealPlayer. Be persistent, however, and you'll have the free version installed before you know it. (After all, this *is* broadband, so it's bound to be a quick download.)

By the same token, you can use the companion product for the Windows version that enhances RealPlayer's ability to handle MP3 files, called RealJukebox. As with RealPlayer, we've got a free (Basic) version, and a version that will cost you a monthly fee to use. RealJukebox Basic adds features such as playlists to make playing collections of MP3 files convenient and, as the name implies, very jukebox-like.

When you install RealPlayer, it appears on your Start menu in the Programs folder (in Microsoft Windows) or on your hard disk in the RealPlayer folder (Macintosh). For Linux/UNIX/other platforms, see the documentation for where the software is installed.

For any operating system, follow these instructions to play an MP3 file:

1. **Open the RealPlayer application (in the RealPlayer folder, or on the Start menu).**

2. **Choose FileÍOpen, and locate the MP3 file you downloaded.**

3. **When RealPlayer opens the MP3, as shown in Figure 6-3, it should begin playing automatically. If it doesn't, click the Play button on the toolbar.**

Figure 6-3:
RealPlayer,
really
playing an
MP3 file.

If you drag a collection of MP3 files onto the open RealPlayer window, RealPlayer collects them as a temporary playlist and lets you work with the files to determine how they'll play back (continuous, shuffle, and so on), in which order, and so on by using the commands on the Play menu.

Using RealJukebox, you can locate and download songs, build and save custom playlists, and even view information about a CD, song, or artist from an online database of facts and figures, as shown in Figure 6-4.

WinAmp

One of the more popular Windows-only MP3 players is WinAmp (www.winamp.com), a free utility that provides lots of features and a wildly customizable interface.

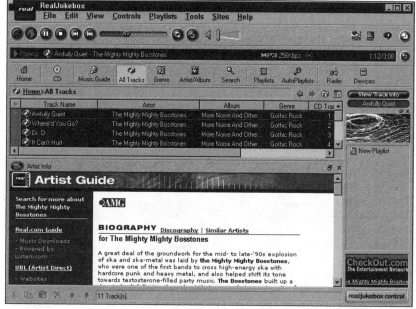

Figure 6-4:
Okay, so
there's no
place to
insert coins,
but here's
Real-
Jukebox.

WinAmp, which supports MP3 files, streaming audio (WinAmp Radio, as they call it) and audio CDs, among other music, prides itself on being quick and easy to load and use. It doesn't put too much strain on your computer's limited resources, such as memory or processing time. The main benefit of that is that if you keep WinAmp running in the background to play music, you won't notice any slowdown while working in other applications, and you won't find your whole system slowing down because you're out of free memory.

WinAmp has also taken the concept of skins, or the customizable user interface, to an extreme. Just check out the Skins menu command on WinAmp's main menu, which lets you browse any skins you may have already downloaded, or to go to the WinAmp Web site to look through and download any other skins you may be interested in. You can download custom skins that make WinAmp all but unusable, or you can download skins that improve the user interface and provide a clean, crisp way to play music. Of course, most of the hundreds of skins fall in-between those two extremes.

WinAmp is free, and comes in two versions: a complete version, and a WinAmp Lite version that has fewer features but still plays MP3 files flawlessly. A comparison chart on their Web site describes the differences between the two versions, but most people will never need more than the WinAmp Lite version.

To use WinAmp to play an MP3 file:

1. **Click the main WinAmp menu (in the upper-left corner of the WinAmp window, on the title bar) and choose Open.**

2. **From the Open menu that appears, choose File to play a single MP3 file, or Directory to select a directory containing more than one MP3.**

3. **Use the Open dialog box that appears to find the file or directory of files you want to hear, then click Open.**

   The file you select, or the first file in the directory you select, starts playing automatically. (See Figure 6-5.)

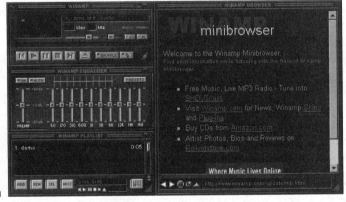

Figure 6-5:
The
WinAmp
window,
ready to
play some
music.

You can create a playlist at any time in WinAmp by clicking the Add button on the WinAmp Playlist window, then adding a file or directory.

Windows Media Player

Microsoft hasn't been ignoring the computer music market, and the evidence of that is their Windows Media Player version 7 or higher. Version 6.x has the ability to play MP3 and other music files, but starting with version 7, Windows Media Player (WMP) has many of the same features as the other more popular MP3 players, including playlists, streaming audio and video, radio station connections, and so on.

Note that contrary to its name, there is a Mac OS version of Windows Media Player. However, as of this writing the Mac OS version 6.3 supports only streaming audio and video, not MP3 or other sound files that reside on your computer. It's possible that Microsoft will add features comparable to the Windows version at some point in the future, so keep checking the Microsoft Web site if the other players described in this chapter don't suit your needs.

WMP is free, and is available from Microsoft's Web site at

`www.microsoft.com/windows/windowsmedia/`

Once installed, you can launch it by choosing Start⇨Programs⇨Accessories⇨ Windows Media Player, or by clicking the Windows Media Player icon on your taskbar.

To use WMP to play an MP3 file, follow these steps.

1. **In the main WMP window, choose Open from the File menu.**

2. **In the Open dialog box that appears, locate the MP3 file or files you want to play.**

   If you select more than one file in the Open dialog box (by control-clicking each one, or by shift-clicking a range), they'll be added to the playlist automatically.

   If you open a playlist from another program, including WinAmp, Windows Media Player imports the entire playlist for you to hear.

3. **Click Open when you have made your selection.**

   The file you selected, or the first file in the playlist, begins playing automatically, as shown in Figure 6-6.

Figure 6-6: The Windows Media Player window playing a song from a playlist.

Note that Windows Media Player supports skins, streaming audio and video, locating and downloading MP3 files automatically, and many other features. See the Windows Media Player Web site for more details.

Portable MP3 players

Instead of a software package that turns your $1,500 computer into a $40 walkaround stereo, why not buy a $150 unit that works like a $40 walkaround stereo? I'm referring here to portable MP3 players.

These devices, which are boxes about the size of a candy bar with head-phones attached, connect to your computer and accept MP3 files into memory. Once you've uploaded music files into the portable player, you can carry it with you and listen to the music you've downloaded wherever you are, as long as the batteries last.

Because the music resides completely in the portable player's memory, there are no moving parts at all in the player. No spinning disks and no tape mecha-nism of any kind. That means you can wear a portable MP3 player while doing jumping jacks in an earthquake without affecting the music playback at all.

The best part is that any MP3 you download from the Internet can be uploaded into the portable MP3 player. You can even copy your own music CDs into your computer (described later in this chapter) and then upload them into the portable player for on-the-go listening without skipping, jarring, or lost tracks.

The first portable MP3 player to hit the market was the Rio, from Diamond Multimedia, but others are available now from many of the major audio manufacturers.

Others

As long as MP3 files — and whichever music format succeeds MP3 — remain popular, you'll never run out of newer and more exciting programs and ver-sions of existing programs available for listening to them. Here are a few short lists of MP3 players available for Mac OS, Windows, and UNIX-like oper-ating systems.

Mac OS players

On a Macintosh, QuickTime and RealPlayer are only the most recent additions to the MP3 market. Here's a short list of some of the more popular players. For more options, visit a Macintosh search site such as www.versiontracker.com or hyperarchive.lcs.mit.edu, and enter MP3 in the search field.

✔ **Audion:** A shareware utility found at `www.panic.com/audion/`.

✔ **SoundApp:** Freeware and available in multiple languages. See `www-cs-students.stanford.edu/~franke/SoundApp/` for details.

✔ **AMP3:** A freeware utility with a healthy array of features, found at `www.applesource.f2s.com/software/amp3/`.

✔ **Player Pro:** A freeware utility from Quadmation that is probably overkill for playing MP3 files because of its high-end sound editing features. Still, it's free, supports playlists and other useful features, and it's available at `www.quadmation.com/pphome.htm`.

✔ **MacAST, formerly MacAMP:** Available in commercial and Lite versions, this is probably the most fully-featured MP3 player for the Mac. See `www.macast.com` for details.

✔ **SoundJam:** A product from Casady & Greene that comes in both a free and a commercial version. See `www.casadyg.com` or `www.soundjam.com` for details.

Windows players

As usual, MP3 has more players for Windows than you can shake a mouse at. Aside from the ones mentioned earlier in this chapter, virtually every one of the MP3 encoders and CD music capturing programs mentioned later in this chapter can be used to play MP3s. For a very short list of popular utilities, try these:

✔ **K-Jöfol** (`kjofol.org`): Free, and easy to use.

✔ **AudioActive** (`www.audioactive.com/download/index.html`): probably the simplest free MP3 player for Windows.

✔ **Lycos MP3 Player** (`music.lycos.com/mp3/sonique`): Kind of over-designed (as is WinAmp, for that matter), but useful and from a major search engine company, for whatever that's worth.

See your favorite search engine for a really long list of players. Fortunately, you have broadband, so downloading all 50 of them won't take you very long.

UNIX-like players

If you're using a UNIX-like operating system (Linux, BSD, Solaris, and so on) you can still find MP3 players available, and some may already be on your system (depending on the distribution you're using). KDE, GNOME, and other graphical interfaces for Linux come with MP3 players built-in, among others. However, if you're looking for a short list, see if any of these have been compiled for your operating system:

✔ **mpg123** (www.mpg123.de). It's free, and has all of the features necessary to listen to music. What more could you ask?

✔ **X Multimedia System** (www.xmms.org). This one's so fully-featured, you'll think you're running WinAmp. Supports playlists, skins, graphic equalizer, shoe shiner (well, not that last one).

✔ **FreeAmp** (www.freeamp.org). Also available for Windows, this MP3 player has all of the feature's you'll need, and it's free (as are the others in this list).

I've Got the Music In Me

Fine, now that you've got a dozen different music players installed on your computer, you're all set. Uh-oh, you still need some music to play. Fortunately, you've got two basic ways to fill up all available space on your hard drive with music from your favorite artists: importing the music from other sources (CDs, for example), and downloading it from the Internet.

Because this is a book on Internet access, we'll naturally address that option first.

Finding your muse

The best way to take advantage of your high-speed Internet connection is to download music. That's because text, Web pages, and even streaming audio don't come close to filling up the pipe leading the Internet to your home, but you can use up all of your bandwidth, bringing all other network traffic from your computer to a standstill, by downloading music files.

That said, the issue becomes where to find the music to download. Remember that at the beginning of this chapter you can see a warning to make sure you understand all of the copyright implications of any music you may find to download. Many musical artists just starting out are finding that making their music available on the Internet is a great way to gain attention and exposure, and so these artists are giving permission to distribute their music freely. Other artists who are well established may encourage copying their music for non-commercial use, such as the Grateful Dead or Phish. Be aware of the copyright issues involved before giving or getting other people's music.

You can visit several areas to download music on the Internet:

✔ **File sharing programs:** These include Napster, Macster, Gnutella, and others.

✔ **MP3-oriented Web sites:** MP3.com, emusic.com, CuteMX, and others.

You may also locate numerous trading Web sites, accessible through your favorite Internet search engine. If you're using a newsreader, such as the one built-in to Microsoft Outlook Express or Netscape Communicator, many of the binaries newsgroups carry MP3 files, such as alt.binaries.sounds.mp3, alt.binaries.mp3, and about 50 others. Figure 6-7 shows an example of a partial listing.

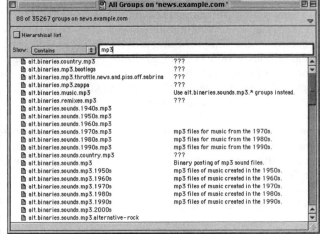

Figure 6-7: Some of the many MP3 newsgroups, as seen in a newsreader on the Mac OS.

The following sections describe how file sharing programs and Internet search sites work so you can find your own music and use up all of the bandwidth you're paying for, every single day.

Hello, my name is Sharon Sharealike

The most popular way to download music today involves joining a community and trading with your newfound friends. That's the model behind file sharing programs such as Napster/Macster/gnapster, SpinFrenzy, and Gnutella/Mactella and other clones. Here's how they work:

- ✔ **Napster, Scour, iMesh, and others:** With the Napster model, you run some software that connects you to a central file server. As soon as you launch the Napster software on your computer, you can search other users' computers for the music you want, and the other users can search your MP3 files for the music they want. Once you download something to your hard drive, that downloaded song can also be made available from your computer for others to find.

  You can find Napster and clones for many operating systems by visiting www.napster.com or opening any Web search engine and entering napster as your search term.

- ✔ **Macster and Rapster:** These two clients are is for Mac users at www.blackholemedia.com/macster or at www.macnews.com.br/overcaster/rapster_.html.

✔ **Gnutella and similar products:** The Gnutella (with a silent "G") model is different, because it has no central file server, and it's not limited to MP3 files. Instead, each Gnutella client searches the Internet for other Gnutella clients. When Gnutella finds the other clients on the Internet, it also finds whatever those clients are sharing, such as MP3 files, movies, graphics, documents, and so on. At the same time, your Gnutella client can begin sharing whichever files you may want others to have.

Because Gnutella has no central server, it has no central authority operating the service. When you launch Gnutella, you're automatically part of the Gnutella community, sharing and trading files with others, in a pretty anonymous way. You can find Gnutella and clones for just about any computer operating system at `www.gnutelliums.com`, `gnutella.wego.com` or by opening any Web search engine (such as Yahoo!, Google, and others) and entering gnutella as the search term.

Both services are free, and both services contain both copyright-restricted and copyrighted but freely-downloadable music. They all depend on users sharing their own files, even as they're searching the Internet for other people's files. It's a great big file cooperative.

To download files using a file-sharing Internet client, follow these steps.

1. **Visit the Web site of the service you want to use, and download the latest version of their software for your computer.**

2. **Launch the sharing software after it's installed as shown in Figure 6-8.**

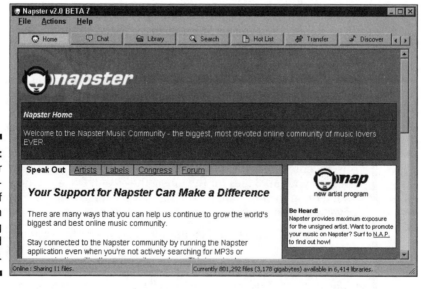

Figure 6-8:
Looking for that long-lost tune of your youth or a song released yesterday.

3. **Enter the search term for the music you want to hear as shown in Figure 6-9.**

   At this point, finding the music you want is like using a Web-based search engine such as Yahoo! or Lycos, but in this case, you're not searching Web pages, but other people's hard drives.

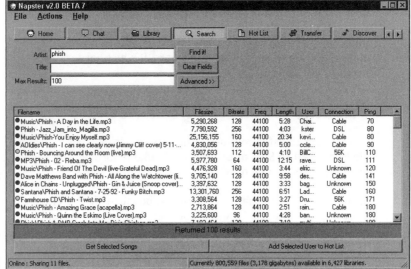

Figure 6-9:
Finding
what you're
looking for
at Napster.

4. **When all of the search results are listed, choose the one with the connection speed that most closely matches your own broadband connection, then download the file.**

   When people with 28.8 Kbps modems are sharing files, it takes forever to download the music, regardless of your broadband connection. You're much better off going for a copy that is shared by someone who's connected as fast as you are, or faster if necessary.

Seek and ye shall find

This may sound as if you've heard it before, but your Internet search site is your friend. Many of the major Internet search sites have jumped onto the music bandwagon, and have added special sections just for MP3 files.

Of course, numerous search sites have sprung up just for music. You'll find a huge collection of music at any of these sites:

✔ **Lycos** (`music.lycos.com`). Music, utilities, music, encoders, music, players, and music.

✔ **MP3.com** (`mp3.com`). The site with the most memorable link of all has a large selection of everything MP3-related, too.

> ✔ **The MP3 Place** (`www.mp3place.com`). Not only MP3 files, but news, software, and more.
>
> ✔ **Oth Net** (`www.oth.net`). This one's slightly different, in that it contains links to people's FTP sites and doesn't provide any of the music itself. Because of this, a great deal of legal and not-so-legal music appears here, and many of the links may be broken as sites come and go. They may have music you want when nobody else does, however.

Bear in mind that most of these sites are upstanding, legitimate organizations and won't carry anything that may be a copyright violation. That kind of thing is for the file sharing community described above (it's no more legal in the file sharing world than anywhere, it's just harder to control).

Putting a song in your heart

So you want to listen to music, but nobody else has already gone to the trouble to convert to MP3 or other downloadable format. The answer to your dilemma is that you'll need to go to the trouble yourself.

Fortunately, it's not that much trouble, because it's pretty easy to convert tracks on an audio CD to sound files on your computer, and from there to MP3 format. Some utilities even skip that intermediate step and go straight from CD to MP3.

Here's what you'll need to do:

1. **Find the music you want to encode in MP3, either on an Audio CD, or already available as a digital file on your hard disk, such as AIFF or WAV formats.**

2. **Launch a utility to copy the sounds (in digital format) from the CD to the hard drive (often called a *ripper*, and the process of copying audio CD tracks is called *ripping*).**

   Most operating systems don't let you simply drag a sound from the audio CD to a folder on your hard drive. Usually, some conversion is needed, and that conversion needs to copy every byte of the sound from the CD to the disk.

3. **Run a utility to convert the digital sounds from the huge CD format into the compact MP3 format (note that some of the rippers in step 2 can save directly to MP3, so this step would be done for you).**

   Remember, the MP3 format throws away a lot of sound that the human ear can't detect anyway, as well as compressing the sounds to fit into even smaller sizes. That can be time consuming, and requires a specific utility to accomplish.

4. **Listen to your MP3 files, or trade them with others (if copyright laws allow).**

All of the necessary tools are available on the Internet, and will work fine on any modern computer. Because even short songs contain a great deal of data, conversion from CD to MP3 can be time consuming, so be prepared to do a lot of nothing while you wait 15–30 minutes or longer for your computer to finish converting a single audio CD.

By now, you're probably an expert at using Internet search sites such as Yahoo.com or google.com to find elusive files on the Internet, but this list of the tools you need may shorten the search slightly.

Some audio CD software lets you export audio tracks to your computer, but the versions of CD players included with your Windows or Mac OS computer probably don't. Download the utilities in the next few sections instead.

Finding the utilities for the Mac

First, you need to get the audio from the CD to the Mac's hard drive.

The simplest way is a tiny utility called Track Thief, available at `homepage.mac.com/blgl/misc/` or any of the Mac search sites. Track Thief grabs the audio tracks from any CD and saves them as Audio Interchange File Format (AIFF) files on your hard drive. Track Thief lets you select a bunch of tracks to convert at once, which lets you leave the computer and do other things while the tracks are copying. Once it's done, you can convert the tracks to MP3 with other software.

You may also want to use Apple's QuickTime to save audio tracks. Open the QuickTime Player, insert an audio CD in the CD-ROM drive, then choose Import from the File menu. Use the Import dialog box to find the CD, then choose each track and click Convert to save it to disk. You'll need to repeat this step for each track on the CD.

Finally, you may be able to use your CD player software to transfer audio. The built-in Apple CD player doesn't provide this feature, but if you have FWB's CD-ROM Toolkit installed, their CDT Remote program lets you save audio tracks as AIFF files, one at a time.

Second, find a utility to encode AIFF files into MP3. As usual, take your pick between free and commercial alternatives.

The free way is to download a utility called mp3 encoder, at `www.dtek.chalmers.se/~d2linjo/mp3/mp3enc.html`. It's not fancy, but it does the trick. Read the documentation for a tip on finding a third-party file needed for the encoding process.

Another free option with few frills is a Macintosh port of a UNIX product, BladeEnc for the Mac. Find it at `www.helsinki.fi/~pkamppur/`.

A couple of other free options include DropMP3, available at `philippe.laval.free.fr/DropMP3/US/DropMP3_US.html`, and MusicMatch Jukebox (available in free and paid versions) at `www.musicmatch.com`.

Commercial products include Mpegger at `www.proteron.com/mpegger`, and SoundJam, mentioned earlier as an MP3 player, but it also does encoding. See Casady & Greene's Web site at `www.casadyg.com` or `www.soundjam.com` for details.

Finding the utilities for Windows

For Windows, life gets a little easier, because you've got the option between several utilities that combine the CD-copying feature with the MP3-conversion feature. Instead of downloading two separate utilities, you get to use one for everything.

For example, try any of these:

- ✔ CDCopy available at `www.cdcopy.sk`. CDCopy is free, with a few features (not related to creating MP3 files) that are enabled if you pay a fee.
- ✔ MusicMatch Jukebox (also available in free and paid versions) at `www.musicmatch.com`.
- ✔ CDex, also a free utility, available at `cdex.n3.net`.
- ✔ AudioGrabber, which can copy the files from audio CDs and can then use any of the free utilities out there (such as BladeEnc) to encode them as MP3. See `www.audiograbber.com-us.net` for details.

For encoding existing WAV or AIFF files into MP3 format, you could try some free options such as BladeEnc, available at `bladeenc.mp3.no`.

For just copying the songs from CD to your computer without using a built-in MP3 encoder, you could use ExactAudioCopy, which claims to be the best utility at preserving the sound quality without errors, available at `www.ExactAudioCopy.de`.

We know sooo many utilities available as commercial, shareware, and free-ware, that we'll just provide you with a few sites that list the ever-changing world of ripping and MP3-encoding utilities:

- ✔ **SoftSeek:** In particular, visit `www.softseek.com/Home_Family_and_Leisure/Music/Audio_Encoders_and_Utilities`.
- ✔ **Tucows:** This software search site contains huge quantities of every MP3 utility you might need. Open `www.tucows.com`, enter MP3 into the Search field, choose the version of Windows you use, then click Go.

- ✔ **Lycos:** The Lycos search site has special sections just for MP3 utilities. Visit music.lycos.com/mp3/ and click the Advanced link under Other Tools.

- ✔ **Google:** As with the other search sites, Google has a special section just for MP3 tools. Check out this lengthy link, or visit google.com and search for MP3: directory.google.com/Top/Arts/Music/Computers/MP3/Software/.

Any of the major Internet search sites will have links to CD rippers, MP3 encoders, and all-in-one tools such as the ones described above.

Finally converting the sounds

Once you have the tools in place, the steps to create MP3 files are pretty straightforward:

1. **Insert the audio CD into the CD-ROM drive of your computer, if you don't already have the audio on disk in WAV or AIFF format.**

2. **Run the ripping utility you've decided to use, and capture all of the audio tracks to your hard drive.**

   Note that this can take up an outrageous amount of disk space, hitting 300–600+ MB of room on your hard drive.

   If your ripping utility can include the track number, album name, or track title in the name of the saved audio files, be sure to enable that feature. Many utilities can tap into databases of CD information on the Internet (called CDDB, or CD Database) that contain all of this information, and can collect it for you automatically when you insert or extract audio from a CD.

3. **Start your MP3 encoder, and instruct it to encode the WAV or AIFF files you've just created. Allow plenty of time for this process, which can take anywhere from 50 to 100 percent of the playback time (that is, 1½ to 3 minutes to encode a 3-minute song).**

4. **Use the MP3 files as you would the music files you download from the Internet.**

   Once you have the files encoded, you can listen to them on the computer, copy them to other computers, upload them into portable MP3 players, and so on.

Chapter 7

Reaching Out to Touch Someone

In This Chapter

▶ Sending recordings of your voice to others over the Internet

▶ Carrying on live conversations with other people's computers

▶ Using your computer to call a regular telephone

*B*ack when you used a modem, you were either tying up the phone line, or people could reach you, but not both. Since most high-speed Internet connections are always connected, that opens up a world of ways you can reach others and they can reach you, without picking up the phone.

Back in the olden days, people would sometimes mail cassette tapes of their voices to friends and family instead of writing letters. You can accomplish this goal in a more modern way by sending a recording of your voice via e-mail.

If you're more interested in live conversations, there are two ways to speak with a real person over your high-speed Internet connection: your computer talking to the other person's computer and your computer talking to a regular telephone. Usually, these methods are free or significantly cheaper than long-distance fees through regular phone lines. This chapter covers the options for using the Internet to carry your voice to the world.

Speaking Out with Your High-Speed Internet Connection

As you may have noticed while downloading MP3 music files (which we cover in Chapter 6), sound can fill up (or *saturate*) your Internet connection faster than almost any other information you can download. About the only other information that is more of a bandwidth-hog than sound is video.

The higher the sound quality is, the more bandwidth it needs to travel over the Internet. However, thanks to data compression and other technological advances, you can carry on a conversation with someone over the Internet even at 56 Kbps modem speeds, although the quality may not be very good.

The slower your connection to the Internet, the more your conversation will contain unexpected pauses, skipped or lost words and sounds, and distortion. Fortunately, you have a high-speed connection to the Internet, so the problems you'll encounter will be limited to busy times of day or when the person on the other end has a slow connection.

The technology used to carry on a conversation over the Internet is called *Voice over IP*, which is usually abbreviated VoIP (and often pronounced "voyp" in conversation). The IP in VoIP refers to *Internet Protocol*, which is the networking protocol used to carry most data over today's public networks.

VoIP as a field is growing rapidly, and it has gone quickly from the realm of computer-to-computer conversations for computer enthusiasts to providing primary telephone service for people in their homes, without a visible computer anywhere in the connection. The quality generally doesn't match a standard telephone connection, although even that may have changed by the time this book is in your hands. (The standard telephone networks of the world are generally referred to as PSTN, *Public Switched Telephone Network*, or POTS, *Plain Old Telephone Service*.)

Why isn't the quality as good as PSTN? Mainly because of the way TCP/IP works. TCP/IP is a packet-based network protocol, which means that each piece of data is sent as a single packet to its destination. When you set up a VoIP call over the Internet, your voice is converted from a continuous stream of sound to a collection of separate packets, which are sent across the public (and often very busy) Internet to their destination. Some of the packets are delayed, or even lost, along the way. If you were transferring files, the computer on the other end would simply request that your computer send the lost packets again. However, when you're transferring voices, any packets that don't arrive in a short amount of time are no longer useful. For example, imagine if you say . For example, imagine if you said "Hi Mom, don't forget to send money" over the Internet, and the word "don't" gets dropped because of network congestion.

For this reason, VoIP requires that each packet of sound arrives as quickly as the rest of the packets in the same sound, or they're no longer useful and are discarded. Significant network congestion, therefore, can cause dropouts in the conversation that wouldn't occur over a PSTN connection.

VoIP is not the only way to send voice over the Internet. Companies often set up streaming audio and video servers (using QuickTime, or RealPlayer, or similar technologies) while other people make recordings of their voices available for download or in e-mail messages. Although the best option for interactive audio is VoIP, exchanging sounds via e-mail is useful for *nearly* interactive communication.

Adding Sounds to E-Mail

One of the easiest ways to get your voice to someone else on the Internet is to insert a recorded voice message into an e-mail message. For example, you might send a birthday greeting to a friend via e-mail, including a recording of you, your spouse, your children, and several pets rendering a birthday song in all its glory. If you want to be more dignified, you could send a snippet of dictation to a transcriptionist, a sample of a song you've written to a record producer, or the correct pronunciation of your name along with your resume to a prospective employer.

Many e-mail programs can record and insert sounds for you automatically, while others lack these features and require you to record the sound elsewhere and send it in the e-mail message as an attachment.

Either way, the recipient should be able to simply double-click the sound in the message to hear it immediately on receiving it.

Getting together what you need

To send a sound via e-mail, you'll simply need a computer with a microphone, or a sound-input port to which you can connect a microphone, and some sound recording software if none is built-in to your e-mail software.

Most PCs come with sound cards already installed that have microphone or sound-in ports on the back. If you don't already have a microphone, you can get one at any computer or home electronics store.

All Mac OS computers sold in at least the last eight years have microphone ports, although you may need to use the PlainTalk-compatible microphone included with your Macintosh to record sounds. If you don't have the microphone included with your computer, you can purchase a PlainTalk-compatible microphone from an authorized Apple dealer, or you can purchase a PlainTalk adapter from Griffin Technologies (`www.griffintechnology.com`) that allows you to use any standard microphone with your Macintosh. Note that PowerBook computers have tiny microphones built-in to the case, usually at the top of the screen, so check your owner's manual for details.

For sound recording software, you can often use the software built-in to your e-mail software, if it supports sending sounds in messages. Qualcomm's Eudora, for example (`www.eudora.com`), provides a small window in which you can record outgoing sounds.

However, if your e-mail software doesn't provide a sound-recording feature, you can always record the sound using the operating system's built-in utilities, and then attach or paste the sound into your message before sending.

The following sections describe how to record and send sounds in several operating systems and e-mail programs.

Sending sounds on a Mac OS computer

If your e-mail program doesn't provide a feature for recording sounds directly into a mail message, you'll need to record the sound separately, then include it in the message as an attachment. There are numerous third-party utilities you can use for sound input, but Apple includes a free utility called SimpleSound with every copy of the Mac OS after 8.5. Here's how to use SimpleSound to record a sound to send in an e-mail message.

1. **Open your Applications folder on your hard drive, and double-click the SimpleSound icon.**

   A window with your current list of alert sounds appears, on the assumption that you want to add a system sound. Close or ignore that window; we're creating a standalone sound.

2. **Choose File⇨New, and a dialog box similar to Figure 7-1 appears.**

Figure 7-1:
Recording
your best
singing
voice with
SimpleSound
box.

3. **Click the Record button, and then speak the message you want to send into the computer's microphone.**

4. **Click the Stop button when you are finished.**

5. **Click the Play button to verify that the sound is correct.**

6. **Choose Save As from the File menu, then enter a name and location for the sound in the dialog box that appears.**

Note that the sound you just created is in a Mac OS-specific sound format often referred to as an .SND file. You can use third-party utilities (including QuickTime Pro, if you have a license for that) to convert the sound to other formats for use on other operating systems, including:

- AIFF (Audio Interchange File Format, used on most operating systems)

- WAV (Windows audio files, used mainly on Windows-compatible systems but often readable on others as well)

- AU (UNIX audio format, but can be heard on most operating systems with add-on software)

Also, Windows users can open the file using Windows Media Player (if it is installed), provided they (or you) first add the .SND extension to the file.

7. **In your e-mail program, create a new mail message to send.**

8. **Specify the recipient, subject, and text of the message as usual, and include the sound you just created as a file attachment.**

9. **Send the message as usual.**

The recipient can either download the attachment and listen to it, or listen to it right there in the message, depending on the e-mail software being used.

Sending sounds using Windows 9x, NT, or 2000

If your e-mail program doesn't provide a feature for recording sounds directly into a mail message, you'll need to record the sound separately, then include it in the message as an attachment. Most versions of Windows include a simple utility called Sound Recorder that lets you record sounds and save them as a file. You can then send the sound file to any other user via e-mail, using these steps:

1. **On your Start menu, choose Programs⇨Accessories⇨ Entertainment (or Multimedia)⇨SoundRecorder.**

   A window similar to Figure 7-2 appears.

2. **Click the Record button, then speak the message you want to send into the computer's microphone.**

3. **Click the Stop button when you are finished.**

Figure 7-2:
The Sound
Recorder
window.

4. **Click the Play button to verify that the sound is correct.**

5. **Choose File⇨Save As, and then type a name and location for the sound in the dialog box that appears.**

Note that the sound you just created is in a Windows-specific sound format (WAV) that can be heard only by other Windows users without conversion. You may be able to use third-party utilities to convert the sound to other formats for use on other operating systems, including:

- AIFF (Audio Interchange File Format, used on most operating systems)

- WAV (Windows audio files, used mainly on Windows-compatible systems but often readable on others as well)

- AU (UNIX audio format, but can be heard on most operating systems with add-on software)

6. **In your e-mail program, create a new mail message to send.**

7. **Specify the recipient, subject, and text of the message as usual, and include the sound you just created as a file attachment.**

8. **Send the message as usual.**

The recipient can either download the attachment and listen to it, or listen to it right there in the message, depending on the e-mail software being used.

Sending sounds using Eudora (any platform)

Eudora includes some technology that Qualcomm (Eudora's publisher) calls PureVoice, but which is a format to encode sounds for rapid delivery using e-mail. If you're sending to another Eudora user, the recipient can simply double-click the sound to hear it. If the recipient doesn't use Eudora, they'll have to download the PureVoice application and plug-in from Qualcomm's Web site to hear the message.

To send a sound to someone using Eudora for e-mail, follow these steps.

1. **Create your e-mail message as usual, choosing Message⇨ New Message.**

2. **Address your message as usual, and type any text message you feel you'll need in addition to the sound you're attaching.**

3. **Choose Attach⇨PureVoice from the Message menu.**

   A recording window appears, as shown in Figure 7-3.

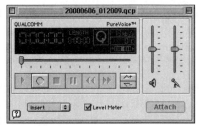

Figure 7-3: Using Eudora PureVoice for recording.

4. **Record your sound by clicking the Record button (the round dot), speaking or singing your message, then stop recording by clicking the Stop button (the square box).**

5. **Send your message as usual.**

When the message arrives, the recipient (using Eudora) can simply open the message to hear the voice message.

Using Your $2,500 Telephone

You spent thousands of dollars to purchase the best multimedia computer, carefully selecting the model with the best sound card, speakers, microphone, subwoofer, and other cool sound-related features. You purchased and set up the perfect high-speed Internet connection, spent hundreds getting connected, installing the hardware, configuring the software, and connecting to the Net. Now, you're ready for the ultimate test of your equipment and setup: emulating a $25.00 telephone.

Yes, just as you can use your CD-ROM drive to turn your $2,500 computer into a $150 stereo system, you can do similar surgery on your computer for *Internet telephony*, or using the Internet for telephone-like communications.

Of course, your computer is still good for other tasks at the same time you're talking on the phone, playing music CDs, or using it as a typewriter, which is the fun part, and the whole reason you paid so much for it to begin with. Acting like a cheap telephone is simply another cool thing your computer can do for you.

Bear in mind that a good computer with a 56 Kbps modem can handle a voice call over the Internet. Why, then, are we discussing voice over your high-speed Internet connection? Because the higher bandwidth provides a much better voice communication than a modem can. Higher bandwidth means you can fit a higher-quality (and therefore larger) sound into the same voice call. Higher quality means a clearer, crisper voice, with fewer delays or dropouts (brief blank spaces in the sound where the sound data has simply been lost). In other words, the faster your Internet connection, the better your voice calls sound.

With that, we'll discuss how to use your computer to call another computer.

Getting what you need

For any voice communication on your computer, you need most of the items discussed in this section.

If you're sharing your high-speed Internet connection using a NAT router or proxy server as we describe in Chapter 13, you may not be able to use many of the VoIP packages. NetMeeting and CuseeMe, for example, use the H.323 protocol, which is almost impossible to operate successfully through a NAT router. For other services, such as DialPad, you may have to change the configuration on your router to allow network traffic on a certain port to get to its destination. Usually, the makers of your NAT router can tell you which voice and conferencing packages work with their product, so check their Web site or documentation for details.

Sound input and output ports

Sound input ports (also called microphone or line-in ports) are built-in to most computers these days, either on sound cards that are bundled with your computer or built on to the motherboard of the computer. If you can find the sound-in and sound-out (speaker or headphone jack) ports on your computer, skip to the next section.

If you don't have one or both of these ports, however, you can purchase and install sound cards for most Windows-compatible PCs from many companies, such as Creative Technology (www.creative.com, makers of the SoundBlaster line of sound cards).

If you'd rather not open up your computer but it already has a Universal Serial Bus (USB) port, you can buy a USB-compatible microphone, speakers, or both from your local computer dealer or Web site.

Why get half duplex when you can have full?

The sound input connections on a computer are either *full duplex* or *half duplex* connections. These phrases indicate whether the connection lets you talk and listen at the same time (full duplex, like a standard telephone) or whether you have to stop talking to listen (half duplex, like a walkie-talkie or inexpensive speakerphones).

Half duplex sound cards may not be noticeable if you're simply recording sounds and playing CDs in your computer, but they're very annoying when you're trying to have a live conversation. Just as when you're using a cheap speakerphone, one

person in the conversation is always getting cut off and words drop out whenever the other person speaks.

If you're using a computer purchased in the last couple of years, the sound card is probably full duplex, but you can check the manufacturer's Web site to be sure. Sometimes, a card that operates in half duplex mode can be upgraded to full duplex by installing new driver software, so make sure you're using the latest drivers (again, on the manufacturer's Web site) before trying voice over the Internet.

On your mark, get headset, go!

Many computers with sound cards already installed also come with a microphone and speakers. Most modern laptops have one or two speakers and a tiny microphone hole built-in to their housing, letting you record and play sounds without lugging around any extra equipment.

There are several drawbacks to using the bundled equipment for voice communications:

- **Microphone quality.** The microphone that may be built-in to your computer may be adequate for voice communications, but the quality will improve with even a US $20 external microphone. Your local appliance or stereo store should be able to sell you an external microphone, but make sure the microphone's plug matches your computer's microphone-in socket.

- **Speaker quality, feedback, and echo.** The speakers are probably excellent quality, or at least better than a telephone's speaker. However, using external speakers can cause feedback or echoes while you're talking to people on your computer. This happens because the external speakers play the incoming sound into the room at large, where it is picked up by the microphone and re-broadcast. After a delay, it comes out the speakers again, only quieter, and this repeats until the sound can no longer be heard.

The solution to this problem is to bypass the external speakers while you're talking. You can do this by plugging a simple set of portable stereo headphones into the speaker jack on your computer (after unplugging the external speakers), or by installing a computer-compatible telephone headset, which gives you a pair of headphones and a boom microphone in the same unit. No change in your computer or software configuration is needed when you replace speakers with headphones, or speakers and microphones with headsets.

If you're going to be making occasional calls with your computer, you'll probably be fine with the bundled speakers and microphone, or with the built-in microphone and an external pair of headphones.

However, if you're planning on using the computer as a second telephone line, making numerous calls every day, you'll want to get a headset or even an earphone (microphone and speaker combined into a single unit that sits in your ear) such as those made by Jabra (at www.jabra.com).

Sign me up!

The final piece of your attempt to replace your cheap telephone with your expensive computer is signing up for an account, either with a computer-to-computer or a computer-to-telephone voice provider. In many cases, the same companies are providing both services. We list some of numerous sources of free and inexpensive voice services for Windows, Mac OS, and other computers.

Remember that "free" products and services on the Internet always have a hidden price. Much of the time, as in the case of most free Internet calling services described here, the price is your time and marketing data. In exchange for providing you with voice calls over the Internet, the companies display advertising on your screen while you use their service, and often track your movements around their Web pages and through the advertising to which you respond. None of this is necessarily a reason to avoid the free services; just remember the price you're paying, and make your own decisions regarding their value and whether the price is right.

If you don't find the services you want to use in the sections that follow, turn to your search engine of choice. There are companies entering this market all the time, with VoIP services becoming more and more popular as broadband becomes more and more popular.

Computer-to-computer communication

If you can get your voice into a computer, it stands to reason that others can hear it on their computers as well, provided you can just get it to them. Software companies are adding voice technology to almost every kind of product. Microsoft Word, for example, has been able to store voice notes since 1990 or so. Many e-mail programs can embed sounds, as described earlier in this chapter.

Those options, while useful for storing short voice notes, are a long way from interactive voice communication (also known as "talking"). For that, you need an Internet-ready program designed for interaction with another live person. Voice abilities are included in numerous kinds of Internet applications, including the following:

- ✔ Chat programs (AOL Instant Messenger, Yahoo! Messenger, and so on).

- ✔ Standalone voice programs, whose sole purpose in life is to provide computer-to-computer voice or video communication, such as

     ClearPhone (www.clearphone.net)

     iVisit (www.ivisit.com)

     SpeakFreely (www.speakfreely.org)

  In many cases, other interactive programs, such as chat programs, can use these stand-alone programs as voice helpers where they don't provide voice services themselves.

- ✔ Conference packages, such as Microsoft NetMeeting (www.microsoft. com) or White Plains Software's CuseeMe (www.cuseeme.com), which have voice communication in addition to their shared whiteboards, file exchange, text chat, and other features.

Voice programs that communicate directly with other computers are often free, or very inexpensive. For some computer-to-telephone packages, such as Net2Phone or NetSpeak's WebPhone, the companies charge you money to call a telephone but provide computer-to-computer calls for free.

Bear in mind that you can usually use a video conferencing program in voice-only mode, without a camera or other video input, to have conversations over the Internet. With these services, you're connected to a central server that connects you to other users, rather than connecting directly to the other users' computers, but the effect is the same.

Generally, you can use a voice program to speak only with other users of the same program. The only exception is when the product uses an accepted standard for carrying voice over the Internet. For example, Microsoft NetMeeting uses a standard called H.323 to carry voice, which is also used by White Pine Software's CuseeMe. NetMeeting users can talk to CuseeMe users, and vice-versa.

There are other standards for voice on the Internet, such as Real-time Transport Protocol (RTP). The documentation for your product or the developer's Web site may indicate the networking protocol used to carry your voice over the Internet as well as any other products that may be compatible with the software.

Computer-to-computer voice programs let you find people by logging on to a Web site or other server that contains a directory of available users, but when you connect to start talking, you're usually connecting directly from your computer to the other user's.

Typically, you fire up your voice software and connect to a central server that contains a directory of everyone who's currently logged on and ready to talk, as shown in Figure 7-4.

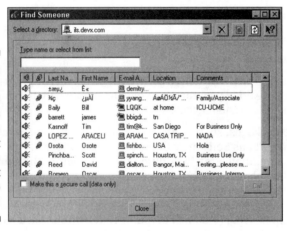

Figure 7-4:
Finding someone who's available doesn't guarantee they'll want to talk to you!

NetMeeting directories let you connect to other users with either NetMeeting or CuseeMe, while other voice-over-Internet applications provide other ways to connect to users. For example, in DialPad you can simply enter the account name of the person you want to talk to, and if that person's logged on and answers the call, you're connected.

To initiate a voice conversation over the Internet, you'll follow a set of steps similar to the following:

1. **Launch the voice software and log on to the central server, or another directory server if available.**

2. **Locate the person you want to talk to in the directory, or enter that person's name or unique number, just as you would a telephone number.**

3. **Try to connect. If the person's logged on, a connection is set up between your computer and the person you're trying to reach, and you can begin talking.**

At that point, it's just like a regular telephone call, and you can usually continue using your computer (to play Solitaire, same as when you're on the telephone other times) while you're on the phone.

Once you're used to the idea of calling another computer over the Internet, it's time to start calling everybody else over the Internet, too.

Computer-to-telephone communication

There are numerous services appearing on the market that let you speak into your computer and have the sound come out on a regular PSTN telephone, where the person you're calling doesn't even have to know you're on a computer or that your voice is traveling over the Internet. Stranger still, that call may be free, depending on the service you use.

For example, a company called DialPad (www.dialpad.com) has made its service available (currently for Windows users only, but that may change) so that you can call anywhere in the U.S. for free from your computer. How do they do it? They display advertising while you're using their product. Their theory is that the advertisers will pay more for your eyes watching their ads than you would pay to make telephone calls. Of course, we all know that ads are pretty easy to ignore, especially while you're talking on the telephone, but who are we to question the plans of advertising professionals? The DialPad dialing window is shown in Figure 7-5.

Other services, such as that provided by Net2Phone (again, Windows only at the moment), cost money to use, but even those often include advertisements.

Even the services that cost money, however, may provide calls to toll-free numbers (in area codes 800, 888, 877, and so on) for free. They may also provide free computer-to-computer calls as a way of enticing you into using the service for *all* of your calls, and you would start paying for calls to standard telephones.

Figure 7-5:
The DialPad
dialing
window.

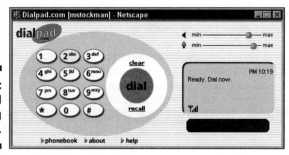

Computer-to-telephone calls fall into the following categories:

✔ You hear the caller through your computer speakers, and you talk into the computer's microphone. You can improve on this kind of connection by using a headset microphone instead of your computer's microphone and speakers, but you're still using the computer's sound card to talk.

✔ You install a card into your computer into which you can plug a standard telephone. The call goes out over the Internet through your computer, but you pick up the handset and dial the number as if the call is on a regular telephone. (This is different from a standard modem card in your computer. When your telephone "passes through" your standard modem today, the telephone is still using the phone line to make calls. With these computer-to-telephone cards, your phone plugs into a card, which connects to the Internet and provides a usable dialtone for your telephone to use, but the calls aren't carried by your local phone company.)

✔ You plug into your phone line a regular-looking telephone with an embedded computer that sets up its own Internet connection, with no additional equipment necessary. Your regular computer(and your broadband connection) doesn't even enter into the picture. The telephone uses your regular telephone line to place a local (and therefore free) call to an Internet provider, then uses a VoIP provider (such as Net2Phone) to make your long-distance calls at a low rate. Even better, self-contained phones are heading to the marketplace that will plug into your high-speed Internet connection instead of a phone line, providing VoIP long-distance that is fast, instantaneous, and inexpensive.

Whichever solution you use, here's how the call works (as illustrated in Figure 7-6):

1. **You install and launch the VoIP client software on your computer.**

2. **You log on to your account and dial the number you want to reach.**

3. **The VoIP service sends your call to a central telephone switch that provides the link between the Internet and land-based telephone lines.**

4. **Your call is sent to the standard telephone network, which switches it to the telephone number you entered.**

Setting up a call to a standard telephone line over the Internet can sound indistinguishable from a regular phone call — if your computer is fast, you use a good headset microphone, and you have a fast connection to the Internet. Even if your connection, computer, or speakers reduce the quality, you'll be able to make calls that are comparable to a speakerphone or cellular phone call.

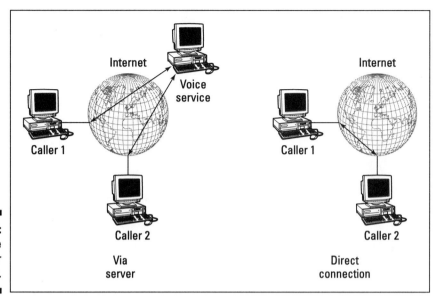

Figure 7-6:
Tracing the
path your
call takes.

Chapter 8

Live, from Your House: Using the Web Cam

ou may remember watching cartoons about the future on Saturday mornings during your childhood. Or maybe you still watch cartoons on Saturday mornings — who are we to judge?

In any event, one of the hallmarks of all such futuristic cartoons has always been the video phone. In this chapter and the next, you find out how today's technology this vision almost a reality . . . almost!

The Web Cam: Another Toy You'll Want to Buy

A Web cam is a camera that you attach directly to your computer. Unlike other kinds of cameras, these cameras don't use film. Instead, when you take a picture, the image you capture is saved directly into your camera's memory chips.

Where computers are concerned, there are two kinds of memory: ROM and RAM. ROM is where the people who built your computer and camera stored all of their most important programs. These are the programs without which your equipment cannot operate properly. For this reason, you are not allowed to ever write over software that is stored in ROM. This is why it's called Read Only Memory (ROM). On the other hand, the kind of memory that stores your pictures and other files you may create on your computer is called RAM. This stands for Random Access Memory, which is just a fancy way of saying that you are free to write to this memory.

Once your picture is saved to your camera's RAM, you may elect to send it on to your computer. In fact, as you see later in this chapter, many of the Web cams currently being manufactured don't even have any RAM of their own! Instead, they rely on a constant connection to your computer in order to save the images that they capture.

Once your images are on your computer, you may use them for a multitude of purposes such as adding them to e-mail or showing potential tourist the view from the porch of your bed and breakfast. This section describes some of these possibilities.

Livening up e-mails

It seems like friends and families are moving further and further apart nowadays. Perhaps you have parents living in a different state or province. Maybe you have friends living in completely different countries. Whatever the case may be, it's clear that instantaneous, long-distance communication is a necessity for great numbers of people today.

Fortunately, the Internet has made such communication commonplace. The Internet's killer app, e-mail, is the glue holding together many modern business and personal relationships.

But e-mail, for all its wonders, often lacks the excitement that accompanies actually seeing a friend or relative in person. At the end of the day, such messages are, after all, only words. With a digital camera, you may now include pictures in your e-mails. These may be photos of yourself, your house, your car, or anything else that you think the recipient of your message may be interested in seeing.

Some digital cameras default to taking pictures in the absolute best, clearest, most colorful format possible. Unfortunately, this is also usually the format that results in the largest file size. If you try to attach such a file to your e-mails, it may take a very long time to upload your messages — even with your fancy, new broadband Internet connection! For more information on this problem and how to resolve it, see the section on Troubleshooting later in this chapter.

Illustrating documents

You aren't limited to putting the pictures that you take with your new Web cam just into e-mails. You can also put them in word processing documents, presentations, and many other kinds of files that you may create.

Sharing live images

You may have wondered what the difference is between a digital camera and a Web cam. Well, you've already noticed that they have different names, so there's one thing for you!

The chief difference between a regular digital camera and a Web cam is simply how it's used. Calling a device a Web cam seems to imply that you have connected it in some way to the World Wide Web. This is different from an ordinary digital camera, which may or may not even be attached to a computer at any given point in time! This difference is illustrated in Figure 8-1.

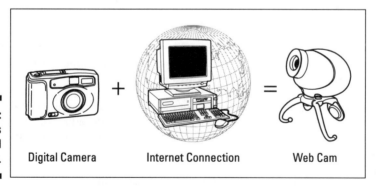

Figure 8-1:
Web cams
vs. digital
cameras.

Digital Camera   +   Internet Connection   =   Web Cam

By attaching a Web cam to the Internet, you gain the ability to instantly share live images of your current location with friends in completely different locations around the globe. Of course, if you live in a location that you would rather not let people know about — a top-secret government base for captured UFO's, for example — then you should carefully control the images that you share!

In the section on software later in this chapter, you find out all about setting up your camera to share images whenever, and only when, you want.

Keeping an eye on things

The flipside of being able to share live images across the Internet is being able to *see* live images across the Internet. This means that, theoretically, you can monitor any place that has an always on Internet connection from any place on the globe.

There are many examples on the Internet of people who have already done exactly this. Some of the better ones include

- http://www.adlerplanetarium.org/skyeye — images of the Chicago skyline

- http://www.videoranch.com/html/cam.html — images of former-Monkee Michael Nesmith's New Mexico ranch

- http://www.educe.com/tower/tower.jpg — pictures from the top of Tokyo tower

- http://www.ireland.com/dublin/visitor/live_view/index.htm — constantly updated view of a bridge in Dublin, Ireland

- http://www.kremlinkam.com — keep an eye on the Kremlin 24 hours a day

Besides watching the images that other people have made available to you, you may like to make images available to yourself from remote locations. For example, you may like to install a Web cam at your home or office and check it occasionally while you're away to see what goes on when you're gone.

Keep in mind that possible does not mean legal. In many countries, photographing people without their knowledge is considered a breech of their right to privacy. Consult a lawyer in your area before attempting any such covert surveillance.

Some reasons why you may consider this surveillance:

- Verify that appropriate care is being given to dependents

- Check to see if janitors are really cleaning after hours

- Making sure your employees don't throw parties in your absence

Videoconferencing

At the start of this chapter, we mentioned the futuristic dream of holding conversations over the telephone in which you could actually see the person on the other end of the line. With a broadband Internet connection and a Web cam, you can come reasonably close to achieving this goal. We discuss this at great length in Chapter 9.

Peeking under the Hood

Before we delve into the many varieties of digital cameras that you can use for Web cams, it seems like a good idea to tell you a bit about how they work in general. After all, most piloting students spend time learning all about the physics of flight before they are ever allowed to climb in a cockpit.

To begin with, all digital cameras have a lens in front that captures light rays from their surroundings. Most cameras have lenses that only capture light rays from directly in front of the camera. Some new digital cameras can actually capture pictures in 360 degrees!

After the light rays are inside the camera, the lens focuses them on a chip at the back of the camera that is extremely sensitive to light. Whenever light hits this chip, it generates electrical impulses. Depending on the exact color and brightness of each ray, these impulses vary in intensity and duration. Figure 8-2 illustrates this process.

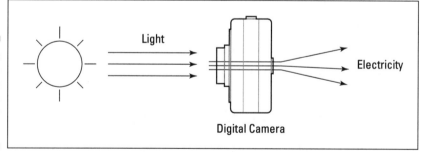

Figure 8-2:
Your Web cam turns light into electrical impulses.

Light

Electricity

Digital Camera

The software stored on the ROM inside of your digital camera understands these electrical impulses and is able to translate them. On the other hand, the computer to which your computer is or soon will be attached hasn't the slightest idea what they mean. For this reason, your camera translates the impulses into a series of binary signals that your computer can understand.

TWAIN is the name of the standard language that digital cameras and scanners use to talk to computers and other devices. Such big-name companies as Kodak, Xerox, and Adobe (just to name a few) have all endorsed its use for this purpose. Interestingly enough, TWAIN isn't an acronym. It doesn't stand for anything. It just is.

Once your camera has translated all of these impulses into a form that your computer can understand, it does one of three things with this information:

- ✔ Sends it down a cable connected to your computer
- ✔ Stores it in its own RAM memory chips
- ✔ Stores it onto a floppy disk

As you see in the next section, the more expensive the camera, the more of these options it supports!

A Web Cam for All Seasons

There are many different kinds of digital cameras available. Some of these support a wide range of features for every conceivable need or requirement. Others offer a reduced set of options in exchange for greater affordability. Ranked from cheapest and most limited to most expensive yet also most useful, your options are

- ✔ Internet-specific cameras
- ✔ Affordable multi-purpose cameras
- ✔ Expensive multi-purpose cameras

Internet-specific cameras

At the most affordable end of the spectrum are the cameras that are sold specifically for the purpose of capturing live images for transfer over the Internet. Some of the best-known current models of Internet cameras are

- ✔ Intel PC Cameras
- ✔ Umax Astra 1000

You can usually recognize these products by a few specific features.

No internal storage

In the previous section, we mentioned that some cameras store images on RAM chips, while others store them on floppy disks. Digital cameras that are made specifically for use with the Internet tend not to store their images themselves at all. This is because once they capture an image, they pass it immediately along the cable connecting them to your computer.

Once the image gets to your computer, you have several options for what to do with it. You may elect to store it on your local hard drive for remote access by other computers. Alternately, you may use software designed to immediately forward the image onto another computer on the Internet for use in a Web page or similar Internet site.

The primary benefit to this design is the lower cost of the final product. RAM and floppy drives are the most expensive part of many of the other cameras you check out in this section.

Fixed focus lens

Most of the cameras with which most people are familiar can be focused at various distances from the person taking the picture. For example, you can zoom in with most cameras to make distant objects appear much closer. In contrast, you can zoom out for situations where you need to get more of a certain image — such as the Grand Canyon — into a picture than is possible at your current distance. See Figures 8-3 and 8-4 for illustrations of zooming.

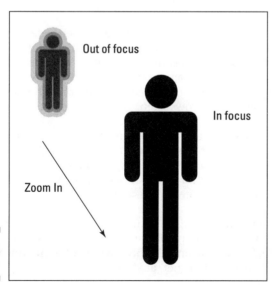

Out of focus

In focus

Zoom In

Figure 8-3:
Zooming in.

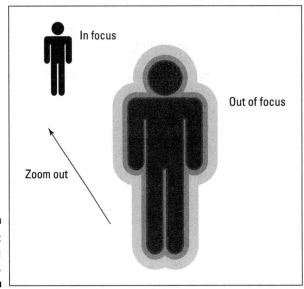

Figure 8-4:
Zooming
out.

Most of the cameras that are manufactured specifically for Internet use, however, don't allow you to zoom in or out. Instead, they provide a certain pre-set focus at a specific distance from the camera lens. You can still see objects that are closer or further than this distance, but with less clarity.

Low resolution

The resolution of a device, such as your computer screen, refers to how many little dots are crammed together on its surface to make it function. When you first bought your computer monitor, you may remember someone saying that it was 1024 x 768, for example. This was just their way of saying that there are exactly 786432 dots (or *pixels*) on your computer screen, arranged in 1024 columns of 768 rows each.

The chip inside of your camera that receives the light rays also has a certain number of dots on it. Each one of these dots is a separate light-receiver that is capable of generating a distinct message for your computer. The more of these dots that there are, the better the quality of the image your camera can produce. This is known as your camera's resolution.

Most of the Internet-only cameras have relatively low resolutions in comparison to some of the other kinds of digital cameras that are available. This is usually all right, though, because images with high resolution typically take too long to transfer across the Internet, anyhow.

You should, however, bear this point in mind before you use any of the pictures taken by such a camera in a document or presentation where the images must appear top-notch. If this is the purpose for your new digital camera, then you should seriously consider investing in one of the models described in the next section.

Multi-purpose digital cameras

All of the cameras discussed in this book are capable of capturing images for use with your new broadband Internet connection. Some of them, however, have capabilities that make them desirable for other purposes as well. Digital cameras of this variety tend to be priced at two levels.

For mere mortals

The first, and most affordable, kind of multi-purpose digital camera tends to provide functionality best described as a regular camera, minus the film. Two of the best-known cameras of this variety include:

- Kodak DC280
- Epson PhotoPC 700

These cameras almost always provide some mechanism for storing the images you gather internally, rather than requiring that they be sent immediately to an attached computer. Typically, these computers don't feature floppy disks or any kind of permanent storage for your images. More likely, they have some amount of RAM within them that allows you to store a certain number of images.

The problem with this approach is that eventually you will take more pictures than your camera is capable of holding. At this point, you must either transfer some pictures to your computer via a cable connection or erase them.

These cameras do have benefits, however. All of these cameras allow you to adjust their focus for objects that are further or closer to you. Also, their resolution tends to be much better than that of Internet-only devices.

For the filthy rich

At the absolute opposite other end of the spectrum from the Internet-only cameras are the top-of-the-line digital cameras. A good sampling of these cameras is

- Sony Mavica MVC-FD81
- Nikon CoolPix 900s
- Nikon D-1

The resolution on these cameras is comparable to that of a regular film camera. In actuality, because a regular camera doesn't even use pixels, you could never get a digital camera that creates pictures 100 percent as good as a traditional camera. You can, however, get a camera that comes so close that the unaided human eye cannot tell the difference. Now, that's good!

Some of these cameras, such as the Mavica, also support the creation of short videos with motion and sound. Think of how happy grandma will be when not only is she able to see her new baby in your e-mail but also watch it move and cry. (Crying, most likely, from the stress of having digital movies taken of it at every turn!)

Top-of-the-line digital cameras almost always support some kind of removable media for saving your pictures. This way you can take as many pictures as you like and, when your diskette is full, you can simply pop in a new one and continue taking pictures!

You may think to yourself that having a floppy disk built into your digital camera doesn't sound like that much of an advantage. After all, you could just upload all of your pictures to your computer whenever your camera's internal storage fills up. This is true, but fails to take one vital fact into account: time is money. Uploading images from your camera to your computer via a normal cable connection takes significant amounts of time. If these pictures were on a floppy, all you'd have to do is pop it out of your camera and into your computer. This is much, much faster and easier!

The final benefit that you typically see in high-end digital cameras that you don't see anywhere else is digital effects. Using these tools, you can make an otherwise normal image look like a film negative or an oil painting with just the press of a button. You can also do useful things with these effects, like removing blur and the famous red eye problem!

Setting Up Your Web Cam

Now that you know all about the different kinds of Web cams that are available to you, you get to choose which one you want to buy. There's no way we can tell you exactly which camera is best for your particular circumstances, but when you've made the purchase, we can even give you some advice about setting up your hardware and software!

Hardware

The hardware for your new Web cam is the simpler part of the equation to setup. Typically, the camera itself ships as a single piece, so you shouldn't need to do any pre-assembly.

You may have to decide between multiple power sources for your new camera. Typical power sources include:

- Disposable batteries
- Rechargeable batteries
- Power adapters

The advantage to using batteries is that when you want to take your camera with you, all you have to do is pick it up and go. Disposable batteries tend to be cheaper than rechargeable batteries initially. However, as you go through battery after battery, rechargeables tend to pay for themselves.

A power adapter is a good source of continual power for your camera, and it's the only source you should use if you intend to transmit pictures continually across the Internet.

 UPS, unless your electric company is perfect . . . and nobody is perfect! If you don't already have one, you should consider investing in an Uninterruptible Power Supply (UPS) for your computer hardware. A UPS is a device into which you plug all of your equipment's power cables. You then plug the UPS into a power outlet. Figure 8-5 illustrates the function of a UPS.

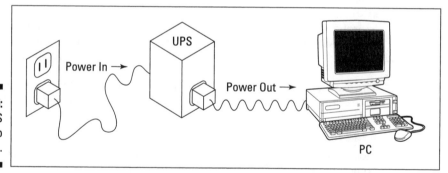

Figure 8-5: Using a UPS to stop surges.

The UPS features a short battery that kicks in if the power from your outlet should fail. This won't keep your system running long, but does give you a chance to shut it all down properly, rather than just having it die suddenly. Most UPSs also feature surge suppression to protect your computer from sudden increases in the power coming out of your outlets.

Once you have your camera unpacked and supplied with power, you are ready to connect it to your computer. Almost all digital cameras make this connection by way of a short cable running from your camera to a port on your computer. This port may either be a traditional serial or parallel port, or it may be a modern USB port.

You should consider the ports that are still available on your computer when making your purchase decision for your new Web cam. If your computer has a USB port free, but your printer is plugged into your parallel port, then you should get a USB Web cam so that you can use it at the same time as your printer. On the other hand, if you have no ports free at all on your computer, then you may consider buying a board for your computer that can provide you with additional ports.

Once you have connected your camera to your computer, you are ready to begin installing the software needed to operate it!

Installing the software

Your camera should come packaged along with some software, either on floppy or compact disk. While some of the applications contained on this media may be optional, you can be just about certain that at least some of it's absolutely required. The software that is absolutely required is known as a driver.

A driver is a piece of software that sits between a given piece of hardware and your operating system. Its function is to translate between the special language spoken by your hardware and the language of your operating system. In the case of your camera, you saw earlier that this special language is probably the TWAIN protocol for image transfer. Without a driver to translate TWAIN into something that your operating system can understand, it would be impossible for your computer to talk to your digital camera!

The exact steps required to setup software vary widely from one digital camera to the next. There are certain principals, however, that always hold true.

Read the README

Most software distributions include a special text file called README.TXT or something similar. This file is usually found at the very top level of the software's folders and directories and is (hopefully) somewhat small. You can, and should, open this file for viewing in your favorite text editor.

README files traditionally include any information about your camera that has:

- ✔ Changed since the manual was printed
- ✔ Been discovered since the manual was printed
- ✔ Been accidentally left out of the manual

Many people skip the README file figuring "If it was anything important, it would be in the manual." This is very, very wrong. Not morally wrong, mind you — I mean, we aren't suggesting it's sinful or anything. it's just a mistake that could lead to absolute disaster.

Manuals are usually printed well in advance of a product being 100 percent finished and tested. Quality assurance people tend to discover lots of little bugs and eccentricities between the time that the manual is printed and when the camera actually ships for purchasing. These kinds of things can drive you crazy unless you know about them.

Fish for updates

Companies don't usually stop working on the software for their products simply because they have already released it to the public. Instead, they use the feedback that they get from the people who buy their cameras to improve their software. Only in the case of the worst software problems will they mail new versions of their software to existing customers.

Instead, new version of existing software are usually posted to the company's Web site for free download by registered customers. This is why you should always do two things when installing a new digital camera:

- ✔ Register your product
- ✔ Visit the camera company's Web site

Visiting the Web site enables you to find the latest versions of whatever software is included with your camera. By registering, you can make sure that you will always be allowed to download it!

When in doubt, reboot!

The software required by most digital cameras requires a system restart in order to take effect. This is because most computers take a snapshot (called a System Inventory or System Profile) of all connected hardware when they are first powered-on. Any change to this collection of hardware may or may not be detected immediately by the operating system.

By restarting your computer, you give it the opportunity to re-compile its list of connected hardware. A restart guarantees that the computer notices the addition of your digital camera and/or the removal of whatever piece of hardware was previously attached to its port.

The development of technologies such as Microsoft's Plug'N'Play architecture has greatly reduced the need to restart your computer whenever adding or removing a new piece of hardware. Nonetheless, this can be a useful trick to know about if you experience problems during initial setup of your digital camera.

Putting Your Pictures on the Web

Once you have your camera set up and operational, you may want to start sharing your pictures over the Internet. After all, that's why you're reading about digital cameras in a book about high-speed connections to the Internet!

One picture at a time

Sending an e-mail to a friend or a relative is much more interesting when you can include a picture or two along with your text. The trick to doing this generally involves including your picture(s) as a file attachment.

Under many e-mail programs, including Microsoft Outlook, the paperclip icon has come to represent a file attachment. Paperclips are used to attach things to ordinary messages, so why not e-mails? By clicking the paperclip button, you can generally begin the process of attaching your picture(s) to the e-mail you're sending.

Once you have located the Attach File command in your e-mail program, you should be allowed to select the file on your local hard disk containing the picture(s) that you want to include. Once you have selected this file, the image may actually become visible within the window where you have typed the text of your message.

Always on = always visible

Many people like the idea of living in a fishbowl by leaving their digital cameras constantly on and constantly transmitting live pictures to the Internet. If this sounds like your cup of tea, then there are many paths you can follow.

Scheduled picture uploads

If you have space on a Web or FTP server at another location, then you may elect to have your camera take pictures at a given pre-set interval — every 10 minutes, for example. Software may be included with your camera that can automatically upload these pictures to a pre-defined Web or FTP site.

If such software was not included with your camera, then you may download and/or purchase it separately from several different vendors. Here is a short list of Web sites offering such software to get you started:

- http://www.thegeek.com/chillcam
- http://www.camcatcher.com
- http://members.xoom.com/LG_developer

Motion-sensitive picture uploads

A slightly more sophisticated variation on the above approach is to take and transfer pictures only when something is happening. In the case of digital cameras, something happening most probably means motion of some kind.

The list of cameras that currently support motion-sensitive capture is rather restrictive. Make sure that your capture software supports your camera before you buy it!

The current de facto standard in motion-sensitive capture software is a program called *Gotcha* from Prescient Systems. You can download a free trial from their Web site at `http://www.gotchanow.com`.

Running your own web server

If you decide to run a Web or FTP server on your own computer, then you can save the trouble of having to upload your pictures across the Internet every time a new one is captured. Instead, your software can simply drop the pictures it creates into a Web-accessible folder on your local computer. This has the notable advantages of:

- ✔ Greatly increasing your choice of cameras
- ✔ Significantly reducing the cost of software

For more information on running your own web server, see the chapter all about this topic later on in this book!

Troubleshooting

The course of true love never did run smooth — and neither did setting up a Web cam. Fortunately, knowing about some of the more common pitfalls can steer you clear of about 90 percent of the problems you are likely to face.

Hardware checklist

The hardware issues are usually the simplest to sort out. Verify the following:

- ✔ Is the camera plugged into the wall for power?
- ✔ Are the camera's batteries run down?
- ✔ Is the camera plugged into the computer?

✔ Is the camera turned on?

✔ Is the diskette or other storage filled to capacity?

✔ Is the lens cap still on?

Putting your big, fat pictures on a diet

Sometimes, the pictures taken by digital cameras can take up much more space on your disk than they should. For example, a typical graphic on the World Wide Web is less than 100k. Conversely, a top-quality image taken by a top-of-the-line digital camera can often exceed 1MB in size! What's wrong with this picture? (If you can forgive the pun!)

The first problem here may be that the quality of the image being captured is just too good. Yes, you read that correctly — it's just too good. Recall our discussion of pixels from earlier in the chapter. A picture captured at 1024 x 768 pixels is much clearer than one at 640 x 480. However, it also takes up almost twice as much storage space.

The number of colors used in your image can also cause picture bloat. In general, the more colors supported, the larger the resulting file size. The absolute smallest pictures are taken in black and white. However, this may not be a sacrifice that you feel comfortable making just to get your pictures smaller.

You can often reduce the size of your images simply by converting them to a more efficient file format. If you have a picture on BMP format, for example, converting it to either GIF or JPG format can result in a file of as little as 1 percent its former size! For more information about various file formats and how to convert between them, consult the experts at `http://www.jpeg.org`.

Call tech support anything you like — just call them!

Asking for help is always a good last resort. The only problem is that sometimes it costs money. The best time to address this issue is while you are still deciding what digital camera to buy. Don't be afraid to ask if the camera comes with free technical support.

When you phone technical support, they are likely ask if you have registered your product yet. They may also want to know your name and the serial number on your Web cam. Having this information readily available should aid in getting your problem resolved more quickly.

Chapter 9

Visiting Mom in a Virtual World

*W*hen was the last time you saw your mother (father, sister, brother, second cousin, once-removed) anyway? How many times have you leaned over a speakerphone for a meeting trying to figure out who said something when you can't see the folks in the other room? Thanks to your broadband Internet connection and the surrounding techno-gadget craze, you can see and be seen by those you know. Soon, we'll all be making virtual visits to Mom or the office without leaving home. For now, we work with new technology to at least get in the door.

In Chapter 8, you can find out how to attach a digital camera to your computer. These nifty devices allow you to share pictures over the Internet using such traditional applications as e-mail. In this chapter, we turn our attention to videoconferencing over your broadband Internet connection, tips for maximizing the available technology, and the things you need to see and be seen.

Tuning Up for Your Video Conference

The ideal with video conferencing is to have a conversation with someone 4,000 miles away that is every bit as life-like as if they were in the same room with you. This scenario would mean video that is at least as good-looking as a television — even if the person you are talking to isn't ready for prime time! Also, you'd like to be able to hear the person that you're talking to clearly and without much lag between when they say something and when you hear it, otherwise known as the audio quality of your conversation.

A number of elements factor in for evaluating and improving modern video conferencing. Some of the most important are

- ✔ The speed of your connection
- ✔ The quality of your equipment
- ✔ The speed of your friend's connection
- ✔ The quality of your friend's equipment

The speed of your connection

Chances are you bought your broadband connection to the Internet because you already had some experience with slower alternatives. In this case, you are already familiar with the hours that it can take to download a simple utility from a free software Web site. Or, maybe you were sick of waiting for changes to your Web site to go across the Internet.

Whatever your past experiences, it should come as no surprise to you by this point that a faster connection to the Internet usually means a much better experience with any kind of transfer. Videoconferencing is the perfect case in point. If the kind of broadband you have chosen has limitation on the speed it provides either with upload or download, the conferencing is affected.

Most users tend to focus on the speed of their downstream when making their initial broadband purchasing decisions. If your broadband has a limited upstream, such as satellite access, then you might be able to *receive* audio and video just fine. Friends that chat with you, however, might have a very hard time receiving the audio and video that you transmit! Chapter 3 explains the limitations of satellite uploads.

The quality of your equipment

The hardware that comprises your videoconferencing setup can also undermine your conversations in a number of ways. A cheap microphone may not pick up all the sounds that you make while talking (or singing, or whatever else it is that you choose to do while on the Internet!). On the other hand, it might pick up the sound of your computer's fan and other machinery so well that your voice is all but drowned out.

The quality of your digital camera can also be a source of dissatisfaction. A cheap camera can have less-than-stellar results:

- ✔ Images look fuzzy because it isn't taking pictures at high enough resolutions.
- ✔ Your movements look jerky because it isn't taking pictures quickly enough.

Of course, the person you are chatting with might think you are jerky even if you have the best digital camera around. The authors of this book take no responsibility for the effects of a poor personality!

The speed of your friend's connection

Imagine this: you go out and buy a top-of-the-line multimedia computer and the fastest DSL connection that money can buy. What's your motivation? You've decided to make your dear mother happy by staying in touch via videoconferencing, even though you are living on a completely different continent.

When the time comes to try everything out for the first time, you find that she is able to hear you fine. You, on the other hand, are completely unable to hear her. Furthermore, neither of you can see each other. What's the problem here?

The problem may very well be that your mother's connection to the Internet is too slow to support videoconferencing. Makers of digital cameras and videoconferencing software are fond of asserting that their products work just fine with 56 Kbps telephone lines. This is, as Colonel Potter on *M.A.S.H.* would say, "Horse hockey!" Figure 9-1 shows the trouble spots.

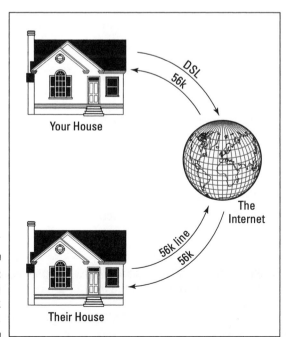

Figure 9-1: The weakest link in the chain.

Always remember, a video conference is only as strong as the weakest link in its chain. If you have a 640 Kbps connection to the Internet, but your friend has only a 56 Kbps connection — the fastest that you can exchange information is 56 Kbps!

The quality of your friend's equipment

Sometimes you may find yourself video conferencing with someone who has spent plenty on their Internet connection but then completely skimped on their computer system in every way possible. Many pieces of equipment can adversely affect video conferencing if they are underpowered. Some of these are

- ✔ CPUs that are too slow
- ✔ Cameras that have low resolutions or slow refresh rates
- ✔ Microphones that are insensitive or that don't filter noise
- ✔ Something that has too little RAM

You can usually tell when this is the source of your problems because you can chat with other people just fine. In these situations, all you can do is suggest in the nicest way possible that your friends upgrade their computers so that they can chat better with you. What better incentive could anyone need than that, right?

Getting Started

Besides your own computer you need four things in order to video conference (or show your live home movies) over the Internet:

- ✔ An Internet connection
- ✔ A Web cam
- ✔ A sound system for your computer
- ✔ The software or medium to show your video

We show you several varieties of Internet connections in this book. You may remember that the three most popular kinds of broadband connection are cable, DSL, and satellite access. For the best results with video conferencing, you should get the fastest connection available in your area that you can afford.

In Chapter 8, we show you all about digital cameras. You might remember from that discussion that a digital camera becomes a Web cam as soon as it's connected to a computer with an Internet connection. Using a digital camera, you can transfer live images from where you are to any other point on the Internet.

Being heard as well as seen

The principles and equipment you need to include audio along with your video are the same as working just with audio, as in Internet telephoning. You need these items to sound off:

- ✔ **Sound card:** Your computer probably has a built-in sound card, but if not, check out these sites:

    - http://www.creative.com

    - http://www.waveforce.com

    - http://www.digitalaudio.com

- ✔ **Microphone:** If your computer is relatively new, it probably has a small built-in microphone, or you can purchase a standalone microphone that fits your input jack. If you're interested only in showing silent footage, this piece is optional.

- ✔ **Speakers:** Many brands are available if your system didn't come with speakers. Just make sure they work with your sound card.

Chapter 7 gives you details on setting up an audio system good for conversations.

Choosing a medium

You can use your broadband connection for video in a number of ways besides video conferencing, such as publishing your home movies or a neighborhood tourist attraction on your Web page, which we discuss in Chapter 8. You can also send clips with e-mail or chat software, which we cover thoroughly in Chapter 10 in the section on Internet Relay Chat (IRC). For video conferencing, though, you need a client software package such as CUSeeMe. CUSeeMe also offers a package of software for putting voice and video on your Web page.

Using CUSeeMe

One of the oldest and most established true videoconferencing software packages is known as CUSeeMe (pronounced as "See you, see me" — if you are a Lionel Ritchie fan, this may have you humming "Say you, say me" for the next several hours). In this section, we show you how to get this package up and running.

Getting what you pay for

CUSeeMe and its premium version CUSeeMe Pro are not free software, which means you have to purchase a copy of the software in order to use it. One obvious place to make this purchase might be the manufacturer's Web site at

```
http://www.cuseemenetworks.com
```

If you already own a digital camera, then you will want to take a look at the CUSeeMe Pro software first. Using this, you can see and hear other people across the Internet, as well as make yourself seen and heard by them!

You may have wondered to yourself already, "What if I want to chat with someone who is using different software?" Well, you may or mayn't be able to, depending on whether or not their software is able to speak the same language as yours. The Internet standard for video conferencing is known as H.323 and is, indeed, used by CUSeeMe. If your friends' software also uses H.323, then you should be able to conference with them without problem.

Currently, the software for CUSeeMe is available for immediate download for under $100. Alternately, you can pay a little more to have the software mailed to you on CD. Table 9-1 outlines the pros and cons of either approach.

Table 9-1	Download versus CD	
Benefit	*Download*	*CD*
Immediate access and use	Yes	No
Backup copy of program	No	Yes
Returnability	No	Yes
Enjoyment	Yes	Yes

Software requirements

CUSeeMe Pro requires

- ✔ An Internet connection
- ✔ 10MB of hard drive space
- ✔ 166 MHz (or better) processor
- ✔ 64MB of RAM

If you want to do video and audio as well, you should also have:

- ✔ A digital camera attached to your computer
- ✔ A sound card, microphone, and speaker

If you don't want to do audio and video, then I strongly recommend that you use mIRC instead because it's free and provides you with everything except streaming video and audio.

CUSeeMe Cam Kit

For just a little bit extra, you can get a digital camera along with the CUSeeMe software. At the time of writing, the CUSeeMe Cam Kit was available for about $100. The immediate download option isn't available for this package because, after all, whoever heard of downloading a camera?

If you haven't already bought a camera or software, this might be just the right choice for you. Mind you, the quality of the camera included in this package isn't exactly top-of-the-line, but it's quite adequate for the intended purpose.

Just add water . . .

Once you buy the software, installing it should be fairly straightforward. At the time of writing, versions are available for both Windows and iMac (sorry, no Linux!). The CUSeeMe installation software needs to know the kind of camera you're using with it. So, have your camera attached to your computer and ready and follow these steps:

1. **If downloaded, unpack the file archive.**

   This file archive usually comes as a self-extracting executable. So, you can just unpack it by double-clicking.

2. **Run the setup program.**

   When you unpack the archive, find and double-click the setup program to run the installation wizard.

3. **When the installation finishes, restart your computer.**

   This gives your operating system a chance to finalize all of the changes requested by the installation software as it ran.

4. **Begin chatting.**

Chatting the night away

After you install the software, you are ready to begin video conferencing on the Internet. When you first start the software, notice that it consists of two windows: a phone book and a conference room.

The phone book

The phone book contains a list of contacts. Most of your conversations will begin when you double-click a name in this list. For example, you might have entries here for Grandma, Boss, and Alien Menace if these are three people with whom you often video conference. A sample phone book appears, as shown in Figure 9-2.

You can add entries (known as contact cards) for each new person you want to chat with. These contact cards must contain at least a name but should ideally also contain an IP address.

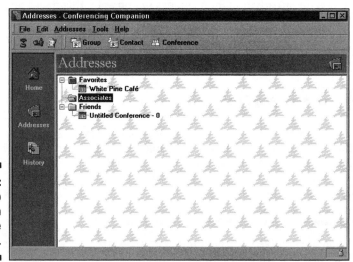

Figure 9-2:
Looking up someone in your phone book.

Don't forget that some of the people in your chat list might not have broad-band connections to the Internet like you do, which means that they must dial their ISP whenever they want to go online. Every time they do this, they get a different IP from the time before. For this reason, you should not rely on IP alone for finding the people to whom you want to talk.

The conference room

You use the conference room whenever you want to have a point-to-point conference. In these cases, your machine connects directly to the your friend or co-worker's machine. The conference room lets you actually see and chat with the people on the other end of the line. A sample conference room is shown in Figure 9-3.

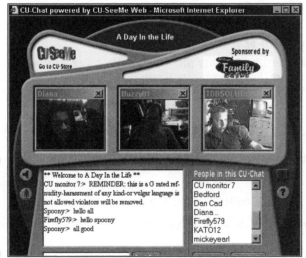

Figure 9-3: Meeting in the conference room.

You also use the conference room to participate in group conferences facilitated by servers known as *reflectors*. A reflector is a computer that has agreed to accept and send (reflect) all the audio and video transmitted by each participant in the conference, meaning everyone involved gets to hear and see more-or-less the same things.

Tips and tricks for using CUSeeMe

You're bound to want to perform few tasks sooner or later while using your video conferencing software. Here are a few tips and tricks to get you started.

Finding your friends

We noted earlier in this chapter that IPs can be a horrible way to try to stay in touch with friends who use dialup connections to the Internet. Fortunately, the Who's Online function offers a better way.

Click the Who's Online button on the toolbar of the phone book window to show a list of everyone currently available for chatting. Double-click a name in this list to connect with that person. To appear on this list, your friends must also use CUSeeMe (a registered copy) and register with the Four11 directory.

Don't be surprised if you don't see some of your friends online when you look for them using this tool. Compared to the total number of people on the Internet, very few register with Four11. Visit Four11's Web site at `www.four11.com` for information on how to register.

Avoiding too much of a good thing

Remember that a higher quality picture requires more bandwidth to send it across the Internet. For this reason, if you find the video under CUSeeMe terribly slow, you might consider reducing the quality of the images you are receiving, like so:

1. **Activate the conference window.**

2. **Click Customize.**

3. **Click the Configuration tab.**

4. **Find the Video Quality control toward the bottom.**

5. **Slide the control to the left to decrease image quality.**

6. **Click OK to confirm your changes.**

Note that this only decreases the quality of the video that you are receiving, not the quality that you are sending.

Do you hear what I hear?

With CUSeeMe on, you can receive video conference calls as well as make them. Sometimes, though, you may want to be on stand-by to receive calls while you work on other projects. For these instances, CUSeeMe comes with a software application called a Listener, which does nothing but wait for incoming calls and notify with a pop-up window or a bell sound when they come in.

To make the Listener start automatically whenever you turn on your computer:

1. **Activate the phone book window.**
2. **Click the Call Options button.**
3. **Make sure the box labeled Run Listener at Startup is checked.**
4. **Click OK to confirm your changes.**

Chapter 10

Chatting with Global Neighbors

● ●

In This Chapter

▶ Contacting others faster than e-mail

▶ Letting others contact you instantly

▶ Downloading chat software

▶ Adding sights and sounds to your conversation

● ●

*Y*ou may think that you'll be so busy gathering data off of the Internet that you won't have any time to interact with real people. Fortunately, we've got a solution to that: Turn off the computer and go outside. No, no, just kidding. In fact, several different technologies make it easy to carry on typed conversations, exchange files, and even carry on voice interactions (often called *talking*) over your high-speed Internet connection.

This chapter discusses how you can use software that lets you carry on typed conversations with others in real-time (called *chatting*, or *instant messaging*). Chatting is similar to sticking your head into someone's office at work or running into someone at the store and having a quick discussion.

You can also join or start a *group chat* with a whole bunch of people sending messages to a single window that everyone can see. Think of it as having a discussion around the dinner table, or around the water cooler, or having an impromptu meeting in the hallway at work.

When you used a modem, chatting may have been more of a nuisance than anything else. You might have been so busy trying to use your dialup account quickly and efficiently to free up your phone line, and who has time to chat during that kind of rush?

Fortunately, you're always on with most high-speed Internet connections, and that means you can chat whenever you want to, without interrupting any other services you may be using. In addition, most chat and conferencing packages let you put up a "Do Not Disturb" sign whenever you need to, and to be selective about who can and cannot bother you.

Conferencing by Internet is usually more involved, including features such as voice, video, shared whiteboards, and even application sharing. Conferencing applications usually include a chat feature of some kind, but that's not their main purpose in life. For a discussion of audio conferencing and voice conversation packages, see Chapter 7; for video conferencing, see Chapter 9.

Why Broadband Is Great for Chatting

Text doesn't take up very much storage space, and can be sent quickly over even the slowest modem. More bandwidth doesn't make text travel better, or even much faster. So why is a broadband Internet connection more useful for chatting than, say, your old modem?

The biggest reason is that most broadband connections are always on. Chatting is mainly useful for keeping in touch with people in a fast, easy, and casual way. That wouldn't be much use if you were constantly appearing and disappearing on the Internet to your friends, family, and colleagues. They wouldn't know when, they could reach you if ever, and eventually they'd give up watching for you altogether.

With an always-on connection, however, you can leave the chat or instant messaging software running whenever your computer is on. So, even if you're not actually at the keyboard, your friends and co-workers can reach you to see if it's a good time to chat, to leave a message for when you return, or drop you a note to get your attention similar to leaving a sticky note on your computer screen in the office. Having always-on availability offers less confusion for people who need to reach you and who don't want to worry about mail, e-mail, telephone, fax, or bricks through your window. You can narrow their choices to two: If they're not in a hurry or are sending a lot of information at once, they can send e-mail. If they're rushed or sending a one-liner, they can try to chat with you through IM. With clear options, everyone can reach you at their (and your) discretion because you're always on.

If you're telecommuting, chatting can provide a good substitute for the water cooler. Instead of running into people in hallways, the supply room, or around the coffee machine, you can simply send instant messages for quick discussions that might not warrant a phone call.

Keeping in Touch in Real-Time

Chat software gives you several different ways to stay in touch and most, but not all, of them involve extensive typing. Unless you can install some really good voice-recognition software, or convince a secretary to take dictation for your online discussions, you'll be typing a lot while you chat. Fortunately, you'll get much faster over time, and soon typing will feel as natural as speaking, only with a backspace key.

In a one-on-one chat session, you each type your messages and click Send, and your words appear immediately on the other user's screen, as shown in Figure 10-1.

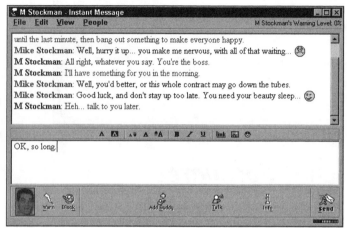

Figure 10-1:
Chatting
one-on-one
in a quiet
little, text-
based
conversation.

In a group chat session, you can imagine yourself in a room with several or even dozens of other people, all of whom are talking at once. In a group chat, you type your message and click Send, and your words appear immediately in the window that you and the others are sharing.

Group chats may be called *chat rooms*, *channels*, or other phrases that all suggest a bunch of people sitting around typing to each other, as shown in Figure 10-2.

Everyone in the room sees your message as soon as you post it, so be sure you know what you want to say before you click Send. There's no Unsend feature in chatting.

Most of the one-to-one chat programs provide a way to invite more than one person to a chat room, so if you see several people on line who know each other, you can start a whole group discussion about where to go for dinner that night, or what everyone thought of that wedding last weekend.

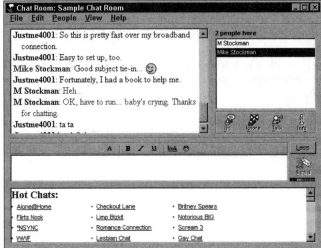

Figure 10-2:
Now,
everybody's
chatting
at once.

Finding Chat Software

Chat or instant messaging software all falls under a generic name, but many of the chat software packages go beyond text conversations to perform additional tasks, such as setting up voice communications, transferring files, and so on.

Most chat software supports one-on-one discussions or group chat rooms, although a chat package usually focuses on one or the other. That is, a package such as AOL Instant Messenger (AIM) provides primarily one-on-one chatting, but it also allows you to enter a chat room with multiple users to have a group chat session.

By the same token, a group-chat package such as most IRC (Internet Relay Chat) packages are designed for entering chat rooms for group discussions, but they also allow you to single out a particular user on a channel and carry on a private conversation one-on-one with that user. The package you choose depends on what you want to accomplish:

✔ If you're mainly interested in meeting new people and discussing shared interests with them, you should start with a group chat package, such as any IRC software or some of the Web-based chat software. Virtually all of the group chat packages also allow you to chat one-on-one with the people you meet, but all conversations generally start in a chat room or channel, and can be taken to a private discussion from there.

✔ If you want to use the software like a less-formal telephone, making chat calls to people you know or meeting people who share your interests one at a time, you should start with a one-on-one chat package, such as AIM, Yahoo! Messenger, or MSN Messenger.

The important thing to remember about chat software is that you can set up accounts and install software for as many chat services as you need. Simply launching the application and logging on won't even begin to use up your broadband connection, so you can stay logged on to multiple services all day until you decide which ones suit your needs best.

Sources of IRC and group chat software

The most popular form of group chatting, IRC (Internet Relay Chat) has not only been around for many years, it's also available on almost any computer operating system you can think of, including DOS and Windows, Mac OS, OS/2, BeOS, UNIX, Linux, and most other modern systems.

The IRC software can also be as basic as a command-line package for use in DOS or UNIX-like operating systems, or as extensive as a full-blown graphical application in Windows, X-Windows, or Mac OS. Look for one of the many software packages with IRC in the name, such as IRCle for Mac OS, ksIRC for the KDE environment on Linux, mIRC for Windows, and so on. We show you how to use a sampling of these in the IRC section later in this chapter.

Watch for group chat as an extra feature in your one-on-one chat software. In AOL Instant Messenger, for example, this feature is called buddy chat. In MSN Messenger, you can invite multiple people to chat, but using Microsoft NetMeeting as the group chat location. See the online help for your chat software to see whether group chat is available.

Sources of one-on-one chat software

Chat software for talking one-on-one is available through many sources, including some of the major Internet providers in the world (Microsoft's MSN and America Online) and some of the major portals on the Internet (Yahoo! Messenger). Some of the most popular packages, such as ICQ, started out as independent packages before partnering or being acquired by the big players, as ICQ is also now an AOL product.

Regardless of the power behind a chat package, you can always sign up for more than one, and gradually eliminate the ones that don't suit your needs, either because most of your chatting circle uses one package or another, or because the software lacks the features you need.

Currently, users of a service can chat only with other members of the same service. Yahoo! Messenger users cannot chat with AIM or MSN users, ICQ users can chat only with other ICQ users, and so on.

A popular movement is under way now to establish a *standard* for chat software to use, so that all of the different services could talk to each other. Currently, this movement is slowly but surely defining that standard, but it remains to be seen whether any of the big players, such as AOL and Microsoft, actually begin using the standard once it's available.

You can find one-on-one chat software at any of the following sources:

✔ **AOL Instant Messenger (**www.aol.com/aim**).** The current industry leader, AIM can chat with its own users as well as anyone with an America Online or CompuServe account, providing it with over 25 million potential users. If your goal is to reach anyone at any time, this is the program to use.

✔ **MSN Messenger (**www.msn.com**).** MSN Messenger, which requires that you set up a Hotmail or Microsoft Network (MSN) mail account to use it, has a good set of features and has added features such as notifying you when you have Hotmail mail. MSN Messenger can also link to Microsoft NetMeeting and other products to provide voice, screen sharing, file transfers, and other features.

✔ **Yahoo! Messenger (**messenger.yahoo.com**).** Another companion to an e-mail account, Yahoo! Messenger not only lets you chat with others, it also lets you join discussion groups for Yahoo! News and other information you might want to discuss.

✔ **ICQ (**www.icq.com**).** Although America Online now owns ICQ (a play on the words "I Seek You"), it's still an independent product with millions of users of its own. ICQ provides the same kind of instant messaging services as the others, but has client software that lets you use it from more computer operating systems than most other instant messaging product. ICQ also adds file transfers, voice chat, and other additional features that make it a useful IM program to use.

The question of which chat software to use depends almost entirely on where your friends and colleagues spend their time online. If they're all AOL or AIM users, install AIM. If they're all MSN users, install MSN Messengers, and so on. The goal of the chat software is to reach people, and the only way to do that (at least until the folks in charge settle on a standard that lets you use one program to reach the others) is to pick the software that your targets use.

That said, be aware that you can install one, some, or all of the chat programs you find online. They use very little of your broadband connection to stay on, and you'll be reachable and able to reach users of any service whose software you have running.

After you have the one-on-one chat software, you need to set up an account with the hosting service. Each chat package comes with instructions for doing this, but essentially, here's how you'll set up a chat account:

1. **Go to the hosting service's Web site, and click a Sign Up link.**

2. **Enter varying amounts of personal information, including any information that helps establish your profile to help other users find you.**

   The next section shows you some tips on compiling a profile.

3. **Install the chat software package on your system, specifying the account and password you established on the hosting Web site.**

4. **Use the chat software to sign on.**

When you sign on, your chat software connects you to the central chat server, through which all of your communication with others will flow. At this point, any other users who are looking for you will see that you're logged on, and may begin chatting with you.

No chat software currently available encrypts your chat sessions, so anyone who can tap into the stream of information flowing between you, the hosting chat server, and the person with whom you're chatting will see your entire conversation. Never say anything in a chat session that you wouldn't be comfortable saying out loud on a crowded elevator.

Letting Others Know How to Find You

With an always-on broadband connection, you can leave a chat program running whenever your computer is on and connected to the Internet. That way, people can find you whenever they feel like it. Think of it as sitting on your front porch waiting for people to show up to shoot the breeze, or opening the door to your office so colleagues can come consult on important matters. In other words, you're providing a way for the world to come to you.

Unfortunately, this seldom results in meaningful discussions. How do your friends and colleagues know you're available to chat? They're probably assuming that you're busy working on your stock trading, upcoming project deadline, or first novel, and that you shouldn't be bothered by idle chatter.

Even worse, they may not even know you're using chat software, or how to contact you even if you are. Luckily, you can also make sure the right people know how to reach you on the chat service. Here are some examples.

Showing your best profile

Most chat services let you *register* with their systems, so that people can search their listings for chat partners by name or shared interests. Besides your name or nickname and an e-mail, this registration, called a *profile* on many services, contains whatever topics you want to discuss, including:

- Geographic location (not your actual address, but perhaps the town or state in which you live)
- Your field of work
- Hobbies and interests

Putting up billboards and road signs

Well, perhaps billboards and road signs aren't exactly the way to get your chat information out to the world, but you have the next best thing: your e-mail and Web sites.

Each time you send out an e-mail message, you can include what's known as a *sig* (or signature) at the end of the message. Many mail programs even let you pre-define a signature that's automatically appended onto each e-mail message you send out. (On UNIX-like systems, these are called sig files, while on other platforms they may be called signature files, or simply signature settings.)

If you can include any signature you want in an e-mail, why not include your chat information as well? For example, many people include a signature similar to the following at the end of their messages:

```
------------------------------------------------------------
E-mail: jrodriguez@example.com    http://www.example.com/jr
AOL Instant Messenger: Jrodriguez12345          ICQ:12345678
```

In this example, the user includes an e-mail address, which is standard information to include in a signature, but she also included two ways to reach her on chat services. If you're using ICQ, you could use that number to reach her when she's logged on. On AOL Instant Messenger, you can reach her using Jrodriguez12345 when she's logged on. If you set up this kind of signature, everyone who receives your e-mail knows how to send you instant messages. They may even add you to a *buddy list* to see when you're logged on.

Adding a chat link to your Web page

You can even include hot links on your Web pages that visitors can click to instant message or chat with you automatically. The method of adding this link to your website depends on the chat software you are using. For example, AOL Instant Messenger (AIM) supports an `aim://` URL, so you could create a link on your web page that looks like this:

```
<A HREF="aim:goim?screenname=
   mstockman&message=Hi.+Are+
   you+there?">
```

```
Click Here to Instant Message
   Me Now!
</A>
```

When visitors to your web page click the link (assuming they had AIM installed), their computer would launch AIM and open an outgoing instant message window to you, automatically.

Other utilities may also support embedded chat URLs. See the documentation or Web sites for your chat software for more information.

Another place to include your chat information is on your personal or business web page. Just as you'd include your e-mail address or other contact information on your Web pages, you can also include your chat information for anyone visiting your web site.

My screen name is Bond. JBond5923.

Don't rule out low-tech ways of letting people know how to reach you. The time-tested methods of networking (with people, not computers) work as well for chat information as for any other method of getting in touch. Be sure to try any of the following ways of getting your contact information to potential chat partners:

- ✔ **Business cards.** Place your screen name or other chat information under your e-mail address.
- ✔ **Letterhead.** Anywhere e-mail addresses go, you can also place your chat information.
- ✔ **Anywhere you might normally provide a telephone number or e-mail address.** Hand out flyers at meetings, clubs, and bars if you're so inclined and wait for the instant messages to pour in.

Of course, you might achieve such a thing as being *too* successful about getting noticed in chat software. The next section describes how to get rid of people once they know how to reach you.

Stopping Others from Finding You

As with all services on the Internet, chatting has a downside. In this case, the downside is the potential for harassment. People may send instant messages pretending to be network administrators who need your passwords to solve a problem (they don't). They may think you're their long-lost cousin Alfie, who went to sea many years earlier and was never heard from again (you aren't). Or, they may simply be having a bad day and feel that they're free to dump on the first person they see (they aren't).

The Internet is just as populated with people you want to avoid as the rest of life. The challenge is to allow the people you want to reach you, and prevent the people you don't want from even knowing you're there. Fortunately, most chat software provides a way.

Putting out the "Do not disturb" sign

Most chat software packages provide you with the following features to protect yourself from harassment:

- ✓ **Blocking individual users:** If a person is trying to locate you about that debt, or someone is very persistent about thinking you're someone else, just add that person's chat name to your list of people you want to ignore.

- ✓ **Blocking anyone you don't know:** Just as caller ID on your telephone can be set up to reject calls from anyone not in your personal phonebook, so can chat software be set up to bounce messages from anyone not on your short list of acceptable people.

- ✓ **Blocking everyone:** If you're working and don't want to be disturbed, just block everyone. Why wouldn't you just quit the chat software instead? Because you might want to initiate a chat with someone, even while you don't want anyone starting to chat with you. Blocking everyone while leaving the chat software running keeps your options open.

Your chat package may have other options available for filtering out unwanted chatting, such as blocking anyone with "luv" or "hotstuf" in their screen names, but the options listed here appear in virtually every chat package available. For example, Figure 10-3 shows ICQ's options for protecting yourself from unwanted chatting. Choose Edit⇨Preferences on the Mac OS.

This version of ICQ provides two options: Either anyone can chat with me, or I have to give permission to everyone. Compare that with the screen shown in Figure 10-4 when you choose Preferences (Mac) or Setup (Windows) in AOL Instant Messenger.

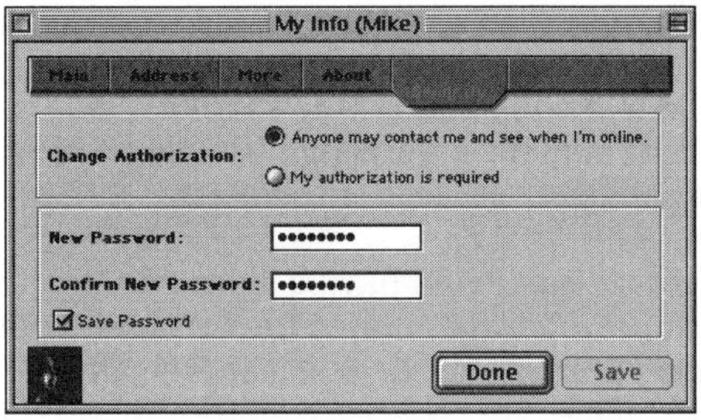

Figure 10-3:
Setting
protection
options in
ICQ's My
Info dialog
box.

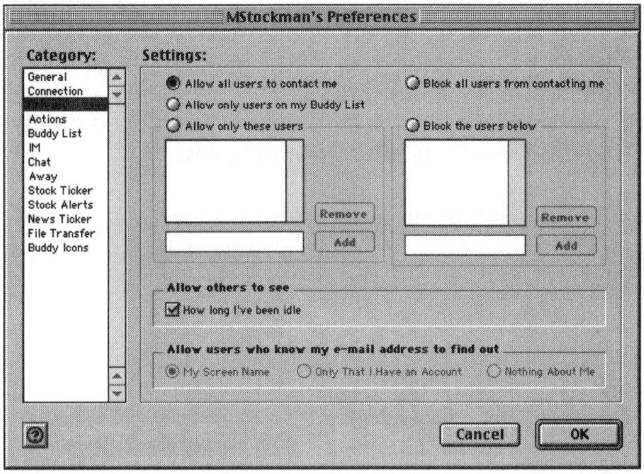

Figure 10-4:
Privacy
Settings for
AOL Instant
Messenger.

AOL Instant Messenger provides very precise control over who can and cannot contact me, providing two separate lists of allowed users (the buddy list, or the list in this dialog box) as well as a list of forbidden users. Microsoft's MSN Messenger software provides a much simpler set of options, providing only an Allowed list and a Forbidden list. Users you allow may chat with you, and others may not.

For information on your chat software's options for privacy, check the Preferences or Options commands, or consult the software's documentation.

Choosing when to show or hide a profile

Often, people who are looking for company, friendship, or someone to vent their frustrations on will search a chat service's database for someone who matches the exact profile they're looking for. Spammers or others with something to sell will search the chat service's database for anyone, whether you match their profile or not.

When these people find you, they'll send instant messages of, shall we say, a delicate nature, try to sell you things, harass you to make themselves feel better, or try to treat you as a lifelong buddy who's interested in their little lives. Worse yet, some people may try several of these practices at the same time.

The easiest way to prevent this is to avoid having a profile altogether. AOL Instant Messenger, for example, has an option in the Create a Profile window that says, "Yes, provide this information." If you clear this option, your information won't be visible to anyone.

The advantage to this is that people can find you only if you give them your screen name or chat ID. The disadvantage to this is exactly the same thing. It's like your telephone number: if you want friends to be able to find your number in the telephone book or on directory assistance, you open yourself up to telemarketers and crank calls. If you have an unlisted number, you have to tell each friend individually what your number is.

Fortunately, we've got a simple solution: Set up a profile if you want one, and if you have to deal with a large number of strangers harassing you, delete your profile and watch the unsolicited instant messages die off.

Using Web-Based Chat

As on the rest of the Internet, all good trends come to the World Wide Web. In this case, many Web sites have set up special pages with real-time chat software embedded in the page. These pages usually work by letting users type a message in, and you see any new messages each time the web page re-loads. This results in a lot of waiting, watching the Web page re-draw itself, and a great deal of flickering. It's slow, and usually not worth the effort.

However, newer Web sites are implementing faster, more efficient chat software that acts more like the standalone applications described earlier in this chapter. These Web sites (using JavaScript, Java, or ActiveX, if you're interested in that sort of thing) let you and other users of the site carry on live conversations just as you would through ICQ, AOL Instant Messenger, and so on.

Generally, people join Web-based group chat sessions when they want to reach out, meet, and converse with large numbers of people. There's very little difference between Web-based chat and IRC, discussed earlier in this chapter. The only real difference is that it's on a Web page instead of in a standalone application.

This section can't provide much in the way of general advice for using web-based chat software, because each Web site uses a different package and each site configures the packages to look and work differently.

However, this example provides an idea of how web-based chat sites work. TalkCity is a popular Web-based community with a busy chat site. Opening the TalkCity chat site (at `http://www.talkcity.com/chat/`) and logging on to a chat session opens a chat window like the one in Figure 10-5.

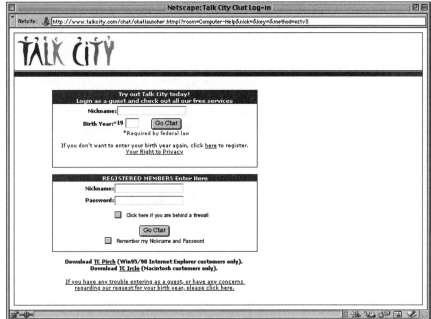

Figure 10-5: A sample TalkCity sign-in window.

You can sign in as a guest, or enter a valid account name and password to log in and join the chat room. Figure 10-6 shows a sample chat window in a browser.

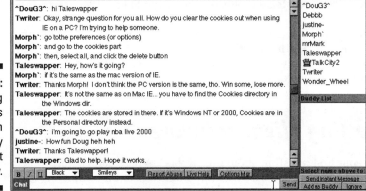

Figure 10-6: Watching the words scroll by in a TalkCity chat window.

The chatting that occurs appears in the main section as a kind of transcript. When you type into the field underneath the transcript and press Return or Enter, your message appears for everyone in the room to see, and everything they type appears on the screen for you to see. I can even send private messages to anyone in the room, or ignore anyone who's being annoying or harassing.

Because I'm using a broadband connection that's always on, I can leave the chat room up and running on a Web page all day if I want to, and join in on the conversation whenever I'm sitting at my computer and have some free time.

The only drawback is that virtually all Web-based chat is group chat, and that's not very useful for keeping in touch with people. Because all of the messages in the chat room scroll by constantly, you'd have to keep reading the discussion to see whether any messages are directed at you in particular. With a one-to-one chat program, a message pops up only if it's directed at you.

Using Internet Relay Chat (IRC)

The granddaddy of all conferencing on the Internet is called IRC, which stands for Internet Relay Chat. Many Web-based chat programs are actually IRC client software that runs in your Web browser, so these two chat categories overlap in some ways.

IRC gets its name from its multi-server method of passing your conversation along. IRC works by stringing together multiple computers, called IRC servers, that all agree to provide users with a common place for chatting. Several thousand users can share the same chat environments — more than would ever be possible using only a single server. This benefit is illustrated in Figure 10-7.

The only problem with this approach is that whenever you type something in for everyone else in your chat area to see, it must be transferred from your IRC server to every other IRC server in the same network. This is where the relay in Internet Relay Chat originates, and Figure 10-8 illustrates the relay.

Probably the strongest point in favor of using IRC for your Internet conferences is the fact that it's the most established Internet chatting standard. You can use any of several, free clients to chat using IRC, and as we show you in this section, you can also use IRC to show off your audio and video files.

Getting client software

So, your first question about IRC may be "Where can I get it?" Fortunately, you are in luck: IRC clients and servers both tend to be completely free on the Internet. The two most popular freeware clients currently are mIRC and PIRCH.

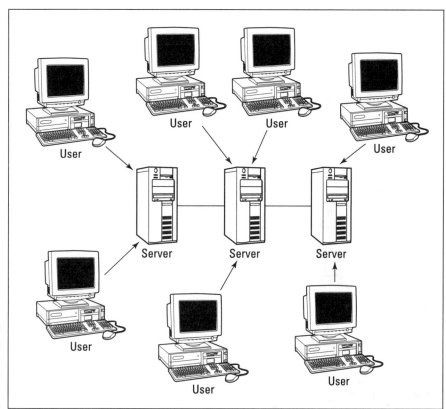

Figure 10-7:
The more
servers, the
merrier!

mIRC

mIRC is a free client for Internet Relay Chat that was written by Khaled
Mardam-Bey. As one of the oldest, most-established IRC client programs, it is
definitely worth a look.

You can download the latest mIRC client software for free from several sites
on the World Wide Web:

- http://www.mirc.com
- http://www.mirc.com.ar
- http://mirc.eon.net.au
- http://www.mirc.co.za

After you locate and download the right file for your system, simply double-
click it to begin the installation process. When the software is installed, you
may begin running it immediately to begin chatting.

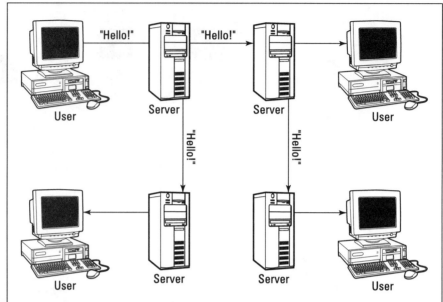

Figure 10-8:
Running the
Internet
relay race.

mIRC clients have been prime targets lately for crackers on the Internet; because they can be run automatically to some extent by small programs known as scripts, crackers have discovered that mIRC often provides an ideal entrance into unsuspecting users' computers. If you are the sort to worry about your computer's security (and who shouldn't be?), then make sure that your anti-virus software is properly installed and up-to-date before using mIRC for chatting on the Internet!

PIRCH

The primary source of competition for mIRC is a program known as PIRCH, written by Northwest Computer Services. You can find out all about PIRCH and download it for free from several sites on the World Wide Web:

- http://www.pirchat.com
- http://www.pirch.com
- http://www.dm.net/~christinag

One of the niftiest things about PIRCH is the GUI interface to its notification tool, which works like instant messaging. For more information on this feature, consult PIRCH's documentation.

Like mIRC, you can install PIRCH as soon as you have finished downloading it simply by double-clicking on its icon. The main difference between mIRC and PIRCH is that PIRCH is a little newer and offers a slightly different mix of features than mIRC. It's not, however, generally regarded as being quite as stable as its older counterparts.

Finding a suitable place for a chat

Once you have installed a chat client on your computer, you are ready to fire it up and begin talking. To chat on the Internet via IRC, you must find a server and join a channel.

Finding servers

The IRC client that you download should come with a list of IRC servers. These servers may be loaded into the client program when you first start it up so that you may pick one from a list of choices, as shown in Figure 10-9.

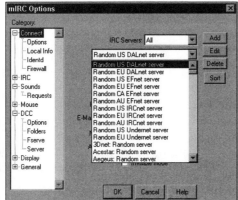

Figure 10-9:
Pick a
server, any
server.

Alternately, you may find a list of servers in a text file that is included with your client software. But, you should be aware that IRC servers are grouped into several large networks of servers. The machines within each group communicate with each other but not with computers from other groups. They're kind of like high school cliques.

The significance of this to you is that some of these groups are larger than the others and, therefore, offer more opportunities to meet more people and discuss a wider range of topics. Furthermore, some groups feature only servers from a certain part of the world (like Australia). If you connect to this group from a place that is very far away, you'll notice messages taking much longer to travel to and from your machine!

Finding channels

Once you have connected to an IRC server, you have to join a channel in order to start having any kind of public conversation. Channels are like meeting rooms — people gather in them to discuss specific topics. The topic being discussed is usually indicated by the name of the channel.

Once you log on to the chat server, you'll see a list of possibly hundreds of different channels, which are simply another name for chat rooms. Figure 10-10 shows a sample listing.

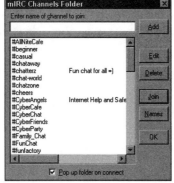

Figure 10-10: Selecting channels, or chat rooms, available on one server.

In most IRC software, you enter a nickname, or handle (to use an old CB radio term) by which you want to be known, connect to the IRC server you want to use, select the channel you want to join, and connect.

You're sure to find that some of the channels on IRC are intended solely for discussing adult themes. In fact, it may seem at first like all of the channels on IRC are intended for discussing adult themes! If these topics bother you, by all means — stay out. More importantly, if you intend to allow your children access to the Internet, make sure that you take steps to prevent them from going to any questionable IRC channels. See Chapter 18 for more details.

To get a list of channels available on your current IRC server, type **/list** **<topic>** at the command prompt. In this case, <topic> refers to some word or phrase that you would like to see in every channel returned by the program. For example, /list bubble would show you every channel currently running on your IRC server that deal with bubbles, as shown in Figure 10-11.

Figure 10-11:
Channels
bubbling up
on IRC.

Notice that this list also gives you a count of the number of people currently in each of the channels. This can be useful when you want to find a channel that is particularly busy or slow.

Tips and tricks

Typing back and forth to other people in a public channel is all fine and well but not really the focus of this chapter. To really get the most out of your broadband connection to the Internet, you need to know about a few more nifty things that IRC can do for you.

Private chats

Sometimes, you want to say something to someone without everyone else seeing (or hearing) it. In these cases, you want to initiate what is known as a private chat with that individual. You can use either of two ways to chat privately under IRC.

Direct messaging

Type /msg <*username*> to send a private message to a given user. For example typing

```
/msg harry You're talking too much!
```

would privately tell Harry what's on your mind.

DCC Chat

Both of the IRC clients we discuss in this chapter support DCC (Direct Chat to Client) capability, which allows private conversation directly between your computer and the computer of the person to whom you are talking. This can be useful for speeding up conversations when you are relatively close to the person you are talking to, but far away from the IRC server. The DCC chat process works as shown in Figure 10-12.

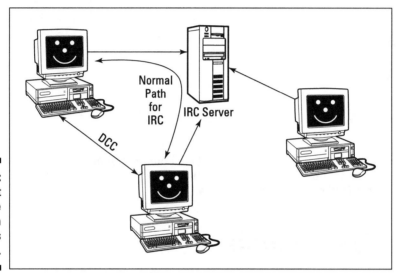

Figure 10-12:
The shortest
distance
between
two points
is DCC.

Sending sounds from an IRC client

Now, we finally start getting into the good stuff! You can enhance your chats by sending and receiving sounds while you type back and forth with other IRC users. This is accomplished via the use of the sound command.

To play a sound for everyone in your current channel:

1. **Copy the .wav or .mid file for your sound to whatever directory your client software requires (in mIRC, for example, this is the /mirc/sounds directory).**

2. **Type** /sound *<filename>*.

   For example, typing /sound tada plays the sound "Ta-da!" (contained in the tada.wav or tada.mid file) for everyone in the channel.

3. **If you want to hear other people's sounds as well, make sure that this setting is enabled in your client's Options settings (it is disabled by default in both mIRC and PIRCH).**

If you enable your IRC client to play sounds sent by other people, it can download any sounds that anyone attempts to play. These sounds remain stored on your hard disk until you elect to erase them manually.

Adding a photo or graphic

Finally, the moment has arrived to put that fancy new digital camera to good use! Unfortunately, the capabilities supported by IRC are better for graphics than video conferencing. In short, you may send files to other users over IRC. These files may be pictures, word processing documents, or anything else that you like.

To send pictures using IRC:

1. **Take a picture using your digital camera.**

2. **Save your picture to a file on your computer.**

3. **Enter the command** /dcc send *<username> <filename>*.

For example, you could take a picture of yourself, save it to a file named me.jpg, then type /dcc send nancy me.jpg to send it to the IRC user named Nancy.

Part III
Getting Down to Business

The 5th Wave   By Rich Tennant

NETWORK MANAGER

"YOU'D BETTER GET OUT HERE - ONE OF THE LINKS IN THE NETWORK IS ACTING UP."

In this part . . .

Tired of the monkey business at the office that keeps you from actually getting work done? Are you considering setting up your own network?

If you've ever wanted to work out of your home or set up your own business, you're one of a growing trend of innovative workers and entrepreneurs. Using broadband access makes telecommuting or publishing your own Web site more feasible than ever.

If your home or small office has more than one computer, you've got some special issues related to connecting and using a broadband service. You need to find a way to get all of those computers talking to the Internet any time they need to, without a lot of hassle or the need to hire expensive consultants. You also need to keep your computer in pace with your high-speed access.

This part explains exactly how to set up a shared connection to your broadband Internet service, from networking your existing computers to connecting that network to the Internet. As an added bonus, your computers can communicate with each other even faster than they can with the Internet. And all of this happens without expensive consultants. Read on, and get connected.

Chapter 11

Using Broadband to Stay Home

In This Chapter

▶ Working in the comfort of your own home

▶ Convincing your boss to allow it

▶ Getting everything you'll need to make it happen

*P*icture this scenario: you wake up in the morning fifteen minutes before that big departmental meeting. You throw on a bathrobe, pour a cup of coffee, and sit down at your computer. You connect to the office, read some e-mail, and download some files just before the phone rings. You put the call on speakerphone and say in your most professional voice, "Yes, I've got your presentation up on my screen right now. . . ."

Fantasy? Not with your high-speed Internet connection. And, remember before you had a job, when your primary job was being a student? For that job, too, you can complete the work from the comfort of your own home. You can apply all of the telecommuting concepts in this chapter to a great new concept called *distance learning* to earn college credit or other instruction without ever leaving home.

"Just Mail Me the Paycheck"

Unlike the scams in the depths of weekly newspapers and magazines ("Make a living at home stuffing envelopes! After only thirty thousand, you can buy lunch!"), you can perform many jobs, and make a decent living at them, without setting foot in an office.

The process of working from a distance is often called *telecommuting*, in which you have a job with a real company somewhere, but you perform your tasks at home. You keep in touch with your co-workers and employers by telephone, e-mail, and other methods that don't involve leaving the house. When you need to visit the office, you bring your work in small, portable packages such as removable hard drives, or you send your work electronically and don't carry anything at all to the office.

Maybe your boss won't consider telecommuting, but you have a skill you know can help you earn a living as an independent contractor or business owner. Still, you don't want to take over the living room with boxes of inventory or assemble the latest mail order junk in your garage. Your broadband connection can help you form your own business as a freelance worker in any number of fields using computers.

Sounds pretty good, doesn't it? Either way you want to work, you may have to convince someone else that this is a good idea. Here are some of the more "convincing" benefits:

- **More efficient work habits:** If you're doing it right, you can get a lot more work done by taking advantage of the fact that people can't barge into your office with distractions, additional work, or crises that aren't your responsibility.

- **Less wasted time:** You can combine tasks that don't take too much thought, such as formatting documents during boring meetings, or cleaning your office while the boss is sharing the company vision with your department.

- **Even less wasted time:** If you commute an hour each way to the office, that's two free hours a day saved by working from home. You can then give those hours back to your employer in the form of additional work. Okay, fine, you can use the two extra hours for goofing off. Either way, you're not stuck on the freeway.

- **Flexible hours:** This one may turn out to be more of a curse than a blessing, but if your office is at home, you can go to work at 3:00 a.m. when you can't sleep or Saturday morning when the kids are busy watching cartoons. This flexibility is useful during tough deadlines, but can become an unhealthy habit.

- **Better use of office space:** Here's one you can give your boss when you ask to telecommute. You can set up a cubicle or office time-share system with a co-worker who also wants to telecommute but on different days. That way, two employees are using only one space, leaving more space for other employees to use. In a crowded office, that point alone could get you the permission to work at home.

- **Exploring new ground:** Broadband makes a number of jobs more feasible because of high-speed data transfer and communication. Some examples include graphics design (working with huge files); Web design and analysis (viewing and uploading large volumes of pages); Recruiting and consulting (performing online research and calling global clients via your Internet phone). When you're ready to work for yourself, hundreds of "real" jobs can make that broadband connection pay for itself.

Of course, most people won't just hang up their employee IDs and work from home their entire week. Many people work from home just two or three days a week, or even just one day to catch up on those tasks that require uninterrupted time. Choose a work-at-home schedule that fits your needs and, perhaps more importantly, your employer's needs.

What You Need for Telecommuting

You already have the most important parts of a successful telecommuting plan: a computer and a high-speed Internet connection. There's more to working from home than surfing the Internet, however. Everything you need to telecommute centers around acting as if you're in the office. Software, networking, and contact with co-workers are all a part of working in an office, and you can't give up any of these to telecommute. This section essentially describes how to stay at home while pretending to be in the office.

Cloning your office

You'll want to make your home office as close to your employer's office as possible, except with better food and a more casual dress code. That usually means outfitting your computer and desk with the same utilities you use at work.

Making the work-at-home plan actually work

One of the make-or-break aspects of working from home, especially if you're telecommuting, is the communication factor. You can have all the bandwidth in the world, but unfortunately, when you step out of the office, you often suffer from the "out of sight, out of mind" syndrome. If folks don't see you on a regular basis, they often forget you're there. If they do think about contacting you, they're not sure what times are best or which method to use.

Additionally, you may go through human-contact withdrawal your first weeks out. Sure it's great to work in your lawn chair under a tree or take a walk to the park on your lunch break, but not seeing another human face to face can drive you (and your family) crazy. You have to stay disciplined and motivated on your own. Many people quit working at home if they can't balance the benefits of time alone with maintaining a healthy community life.

Having broadband Internet access means you and your co-workers have no excuse for not keeping in touch, whether it's a simple conversation, an answer to that question you can't solve on your own, or a project meeting.

You'll make your telecommuting life far easier if you use the same software tools as they do at work. For example, if your company has standardized on Microsoft Office or Corel's WordPerfect Office suite, you can install those same tools at home to make sure you can read everyone else's documents and they can read yours.

That doesn't mean you have to have the same computers at home that they use at work. You can install Microsoft Office for Windows or Mac OS and exchange documents with others, and there are versions of Corel WordPerfect Office and other office products for both platforms as well.

Some office applications available for UNIX-like operating systems, including Linux, can read and save most of the common document formats (including Microsoft's and Corel's) so you can stay compatible. These include Sun's StarOffice suite (`www.sun.com`), abiSuite (`www.abisource.com`), and Corel WordPerfect Office for Linux and WordPerfect 8 for UNIX.

Two main concerns with the software tools you use at home include

- **Technical support:** Make sure your employer's help desk or other technical support teams will be able to help you with whichever tools you end up using. If you run into trouble bringing documents back and forth, you don't want to be left out in the cold because they don't like the tools you are using.

- **Licensing agreements:** If you bring home a copy of an office suite to install at home, make sure the software's licensing agreement allows you to do so. Often, you'll need to ask your employer to purchase a second copy for your home computer. Some agreements, however, let you make exactly one copy of the software for use at home, as long as both copies are never in use at the same time. Again, check the software's licensing agreement for the package you want to use.

When you have software at home to match your work environment, you can simply carry (or e-mail, or copy over the Internet) your documents back and forth, and exchange them with co-workers without worrying about whether everyone involved is able to read and edit them.

Hooking up the umbilical cord to the office

An important part of telecommuting is making sure that you have access to all of the networking resources from home that you would have at the office. That includes the office e-mail system, file servers, corporate databases, internal Web sites, and so on. You might even want to have access to printers at the office, especially if you need to provide someone with a printout of a document you're working on. ("Hello, Gail? You can pick up that document at printer number 7.")

The best way to make sure you have access to everything on your corporate network is to set up a *virtual private network*, or VPN, connection between your home computer and the office. When you set up a VPN connection, your computer uses the Internet to hook in to the office network exactly as if you were physically in the office, with your computer plugged in to a network port on the wall. Figure 11-1 shows how this connection is set up.

Using a VPN may sound dangerous, since the Internet is a public network, and you're dealing in confidential corporate data. Fortunately, it's relatively safe, because setting up a VPN connection creates a kind of data tunnel between your computer and the office, where the data is *encrypted* as it leaves your computer and only decrypted by the VPN server at your office. Thanks to the encryption, nobody between you and your office can make any sense of the data you're sending and receiving.

If you've ever used Microsoft's Dial-Up Networking or Apple's Remote Access software, you've already used this kind of technology. The only difference is that when you dial up a remote network, you use telephone lines, and setting up a VPN connection uses the Internet.

Setting up a VPN

To set up a VPN connection to your remote office, you'll need several things. I hope you've been good to your company's network administrator, because she'll be your main source for most of the required information.

- ✔ **Permission from your company's network administrator to connect.** Remember that the Internet can be a source of attacks for your company, so they can't let just anybody in. You need to set up an account and password with your company to give you access to the network from home.

- ✔ **The address and account information for the company's VPN server.** Ask your network administrator for this: It includes the Internet address of the server (as in networkaccess.example.com, or a numeric address such as 192.168.1.53) as well as your user ID and password for the VPN server.

- ✔ **The software needed to set up the VPN connection.** Your network administrator needs to tell you which software is required to make the VPN connection work, since different VPN servers use different protocols and may require special software packages. Your network administrator may even be able to provide that software, but see the next section if you need to provide the software yourself.

When you have these items in place, you can proceed with setting up the VPN connection.

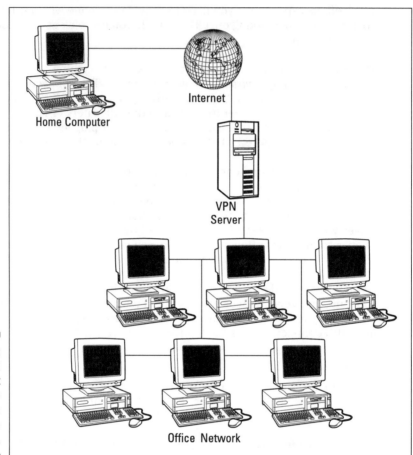

Figure 11-1:
Using a VPN
to connect
to a remote
location
over the
Internet.

Internet

VPN
Server

Home Computer

Office Network

Sources of VPN software

The VPN software you use depends on which VPN server you're connecting to and how it's configured. The best way to get the software you need is to use whatever is included by the VPN server's manufacturer or to get the latest version of that software from the manufacturer's Web site. If you use the VPN server manufacturer's own software, you can feel secure that the software definitely works with that particular server.

If you don't have the manufacturer's software, or if the manufacturer doesn't make software for your computer's operating system (a common problem if you are connecting using a Mac OS or UNIX-like computer), you need to find software that is compatible with the VPN server. Because there are some popular standards for setting up VPN connections, locating compatible software shouldn't be too hard. Check with your network administrator for the right VPN software to use.

Windows 95 and higher computers support these:

✔ **Microsoft's Dial-Up Networking versions 1.3 and higher.** Dial-Up Networking (DUN) has been included with Microsoft Windows since Windows 95 first came out. If you use Windows 95, download the latest version of DUN from Microsoft's Web site at www.microsoft.com/downloads. If you have Windows 98 or higher, the pre-installed version of DUN can already set up VPN connections and works fine.

✔ **NTS TunnelBuilder** (www.nts.com/products/vpntnnlbldr.html). This package works with almost any VPN server. It works with Microsoft and Cisco VPN servers, just to name the two most common, and with any servers that use PPTP, IPSec, and other VPN protocols. If your network administrator can't provide you with VPN client software for the equipment your company is using, ask him to buy this package for you instead. TunnelBuilder comes in a Windows or Mac OS version.

✔ **F-Secure VPN from DataFellows** (www.datafellows.com). Another versatile VPN client that works with many kinds of VPN servers.

If you are using a Mac OS computer, the following list contains some of the VPN software packages available:

✔ **NTS TunnelBuilder** (www.nts.com/products/vpntnnlbldr.html). See the list of Windows-compatible VPN clients for the details on this package, which is available for both Microsoft Windows and the Mac OS. If you need the most versatile and powerful VPN solution for the Mac, buy this package.

✔ **PGPNet** (www.pgp.com). Available in both a free and a commercial version, PGPNet can set up a VPN connection with any server that follows a standard called IPSec. If you're not sure of the VPN server your employer uses, check with your network administrator. Note that the free PGPNet software is part of the PGP Freeware package, although the Web site doesn't mention that.

✔ **Compatible Systems** (www.compatible.com). Now part of Cisco, Compatible Systems makes an IPSec-compatible VPN client that should work with many different VPN servers. Contact your network administrator or the maker of your company's VPN server to see whether the Compatible Systems client will work.

For Linux and other UNIX-like operating systems, you may be able to connect to Microsoft's VPN servers using PPTP-linux, available from your favorite download site or at this location:

www.pdos.lcs.mit.edu/~cananian/Projects/PPTP/

For a thorough discussion of other VPN clients for these operating systems, see

```
securityportal.com/lasg/vpn/
```

Connecting to a remote network

The concept of setting up a VPN connection is the same no matter which products you're using. You open some software on your computer, tell it to connect to the VPN server in the office, the software creates an encrypted connection across the Internet to the office, and presto, you're on the remote network as if you were physically present in the office.

The details of opening this connection differ from product to product. This next set of steps shows how to set up a VPN connection using Microsoft's Dial-Up Networking, which may be the most commonly used VPN software. If you use a different product, the screens may be different, but the ideas should be the same, so follow along with these steps.

If you're using Windows 95, you may need to install a newer version of Microsoft's Dial-Up Networking software before you can set up a VPN connection. You can find the upgrade on the Microsoft Web site by opening article ID Q191494 in the Microsoft Knowledgebase, by clicking the Downloads link on the Microsoft home page and searching for DUN, or by visiting this link:

```
http://support.microsoft.com/support/kb/articles/Q191/4/94.asp.
```

To set up a VPN connection using Microsoft's Dial-Up Networking (DUN) in Windows 95 or 98:

1. **Open My Computer and double-click the Dial-Up Networking icon, which opens the screen shown in Figure 11-2.**

Figure 11-2:
The Dial-Up Networking icon in its natural habitat.

2. **In the window that appears, double-click the Make New Connection icon to reach the screen shown in Figure 11-3.**

   Notice how the Microsoft VPN Adapter is selected in the drop-down list instead of a modem.

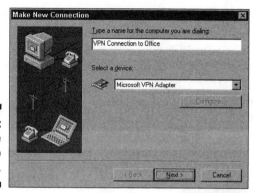

Figure 11-3:
A sample
setup
screen.

3. **Type a meaningful name for this VPN connection in the Type a Name field.**

You can enter any name here, just so you don't forget what this connection does in the future.

4. **Choose Microsoft VPN Adapter from the Select a Device drop-down list; then click Next to continue.**

This tells Microsoft Windows that you're not dialing up using a modem, but rather connecting to another network over the Internet.

5. **In the window that appears, shown in Figure 11-4, type the name or Internet address of your employer's VPN server in the Host Name or IP Address field and click Next.**

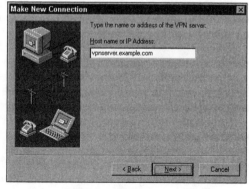

Figure 11-4:
Providing
DUN with
the address
it can use to
find the
remote
network.

Your network administrator should be able to provide this information for you, if you don't already have it.

6. **When the DUN wizard confirms that you have created the connection, click Finish.**

   The wizard closes, and your DUN connection is ready to use. You should see the new connection in the Dial-Up Networking window, right next to the Create New Connection icon.

7. **In the Dial-Up Networking window, double-click the new connection icon and the Connect To window opens, as shown in Figure 11-5.**

8. **Type your account name (if the default name isn't already correct) and password for the VPN server, then click Connect to continue.**

Figure 11-5:
Entering
your name
and
password
while
opening
the VPN
connection.

If you're the only one who has access to this computer, or if you trust everyone who has access to this computer with your data, click the Save Password checkbox before you click Connect. That checkbox saves you the step of entering the password every time you connect to this remote network. It also means that anyone with access to your computer also has access to the remote network, so be cautious about selecting this option.

If everything is correct when you click the Connect button, you'll see a series of status dialog boxes flash by, and then you'll be connected to the remote network. The VPN information fades to the background, but you can open it to view the connection status or close the connection by double-clicking the VPN icon on the Windows taskbar.

When you are connected, you can do anything you would normally do on a computer in the office, including browsing the Network Neighborhood, logging on to your e-mail, copying files from a server, and so on.

Announcing your absence

If you don't let your co-workers know when you're available and when you're not while telecommuting, one of two things will happen:

- ✔ Nobody will ever call you, thinking you're busy and can't be disturbed.
- ✔ People will call you early in the morning, late at night, and basically at any time you've decided you're not working and you're on personal time.

To avoid those situations, you need to provide a foolproof way to keep fools from bothering you at the wrong time, while at the same time making sure your quality co-workers keep in touch with you as regularly as they would with you in the office.

Posting your last-known whereabouts

If you have an office, cubicle, or comfy chair at work where people are used to finding you, post a sign on the door (if you're fortunate enough to have one) or at the entrance with the following information:

- ✔ **Your telecommuting schedule.** Make this clear, so even your slowest co-worker looking at it can say "On Tuesday and Thursday, he works here in the office. Today is Wednesday. He is, therefore, not here in the office."

- ✔ **Your contact information.** List your telephone numbers for your home office, cell phone, or IM account number so that people can call you before they forget what the question was.

- ✔ **Your hours of operation.** Don't account for every minute of your day, but give people guidelines for when it's safe to contact you. A basic range of hours is all most people need, such as 8:30 a.m. to 6:30 p.m. If you omit this information from your sign, you'll almost certainly get calls at 11:00 p.m. asking about some trivial piece of information that you don't even have.

- ✔ **Some encouragement to get in touch.** No matter how many times you tell people that you're really and truly working when you're at home, some people just plain won't call you at home to talk about work. For those people, include a note on your sign that says "If you want to talk about work, or even talk about *people* at work, don't hesitate to call me, right now." That little bit of encouragement could help people keep in touch with you better.

This sign on your office won't guarantee that the right people will stay in touch, but it helps improve the odds a little bit.

Using a public calendar

For example, I keep AOL Instant Messenger (AIM) running whenever my computer is on, which is pretty much 24 hours a day. Many of my co-workers also use AIM, and during the business day, they'll frequently send me a quick question, a reminder of meetings or deadlines, or a request to chat about an upcoming project. There's a side benefit, too: When you're done with an instant messaging discussion, you can save the entire conversation for future reference. Entering appointments like this serves two purposes: It lets people in the office know why you're not at your desk, and it encourages people to get in touch with you at home. Even if your co-workers don't pay much attention to the shared calendars, you may still want to keep the calendars up to date so your office receptionists and administrators know where you are.

Use your teammates

Unless you're the only one in your department, depend on the others on your team to communicate for you while you're working at home. No, they can't speak for you ("Sure, Bob'll be happy to take on those projects!"), but they can speak up when people wonder where you are, or to suggest dialing you in to meetings by telephone, or to let you know when someone has been looking for you.

Better still, if your teammates are also telecommuting occasionally, you can offer them the same courtesies to *guarantee* they think of you when you're working from home.

Tools to Make Working at Home Easier

Although you should be able to telecommute effectively just by connecting to the office, the fact is that you have to make extra effort to keep in touch with your co-workers and make sure you're communicating effectively with them. That can be as simple as making sure you're dialed in to meetings on a speakerphone and as complicated as setting up video hardware on your computer for that face-to-face effect.

This section discusses some additional tools, including software, hardware, and some items that aren't even computer-related, that will make your telecommuting experience better and let you take advantage of your high-speed Internet access most effectively.

Conferencing, casual style

One of the big improvements available in the telecommuting world is conferencing software. A conference package lets you do some combination of the following activities:

- ✔ **Audio conferencing:** You can talk over the Internet to people in all kinds of different locations. Using audio conferencing, you join a virtual room and talk with all of the people in that room. So, people in scattered locations can use the Internet to talk together to finally agree on those project specs. See Chapter 7 for more details.

- ✔ **Video conferencing:** This works just like audio conferencing, but lets people in each location in the meeting show streaming video of themselves or the room they're in. While you're carrying on a budget meeting by talking using audio conferencing and looking at each other via video, you'll wonder why people *ever* go into an office. Unfortunately for the more casual telecommuters, when you're on video, you have to be presentable, and that means losing the bathrobe and putting on work clothes. Sorry. We cover video conferencing in Chapter 9.

- ✔ **Text chatting:** If you don't have audio, or even if you do, you can carry on a text-based conversation with others in the same virtual meeting. Not only does this include people who may not have audio, it also lets you keep a transcription of the meeting for future reference. When the meeting is done you can save the messages in the chat window as a text file, giving you the minutes of the meeting immediately. We show you chat techniques and software in Chapter 10.

- ✔ **Shared whiteboards:** Many conferencing packages include a virtual whiteboard, which is simply a paint-and-draw program where everyone in the conference shares the same window. That means you can draw something on your screen, and everyone else in the conference sees it appear on theirs, magically.

Examples of conferencing software for Mac OS and Windows users include CUSeeMe from White Pine Software (www.cuseeme.com); ClearPhone from Internet Communications Technologies (www.clearphone.com); and iVisit (www.ivisit.com). Each of these programs supports audio, video, and text chatting. ClearPhone supports shared whiteboards in addition to the other elements.

Microsoft provides a solution for Windows only in the form of Microsoft NetMeeting (see www.microsoft.com/windows/netmeeting). This software has all the bells and whistles — audio, video, text chat, shared whiteboards, even shared applications.

Some of these solutions can work with each other. For example, you can use CUSeeMe to conference with Microsoft NetMeeting users. Check the documentation or Web site for your conferencing software for more information.

E-mail

When you start telecommuting, it becomes even more vital than ever to stay on top of your e-mail, reading and responding to messages quickly and efficiently, like a well-oiled e-mail machine of some kind. People who might normally stop you in the hallway at work for an impromptu meeting need to have a similar way to contact you at home, and if you're using e-mail efficiently, that can be their new method.

The rules of e-mail don't change simply because you're telecommuting. The only difference with telecommuting is that you're likely to become more dependent on your e-mail than you were before.

Here are a few tips for using e-mail effectively:

- ✔ **Set up folders in your e-mail program in which you can file e-mail messages.** For example, you might set up a folder for each project, or even a folder for each stage or aspect of a project, and file all incoming mail (after replying promptly, of course) in the appropriate folders. Without a good way to organize your e-mail, you can get buried under a sea of memos and conflicting instructions and never dig your way out.

- ✔ **Use the office e-mail system for your office e-mail, not your personal account.** If you start giving people your personal e-mail account for working at home, you'll end up with some mail going to the work account, some going to the home account, and some going to a third person you don't even know. Stick with your work account for work correspondence. Check with your network administrator for details. If you can't log on to the work e-mail account from home directly, you may have to set up a VPN connection and log on to your e-mail account after the VPN connection is established. Check out the VPN section in this chapter for how to do this.

- ✔ **Include your e-mail address and both home and work phone numbers on everything you give to anyone.** Remember, your goal is for people to be able to reach you when you're working at home, so include both telephone numbers (home and work) and your e-mail address on any document, e-mail, or presentation you give anyone. Nobody at your office should ever have to ask "Say, how do I get in touch with <your name here>?"

You may also want to e-mail your agenda before holding a meeting, your schedule (when you're working at home versus the office), and other useful information you might not have thought about when you were still working in the office. Remember, there's no such thing as being *too* in-touch with your co-workers.

Ready, IM, fire

We discuss instant messaging fully in Chapter 10, but it has a special place in the telecommuting world. If you have instant messaging software such as AOL Instant Messenger or Yahoo! Messenger running whenever your computer is on, IMs can be a powerful tool for keeping in touch with your co-workers.

For example, I keep AOL Instant Messenger (AIM) running whenever my computer is on, which is pretty much 24 hours a day. Many of my co-workers also use AIM, and during the business day, they'll frequently send me a quick question, a reminder of meetings or deadlines, or a request to chat about an upcoming project. IM helps combat your isolation blues, too.

Files travelling to and fro

One of the keys to being able to telecommute effectively is getting the files you're working with, such as word processing documents, spreadsheets, graphics, and so on, from work to home and from home to work. Broadband makes these transfers speedier than ever.

If you're using a VPN connection to hook your computer at home to the network at the office, you don't need to worry transferring files because you just click the network drive and copy or move the files from home to the office or vice versa. You can use your department's file server, personal (or *peer-to-peer*) file sharing, or e-mail the same way you would if you were in the office.

You can choose from a number of excellent ways to get files back and forth between your home and office, but you'll have to decide which you prefer after reading the descriptions. No method here is better than the others; you simply have to pick the one that best suits your working style.

Virtual or Web-based hard drives

One of the recent technologies made available on the Web is a *virtual hard drive.* The concept is similar to the file servers you may use at work. With a virtual hard drive, a company on the Internet maintains some file storage space, and breaks it up into small sections for individuals to use.

Check out these sites for the features and availability you need:

- **Apple's iTools page** (`itools.mac.com/WebObjects/Tools`). Look for the service called iDisk. When you sign up for iTools, you automatically get a virtual hard disk on Apple's site that appears on your desktop as would any other disk.

- **NetDrive** (`www.netdrive.com`). NetDrive provides a utility that makes the virtual drive (with up to 100MB of storage) appear on your Windows desktop as if it were a locally-connected drive.

- **Xdrive** (`www.xdrive.com`)

- **Driveway** (`www.driveway.com`)

- **iDrive** (`www.idrive.com`)

Most of these virtual hard drive services are either commercial (with monthly or yearly fees) or advertising-based, but if they're on the Internet, you can use them to transfer files. Virtually all of these services let you copy and manage files through any Web browser, anywhere in the world. Figure 11-6 shows an example of Internet storage.

To use an Internet storage drive to transfer files between home and work simply copy from your hard drive to the Web site's virtual drive. Then, at your destination, copy the files from the Web drive to your network or alternate machine.

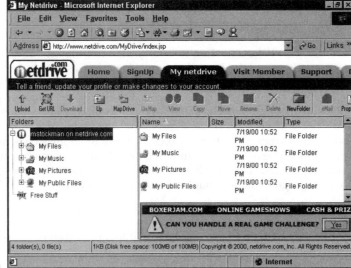

Figure 11-6: Accessing your 100MB of Internet storage available through a Web browser.

As with any account on the Internet, virtual hard drives are subject to cracking or other data theft. You can't even necessarily trust the company operating the service. Be sure to assign a strong password that's difficult to guess or crack to your account. Even with a good password, we don't recommend using this service for very sensitive files, unless you use some security software to encrypt the files before placing them on the Internet.

Remember, the more space you have, the more files you can back up and transfer to the office. But even with a high-speed Internet connection, copying files may take a while, especially if you're copying a large number or very big files.

E-mail attachments

One of the easiest way to transfer files is as attachments to e-mail messages. But you knew that already, right? Here's a trick: Whether you have a single or multiple (work and home) accounts, you can mail attached files to yourself, as long as you wait until you get to the other location to read the messages.

Simply attach the file at one location and send it (don't use a send/receive command). When you get to your destination, either access your account on your provider's Web site, or open your alternate account to transfer the file. This is especially useful if you're sending to more than one person.

Chapter 12

Keeping Your Computer Up to Speed

. . . .

In This Chapter

▶ Knowing how and when to upgrade your Internet software

▶ Adding RAM: Too much is never enough

▶ Troubleshooting poor video

▶ Upgrading your operating system

▶ Choosing your disks: You've got options!

▶ Replacing the processor

▶ Replacing the motherboard

. . . .

So, you think you're the fastest Internet connection in the West, eh kid? Well, it takes a lot more than a fast connection to keep yourself a-whoompin' and a-whompin' down the information superhighway nowadays.

Sooner or later, you just might find that your new super-fast connection to the Internet has put your computer on the fast track to obsolescence! In this chapter, we show you how to figure out which bit of your hardware needs upgrading or replacement, and how to go about this in the cheapest and easiest manner possible.

Also, the more you use your computer, especially your broadband connection, the more your hard drive fills up with files you either don't need or need to store for archiving purposes. We give you clues on how to handle those issues, too.

Keeping Your Software Current and Clean

You can think of your computer's connection to the Internet as being a stream of 1s and 0s moving extremely fast in and out of your computer, as shown in Figure 12-1.

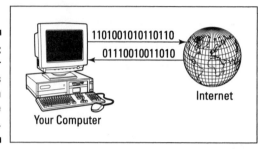

Figure 12-1:
Your computer's connection to the Internet.

1101001010110110
01110010011010

Your Computer

Internet

Now, unless you are Zoldar from the planet Brainiac, you probably aren't going to interact with the Internet directly at this level. Most of us have much better things to do with our time than directly influencing the patterns of high and low voltage that our computer uses to communicate with other computers. For us, software developers create two kinds of software: operating systems (which run the computer) and applications (which the computer runs).

Applications come in a variety of forms for everything from word processing to playing games. These files come and go with every whim and download or when you need to perform a specific project. The operating system, such as Windows, Linux, or Mac OS, is something you don't upgrade as often. This section shows you ways to keep your applications in tune. The section on operating systems in this chapter tells you what you need to know to keep that software in tune.

Upgrading software

When you need to upgrade software depends on a few factors:

- ✔ The kind of software it is
- ✔ Changes in your operating system
- ✔ New versions that offer features you want

Special services — unavoidable upgrades

The software included for use with some large Internet services, such as AOL, is intended specifically for use with their own service. Because these services employ their own, special protocols for communication, you should not expect to be able to use their software with other services. Furthermore, these special protocols have been known to change in ways that absolutely require users to upgrade their software in order to continue using the service.

The good side to this is that, when it comes time to upgrade, the service in question will usually be only too willing to assist you in the process. The reason for this is that their revenues absolutely depend on your continuing to pay for their services. Since you obviously won't pay unless you are able to use, most services are pretty good about making sure they don't upgrade their customers out of the game!

Some applications exist specifically to facilitate your use of the Internet. For example, Microsoft's Internet Explorer browser interprets the stream of 1s and 0s flowing in and out of your computer in the context of various Web pages. E-mail programs are able to use this same flow to send and receive messages all over the world.

It is unlikely that the language spoken by the Internet will ever change. For this reason, you should not worry too much about ever *having* to upgrade the software that you use to connect to the Internet. However, the technologies involved in the Internet are improving at such a tremendous pace that you stand a good chance of missing out on a lot of neat features and benefits if you never even consider upgrading.

Other kinds of software issued by companies that offer a limited-license let you use it free for a while and then ask you to upgrade or register the product — meaning buy it! Some of these products automatically downgrade the features they initially offer if you don't register the product in a specified time.

Other packages, such as some types of shareware offer a free-forever feature-reduced version. If you like it and want more features, you need to upgrade.

The most common form of software before the advent of the Internet came in shrink-wrapped boxes from the store. This commercial software is, perhaps, the simplest to understand:

- ✔ You pay the author a fee (possibly through a third-party, such as a software store)
- ✔ The author gives you one copy of the software (also, possibly through a third-party)

> ✔ You *and only you* are allowed to use this software . . .
>
> • however you want
>
> • for as long as you want
>
> ✔ When the software doesn't fit your needs any more, you stop using it

The problem with these issues is that when you feel the need for new software of this sort, you will have to pay more to get it. Many software publishers cut special deals for people who already own older versions of their software.

The special upgrade prices often offered for current owners of a software package don't typically last forever. If you let a version come and go before upgrading, you will often have to pay full price — just as if you'd never owned the software at all!

RAMming and ROMing More Memory into Your Computer

The sea may have no memory, but your computer certainly does. In fact, it has memory of two particular kinds: ROM and RAM. ROM stands for Read Only Memory. Your computer stores in the ROM its instructions for carrying out only the most basic of tasks, including

> ✔ Checking for hardware errors
>
> ✔ Keeping track of the time and date
>
> ✔ Talking to its ports

RAM is reserved for storing more sophisticated instructions. The programs that go here include

> ✔ Operating systems
>
> ✔ Applications
>
> ✔ Data, such as Word documents and MP3 songs

Upgrading ROM

As mentioned above, the ROM in your computer stores all of the most basic, vital tasks that your computer must perform in order to function. As you might have guessed from its name, it's also impossible to overwrite the contents of your computer's ROM. This is good, because the functions performed by these instructions are far too important to risk the introduction of errors.

ROM upgrades for personal computers are *not* common. The instructions typically placed into computers' ROM are written by their manufacturers to provide for all their computers' needs for as long as they are in use. What are the odds that you would ever need to change something as basic as the way that you turn on your computer?

Whenever you turn on your computer for the first time, you probably see a lot of things scrolling past you on the screen. Many of these things are programs specially designed to test the ROM chips in your computer for errors. If they discover any errors, there isn't much that they can do to resolve the problem. They can, however, alert you to the presence of a problem with your computer's ROM. You may then elect to pursue one of the upgrade approaches described in this section.

One example of an instance in which a ROM upgrade *would* be needed is if some errors are discovered in the programs inside your ROM. This was the case with many computers shortly before January 1, 2000. The way that the ROM in these computers had been programmed meant that, without upgrade, they would revert to January 1, 1999 at the start of the New Year.

In the cases described, many people opted for a software solution rather than upgrading the ROMs in their computers. You can think of this kind of like the difference between getting glasses and going for corrective eye surgery. The glasses don't actually do anything to fix your eyes — they just compensate for whatever is wrong with them. Figure 12-2 shows how a software fix for the so-called Millennium Bug might work.

When software fixes are out of the question, as is typically the case with severe errors in ROM programming, the only alternative is to replace the chips containing the bad ROM. In some cases, replacement chips may be ordered directly from a computer's manufacturer and installed by a reasonably technically knowledgeable end-user. In other cases, the entire computer must be temporarily returned to a service center in order to undergo the operation.

Getting more RAM

After software upgrades, RAM upgrades are probably the single most common improvement most people make to their computers. There are two main kinds of RAM upgrades:

- ✔ Changing the *quality* of your computer's RAM
- ✔ Changing the *quantity* of your computer's RAM

Figure 12-2:
Software to
the rescue!

Quality. QUALITY!!

RAM comes in many different flavors. What they all share in common is that
they will be shipped to you as little silicon chips mounted on silicon boards
that you have to slide into the correct slots on your computer. A few of the
things that they differ in include

- ✔ Size and number of pins on the silicon board
- ✔ Speed at which your computer can talk to the chips
- ✔ Likelihood of failure

Differences in the size and number of pins on the silicon boards where your
RAM chips are mounted will be a primary determinant of whether or not you
are able to use a certain kind of RAM with your computer. In short, if the RAM
is mounted on a board that is too big or too small for your computer's slots,
then you won't be able to use it. This isn't anything terribly advanced — just
basic physics!

The speed at which your computer can talk to the chips is one influencing factor on your computer's overall performance. By replacing very slow-access memory with quicker chips, you can achieve something of an increase in the speed of your computer. In actuality, however, the speed of your computer's other parts (such as the CPU) are so, *so* much more important than your RAM that this is a very rare computer upgrade.

Different flavors and speeds of RAM typically have different names. These flavors are not at all interchangeable and the odds are good that your computer is only capable of working with one or two of these flavors at most. Check with your computer's manufacturer before purchasing any new RAM and never, ever mix and match different kinds of RAM within the same computer!

Maybe it is how much you have, after all

The truly common RAM upgrade operation for personal computers is increasing the overall quantity of available RAM. The effect of doing this can often be as dramatic as buying a brand new computer! On the other hand, if your computer already has plenty of RAM, the effects of any new additions can often go completely unnoticed. Figure 12-3 shows a graph illustrating the impact of adding more and more RAM to a computer.

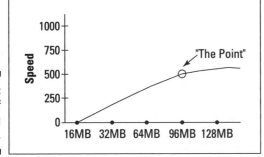

Figure 12-3:
The point of diminishing returns.

There are a couple of tricks to increasing the amount of RAM in your computer. To begin with, you have a limited number of slots in your computer. RAM comes on boards of varying capacities — anywhere from 2MB to 128MB in many cases. Suppose that you have a computer with 4 slots, each of which contains its own 32MB card. This gives you a starting total of 128 MB in your computer (4 $\times$ 32 = 128).

If you want to upgrade at this point, you must be willing to sacrifice *at least* 32MB just to get started. This is because you will have to remove one of the existing cards in order to install a new one; otherwise you won't have any empty slots with which to work!

In some computers, RAM must always be installed in pairs of cards with exactly the same capacity. So, for example, you could never have three cards of 32MB each with one card of 64MB. This is because the 64MB card would be paired with one of the 32MB cards — and your computer would not even turn on this way! Instead, you would actually have to remove *another* of the 32MB cards and install *another* 64MB to replace it.

Keeping Video Free from Jerks

Sometimes, the first sign suggesting that your computer needs any kind of upgrade will come while trying to play the latest, greatest video game on your computer. At best, you might notice that the alien ships and bombs that are supposed to zip and around and explode don't seem to be moving quite right. Rather than zooming smoothly from one place to another, they may appear to be moving more in stop-motion fashion.

In even more dire circumstances, many of the newest games will simply refuse to load onto your computer unless you have hardware that comes up to their standards! You may get an irritating little message such as:

```
...inadequate video equipment.
Go buy a new card, loser!
Bye.
```

Usually, you can resolve these problems relatively cheaply ($100–$200) by simply buying a new video card for your computer. A video card is a piece of special equipment that sits inside your computer and focuses solely on facilitating communications between your computer and your monitor. You can think of it kind of like hiring an assistant for your computer that will do nothing other than deal with the video portion of things — so the rest of your computer can focus on other things.

Video cards come with varying amounts of RAM on them. The more RAM they have, the more screens of video they can store internally before they are ever displayed on your monitor. This allows them to do a much better job of making your video appear smooth, rather than stop motion.

It is important when you go shopping for a new video card to make sure that it's compatible both with your computer and your monitor. If your computer is particularly old, the newest video cards may not work with it. At this point, you will be faced with the prospect of performing significantly more in-depth upgrade operations — or buying a new computer!

The manufacturers of some of the most popular video cards are listed below:

- http://www.3dfx.com
- http://www.videologic.com
- http://www.ati.com
- http://www.intel.com
- http://www.matrox.com

Operating on the Operating System

Earlier in this chapter, we discussed upgrading the application software that you use to communicate with the Internet. We explained that applications are the programs (such as e-mail clients and Web browsers) that actually perform the useful work involved in communicating over the Internet.

There is another kind of software loaded on your computer, however. The operating system is the software on which all of the other programs on your computer rely. Most operating systems need to be upgraded from time to time, just like application software.

Why bother?

The following are a number of possible reasons why you might decide to upgrade your operating system:

- **Desire for new features:** You're tantalized by all the bells and whistles readily apparent in a manufactures marketing scheme or have money burning a whole in your pocket.

- **Need to support new equipment:** Some operating systems are old enough now that new printers, scanners, or that Web cam you want to use simply won't work with it.

- **Required in order to run some software:** Perhaps you need a new application that your current OS can't support; then you may need to upgrade.

- **Need to fix bugs in current version:** Either the OS was shipped a little too quickly, or some brilliant cracker finds a hole, and a buggy OS can cause problems.

Many corporations now follow policies that expressly forbid the installation of any piece of software — including operating systems — until they have been on the market for at least a year. The thinking is, "Let everyone else go out and find the bugs. Then, when they have been fixed, we will reap the rewards right along with them." Although this is an effective means of avoiding many bugs that are present in the earliest releases of software, it also means that, by the time you install your operating system, you will be that much closer to being obsolete once again.

Types of OS offerings

Depending on what operating system you use and on your reason for upgrading, you may have several options available to you.

Upgrade packages

Operating systems publishers are particularly likely to offer special upgrade offers to current users of their products. This is because they have a vested interest in making sure that you continue using their product instead of defecting to the competition. By offering you a special price to continue using their product, they give you an extra incentive to stay loyal.

You can usually buy these OS upgrades at your local software retailer. Beware if you think you can get the lower-priced upgrade without owning the original product, however. Not only is this practice not legal, but also it typically will not work. Most OS upgrade packages are capable of telling whether or not you actually have an older version of the OS installed!

Full installs

If you want to get an operating system that you don't already have running on your computer, then you will need to get a full install. Your exact path to doing this will depend on the specific OS.

Windows

The Windows operating systems are commercial software in the truest sense of the word. You will have to buy this software, in order to use it.

Linux

Linux, and many other flavors of Unix, may be freely downloaded off the Internet. Furthermore, you may buy packages at most software and bookstores that include the OS on CD along with extensive documentation and technical support.

MacOS

The Macintosh operating system is commercial software, just like Microsoft Windows. It is a little confusing because Apple also manufacturers the computer on which most installations of MacOS operate — the iMac.

OS Updates

Updates are a slightly different concept from upgrades. Operating system updates are released for a couple of main reasons:

- ✔ To provide important new features that can't wait for the next version of an operating system
- ✔ To fix bugs too severe to wait for the next version of an operating system

In the case of severe bugs, most of the major OS manufacturers will make fixes available to current owners free-of-charge. If you are experiencing a specific bug with your OS, you should check the manufacturer's Web site for free fixes before making any purchases.

One example of a new feature that couldn't wait for a new version of an operating system might be Microsoft's Internet Information Server. Version 3 of this software represented an enormous and vitally important improvement over the version of this software that was originally included with their Windows NT operating system. There was no way that Microsoft could wait for Windows 2000 to be released before improving on this piece of their software, so they released a free update to their operating system: the Windows NT Option Pack.

The numerous service packs that Microsoft has released for Windows NT would be good examples of bugs that couldn't wait to be patched. At the time of writing, there have been six of these also made freely available to current owners of the Windows NT operating system.

More Disks Than You Can Shake a Stick At

Eventually, it's bound to happen: The files you accumulate will outweigh your computer's native storage capacity. At this point, you will have three options:

- ✔ Get rid of some files
- ✔ Compress some files
- ✔ Buy more storage

The most obvious way to get rid of files is to start going through your hard disk and deleting things. However, you may also elect to get rid of files simply by off-loading them onto floppies or tape storage.

On many modern operating systems, deleting files simply moves them to a trash can or recycling bin on your desktop. Until you empty this trash can or recycling bin, you won't realize any of the space savings associated with having deleted these files. They will still be on your computer, taking up space.

Rather than deleting these files, you might be able to save space simply by compressing them. One of the most popular packages for doing this on the Windows operating system is called Winzip. You can download a free trial of this software from www.winzip.com.

Your final option requires that you neither delete nor archive your files. In this case, you simply go out and buy more storage so your computer's capacity can be increased.

Ye olde hard disks

The old standard for most peoples' storage decisions is the common hard disk. In recent years, it has become possible to purchase enormous quantities of storage — in excess of 20 gigs — for less than $200.

The main disadvantage to purchasing hard disks is that they can be somewhat difficult to install. Typically, you must open your computer's case, connect the new drive to the appropriate cables, and readjust several settings on your computer in order to have the new drive recognized.

In spite of these complexities, hard disks are still a good choice when:

✔ You will be writing to the new storage at least as often as you will be reading from it

✔ You need the absolute best speeds available

✔ You want the best prices available

Floppies on steroids

Since the mid-1980s, storage media has been available which presents a kind of hybrid between hard disks and regular floppy disks. These feature storage capacities lower than hard disks, but significantly greater than floppy disks. The best part, however, is that they can be easily removed for storage or for use in other computers.

Another benefit to these devices is that they are generally easier to set up and get running than new hard drives. Most of these sit outside of your computer's main case, so you can install them without having to perform major surgery!

Sometimes you can choose between purchasing an external and internal version of the same disk drive. All other factors being equal, external drives are better if you think there is any chance that you will ever want to use your drive with more than one computer. Having a drive that is external and merely connected to your computer by a cable makes it much, much easier to move to another computer and reconnect.

Burning CDs without a fire

Optical drives use lasers to read and write electronic impulses on CDs. The idea is that binary 1s are represented by markings on the disks that generate different kinds of light from binary 0s. Because these markings can be infinitesimally small, the storage capacity for CDs can be much greater than that of comparably sized conventional storage.

CDR

CDR drivers are the first commercially available optical drives that allow consumers to record their own CDs! Those in the know refer to the process of creating a new CD as *burning* it. This refers to the action of the laser inside your drive as it etches, or burns, your data into the surface of the disk.

Although a CD looks relatively flat, it is actually composed of several layers of materials that are each remarkably thin, as shown in Figure 12-4. On the outermost layers, there is a clear layer of protective plastic to give your CD (some) protection from scratching. Beneath this is a layer of 24K gold that serves to reflect the light from your CD drive's laser during reading. At the innermost level is a thin layer of green dye, which is what your CDR will actually burn into during writing. This layer gives your CDR a green appearance when you hold it up to the light.

A CDR can hold every bit as much information as a regular CD: about 640MB. CDs are also relatively cheap, retailing for approximately $2 each at the time of writing. There are only two potential drawbacks to CDR storage: speed and permanence.

Speed

The parts in writeable CD drives are several times heavier than those in read-only devices. For this reason, they tend to take much longer to read and write data. Whereas there are so-called 20x standard CD drives available for computers that operate at 20 times the speed of regular CD players, the best you can get with writeable drives are 4x. It takes approximately 19 minutes to fill a CD with information at this speed.

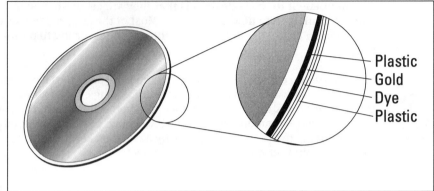

Figure 12-4:
A CD
sandwich.

Permanence

Once you write data onto a CDR drive, it is there forever. Obviously, if you were to scratch the CD beyond usability, then this data would no longer exist. But, then, neither would your CD for all intents and purposes. The important thing to remember is that you cannot write over data once you record it onto a CDR drive.

CDRW

CDRW drives can be thought of as exactly the same as CDR drives with one exception: These drives allow you to erase and rewrite data. For this reason, of course, CDRW drives are slightly more expensive at the time of writing. Whether or not the extra expense can be justified depends on your reasons for wanting a recordable CD drive in the first place. See Table 12-1 in the next section for a comparison of usefulness between all three kinds of optical drives.

DVD

The latest rage in optical disks is the DVD drive. You may already own one of these, but chances are better that it's attached to your television, not to your computer. DVDs' main value advantage over traditional optical disks are their much greater storage abilities: 17GB! This is enough to store entire movies and still have room left over!

Currently, most of the DVD drives that ship with computers are read-only. This means that the only thing that most people are using DVDs with their computers for at the moment is software and movies that they receive this way.

If you have an abundance of cash, DVD writers are available for personal computers. These are still in the advanced technology stages, so you can expect to pay extra for hardware that is still neither 100 percent reliable nor particularly easy to use.

Table 12-1 compares the usefulness of all the different types of optical storage in different scenarios:

Table 12-1	The Many Faces of Optical Storage			
Purpose	*CD*	*CDR*	*CDRW*	*DVD*
Playing games from disk	Yes	No	No	No
Archiving many small files	No	Yes	Yes	No
Viewing/archiving movies	No	No	No	Yes
Use just like hard disk	No	No	Yes	No

Getting a Brain Transplant for Your Computer

The second most extensive upgrade that you will ever have to perform on your computer is an upgrade of its CPU. The CPU is the chip that sits at the center of your computer and is responsible for the computer's thinking. For this reason, you can think of your CPU as being the brain of your computer.

In general, there are three distinguishing characteristics to any CPU chip:

- Manufacturer
- Model
- Speed

One example of this would be an Intel 266 MHz Pentium II processor. In this case, the manufacturer is Intel. The model of this processor is the Pentium II. And, finally, the speed here is 266 MHz — this means that the chip's internal clock ticks about 266 million times per second . . . now that's fast!

It is important to understand these three attributes of your current processor because, in general, the only difference in an upgrade chip may be its speed. This means that, in the above example, it would be perfectly legitimate to try replacing your 266 MHz chip with a 300 MHz CPU.

Some particularly high-end computers have more than one CPU. In these cases, it is important that each CPU be of exactly the same speed as all the others. For this reason, you could never have a computer with one 266 MHz CPU and another 300 MHz CPU.

It is highly unlikely that your computer would tolerate the installation of a different-model CPU than the one that you currently own. So, if you currently have a Pentium II in your computer, it probably wouldn't work if you tried installing a Pentium III. In fact, owing to the changes in size and shape that usually accompany model differences, it probably wouldn't even fit into your computer's CPU socket!

Differences in manufacturer are a slightly more complicated matter, and related to the differences in model described above. Some manufacturers specialize in producing chips that are clones of the chips developed by other manufacturers. These chips function at least 99.9 percent the same as those made by their competitors, but the clones are generally priced lower. These companies are able to offer lower prices because, of course, they didn't have to spend any money researching and developing the technologies that they wind up selling.

Whether or not this practice is ethical is a point left up to the reader's conscience. The important thing for our discussion is that it is 100 percent legal. It can also be a good way to reduce the cost of your upgrade if you are in a limited-budget situation (and who isn't?).

If a clone of your current CPU exists, then there is a good chance that clones also exist for all of the chips that you could potentially upgrade. In these cases, it would be technically possible for you to upgrade from your current processor to one of a completely different model and manufacturer.

In Order to Win This Game, You Have to Fight the Motherboard

Inside of your computer, there is a single, large board on which your CPU is mounted. Any extension cards that you have installed, such as video and sound card, are also plugged into this board. Your memory is attached to this board in some way, as are all of your disk drives.

By now, you might have deduced that this is one extremely important board! It is, in fact, arguably the entire heart and soul of your computer system. For this reason, it's given the suitably reverent name of the motherboard. Without a motherboard, you don't have a computer — you just have a pile of computer pieces.

Replacing the motherboard in your computer is the most intensive upgrade that you could ever possibly perform. This is the point at which you really have to ask yourself, "Wouldn't I be better off just buying a brand new computer?" The answer to this question will vary according to your situation.

Break loose with some of that cash!

The main reason for upgrading your motherboard would be if any or all of the *other* pieces that you need to upgrade will not work with your current motherboard.

For example, suppose that you need a faster CPU because all of your programs are taking way too long to run and you have plenty of RAM, so you know that this can't be the problem. Every motherboard is designed to accept a certain set of processors, as described in the section above. If your current CPU is the fastest that your current motherboard will support, then you will need to replace your motherboard in order to get any better CPU.

Unfortunately, your CPU isn't the only thing that you have inside of your computer. There are RAM chips, disk drives, and all sorts of extension cards to consider. Many of these are only designed to work properly with certain kinds of motherboards. By replacing your motherboard so that you can get a better CPU, you can wind up in a situation where nothing else inside of your computer works any more!

Worse yet, motherboards come in vast variety of shapes and sizes. In general, the older motherboards are smaller than the newer ones — but this is a gross oversimplification. Nevertheless, the chances are good that the new motherboard you need won't fit inside of your existing computer case. This means that you will now have to invest in a new box as well.

If you're getting the picture at this point that it usually isn't worth upgrading your motherboard, then you get the message, my friend! Before committing to this project, always carefully compare the compatibilities between all of the equipment you plan on replacing and ask yourself, "Am I going to be spending as much money replacing as I would if I just bought a new one?" If you even come close, you are better off buying a brand new system.

The place is grilled, but there's life in the old thing, yet

It can be economically expedient to upgrade your computer if:

- ✔ The new motherboard fits inside of your existing computer case
- ✔ Most of your existing hardware will still work
- ✔ You have a reasonably up-to-date operating system
- ✔ You have a reasonably up-to-date video system

We told you all about the problems with getting your new board to fit and work with your existing equipment in the previous section. But, when considering the purchase of a new system, you should also take your monitor and operating system into account.

A new monitor may or may not come as part of a new computer system. If you have a really good monitor currently, then why would you want to buy a new computer system that may also include a new monitor? This is an additional expense that you don't need.

Similarly, if you have just gone to the expense of buying the latest version of Windows, MacOS, or Linux — then why buy a computer that has this included? The cost of this software will be passed along to you in the price of the new computer, whether it's itemized or not.

In these instances, you will definitely want to consider maintaining your current system rather than upgrading.

Chapter 13

Sharing Your Connection

● ●

In This Chapter

▶ Deciding the best way to hook your computers together in a network

▶ Deciding the best way to connect your network to your Internet connection

▶ Comparing NAT, proxy, and direct connections

● ●

*O*nce upon a time, having a computer in your home made you the object of fascination and envy among your friends and neighbors. These days, however, keeping up with the Joneses means having a computer for every member of the family, plus one for guests. Even if you haven't gone that far overboard, you may have more than one computer in your home or you may want to set up two or more computers for your growing business. If so, you can share your high-speed Internet connection.

Sharing the connection means that while you're retrieving your e-mail, your spouse can browse some travel sites for your upcoming vacation, and your 2.5 children can conduct research for their latest school projects, all at the same time.

This chapter provides the information you need to decide how to hook your computers together; because much of the technical information relies on the specific options or products you choose, we don't go in-depth on the nuts and bolts. For that information, check out *Networking For Dummies*, 4th Edition, by Doug Lowe (IDG Books Worldwide, Inc.).

Implications of Sharing the Connection

There are several ways to set up a shared Internet connection. Some require that you to pay your Internet provider more money, and others cost you nothing but the equipment to string your computers together on a local network.

> ✔ **Pay the broadband provider for additional addresses.** The easiest option, paying for more connections involves contacting your high-speed Internet access provider and paying a fee, often $5 to $10 per month.

✔ **Set up NAT/IP Masquerading.** By setting up some software on a computer or a two-port router, you can share your single public Internet connection with all computers on your private LAN.

✔ **Install a Proxy Server.** Setting up a proxy server involves dedicating a computer to act as an Internet server, so that your computers talk only to the proxy server, and the proxy server talks to the Internet on their behalf.

Remember, all methods for sharing an Internet connection involve connecting your computers to a local area network (LAN), so they can all talk to the device providing the Internet connection (and, conveniently, to each other as well). Read the instructions in this chapter for setting up a LAN before you install any of the methods for sharing the connection.

Technical implications of sharing the connection

There are two basic concerns with putting more than one computer on an Internet connection:

✔ Having a valid Internet address for each computer

✔ Protecting each computer from unauthorized access

A short discussion of each subject follows.

What's a valid Internet address and why do I need one?

When you view a Web site, you usually enter an Internet address, such as www.example.com. The Internet, however, works on numbers, not names, so the name you enter has to magically change into the required number. When you enter www.example.com, special servers connected to your Internet account translate the name you enter into the group of four numbers required by the Internet in the form xxx.xxx.xxx.xxx, as in 192.168.12.2. For example, www.whitehouse.gov (the White House Web site maintained by the United States government) is actually 198.137.240.91. You may enter either value into your Web browser to visit that site. These numbers are called *IP addresses*.

What does this have to do with your high-speed Internet account? The answer is that no computer can communicate with others on the Internet without a valid IP address. The IP address identifies you to the entire world, and allows incoming Internet traffic to find your computer. When you try to view a Web page, your request not only contains the page you want (say, www.example.com) but also where to send the requested page (10.19.0.5, if that's your IP address). Without the valid IP address, the page won't come back, because no one knows where to find you, and so the Web page won't load.

When you used a dialup Internet account, you most likely were assigned a different IP address each time you used your modem to connect. You never knew what the IP address was, mainly because you had very little reason to know. All addressing is handled automatically for dialup accounts.

When you get a high-speed Internet account that is always on, your computer is assigned an IP address in one of two ways:

- ✔ **Static IP addressing:** With static IP addressing, the Internet provider reserves an IP address and assigns that address to your computer; no one else can use that address.

- ✔ **Dynamic IP addressing:** If your Internet provider assigns IP addresses dynamically, your computer is assigned an address from a list of available addresses the first time you connect to the Internet. Your computer borrows the address from the list temporarily (usually called a *lease* on that address). That address remains with your computer until you shut down or the lease expires. Each time you start up your computer or enable Internet access, your computer checks to see whether the old IP address is still available. If so, you get the same address again. If not, a new address is assigned.

Under either method, your computer always has a unique IP address, and no one else can use it.

The need for a valid IP address is why you can't just assign a number at random to your computer and log on. If you provide a false or invalid IP address, none of the information you request can reach you, and your Internet connection will not function.

When you plan your network that will connect multiple computers to your always-on, high-speed Internet connection, you have to make sure that each computer you use appears to the rest of the Internet to have a valid IP address. *How* you make sure depends on whether your network uses public or private IP addresses.

Public versus Private IP Addresses

Whenever a computer talks to others on a network using Internet Protocol (IP, the basic networking protocol used to communicate on the Internet), it must be assigned an address by which others can reach it. For computers that are connected to the public Internet, there are very strict methods by which those computers receive IP addresses, to avoid duplicate address. Every computer on the public networks is identified by a unique IP address that nobody else is using.

But what about a private network, as you might set up in your home office with two computers and a printer? If those computers aren't connected to the Internet (or if they connect using a dialup account, which assigns a unique address temporarily each time the computer dials up), you can basically use any addresses you want. There are some standards, however, for numbering private networks that make it easier for you to keep track of your settings:

From	*To*	*Examples*
10.0.0.0	10.255.255.255	10.19.0.1, 10.0.0.145
172.16.0.0	172.31.255.255	172.16.21.4, 172.23.128.1
192.168.0.0	192.168.255.255	192.168.123.61, 192.168.0.2

The first range (10.x.x.x) gives you the highest possible number of private IP addresses. The second range provides fewer possible addresses. The final range (192.168.x.x) gives you the fewest possible addresses (up to 254 unique addresses per network), although far more than any small or home office is likely to ever need. For this reason, the 192.168.x.x range is the most commonly used range for home or small office private networks.

Small offices all over the world are using IP addresses in these ranges on their private networks, often using the same addresses as other small offices. They don't cause networking conflicts because the addresses are *private*, and are never seen by the public Internet.

Computers that have a private address can still talk to the Internet, however, because of a service called *Network Address Translation*, or NAT. When you use a NAT router, you use only the one public IP address given to you by your Internet provider, and assign private addresses throughout your LAN. NAT sits between the privately addressed computers and the Internet, and translates the incoming and outgoing network traffic (swapping private addresses for public ones in all the data and vice versa) to make it all work. For more information on NAT, see *Setting Up a NAT Router* later in this chapter.

Protecting each computer from unauthorized access

One of the biggest risks when you place your network on an always-on, high-speed Internet connection is that someone, somewhere, will break into or damage data on one of your computers. After all, once your computers are on the Internet, they're sitting ducks for anyone with a little bit of knowledge about computer networking and too much time on their hands. As described in Chapter 16, you need to place some safeguards on a network that will be connected to the Internet. A *firewall* is a device that acts like a traffic cop at the intersection of your network and the Internet, letting safe traffic through and holding up its hand to unwanted traffic before it can reach your computers.

Some of the methods for sharing your Internet connection protect your network at the same time, such as NAT and application proxy servers, but you need to take additional precautions to make sure malicious software doesn't sneak past those safeguards.

The risks of break-ins and computer vandalism aren't reasons to avoid sharing your Internet connection on a network; they're just reasons to be careful as you set up your shared connection.

Legal implications

Can you simply share a high-speed network connection with multiple computers in your home or small office? Of course, but although something is technically possible that doesn't make it legal. Make sure what you're doing is allowable under your agreement (usually called an *Acceptable Use Policy,* or *AUP*) with the Internet provider.

If your Internet provider forbids you to share the connection without paying them for each additional computer, you must abide by that agreement, or face loss of service or various penalties that may be spelled out in the agreement. This is true even if, as in some of the cases described here, there is no way for the Internet provider to know you're sharing the connection.

Our advice is two-fold: Know what your provider's license agreement says about multiple users sharing the connection by checking the AUP; to be safe and ethical, simply fork over the cash to add new users or check for cheaper providers. After all, you could take up a collection from those folks sharing your connection. However, many providers include language that says they only *support* a certain configuration, and that if you step outside of their recommended setup, they won't help you when it breaks. If your agreement says this, you're probably free to share the connection as described here, although you're on your own if you run into difficulties.

Before You Share

Sharing an Internet connection requires that all of the computers you want to use the Internet connection be able to talk to each other, which requires some kind of local area network (LAN).

What is a LAN?

A LAN refers to a bunch of computers in a single location (say, a small office or someone's home) that can talk to each other and to some common services (such as printers, file servers, and so on), either through cables or a wireless connection.

If you have ever connected two computers together for any reason, you've most likely created a very small LAN.

LANs can be connected and organized in many different ways:

- ✔ **Wired Ethernet.** Generally, setting up an Ethernet network involves connecting each computer to a central hub with special cables. For the most common type of Ethernet, the cables have connectors that look like very wide modular phone connectors, and this type of Ethernet is called *10Base-T* and operates at speeds of up to 10 Mbps, which is much faster than most high-speed Internet connections can provide. This is the most common and least expensive solution, and many computers on the market come with the necessary connections already built-in.

- ✔ **Wireless Ethernet.** Operating solely using a broadcast signal, this option doesn't require any wires to connect the computers together to the central hub. This option is the most expensive, requiring a wireless network card for each computer and a central base station to receive the signal and connect it to the Internet or wired network, but Wireless Ethernet has been coming down in price while achieving the same networking speeds as a basic wired Ethernet connection (around 10 Mbps). Also, because no wiring is required, a Wireless Ethernet lets you use your network from any location in your home or office, or even outside of the building within a limited distance (at the most, several hundred feet away).

- ✔ **Phone Line or A/C Power (Powerline) Networks.** These connections use special hardware to convert your existing telephone lines or standard electrical outlets into network wiring, without disrupting the phone or electrical service already running. These are by far the easiest networks to set up, because you have a connection anywhere you have a phone outlet or electrical outlet, and no central hub is required. These connections were very slow initially (around 1 Mbps) but recent updates have made these connections as fast as wired Ethernet (around 10 Mbps).

More options will undoubtedly appear, but as long as the network you install allows your computers to talk to each other and to your Internet connection, you can use it to share your Internet hookup as described in this chapter. In most configurations today, computers can speak to each other by way of a central hub to which they are all connected. This isn't the only method of setting up a network, but it's the most common (called a *star topology*). To use a high-speed Internet connection with the computers on the network, you would have to connect your external high-speed connection to that hub as well.

Why you need a Local Area Network (LAN)

Before you installed a high-speed Internet connection, you were probably connecting to the Internet using a modem and a telephone line. In that situation, the modem provided a kind of network connection, and you had no need for any other kind of connection to other computers in your home or office. If your computers have never needed to communicate with each other before, you may not have them connected to each other in any way.

High-speed Internet access usually requires a network connection to talk to your computer. When you installed high-speed Internet access, the Internet provider either used a network connection already installed on your computer, or installed a network port for your computer to use for talking to the Internet.

A network port (also referred to as an *Ethernet connection*) is provided by an internal *Network Interface Card*, or NIC. All Macintosh computers shipped in the past five years or more have NICs already installed, and can be connected to a network by plugging in the correct cable. Most Windows-compatible computers do not include NICs by default, but they can be added for as little as US$30, or sometimes even less. For other systems, contact the manufacturer if you're not sure if a NIC is already installed.

In most cases, a NIC provides an Ethernet port, which is usually an RJ-45 connector that resembles a modular phone port, only noticeably wider. When you connect the appropriate cable to this port, and connect the other end to a central *hub* (to which your other computers are also connected), your computers can begin talking to each other.

Just as you need to have a network port to connect one computer to your high-speed Internet connection, each of your additional computers also needs a network connection before it can speak to the Internet. Once you install network ports into each computer, you could hook each computer up to the Internet connection, but only one computer at a time.

To have them all talking to the Internet at once, they have to be connected together as a LAN, and then the LAN has to be connected to the Internet.

Figure 13-1 shows how it works.

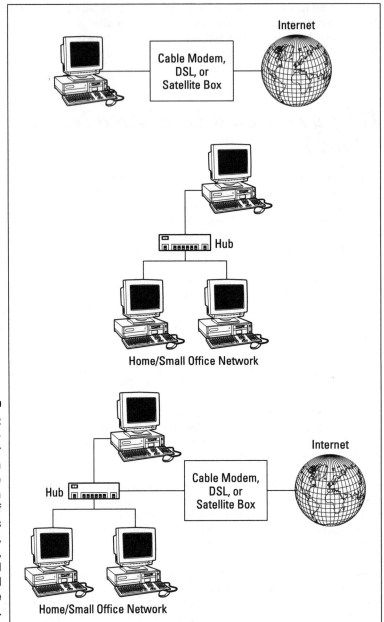

Figure 13-1:
A single-
computer
connection
to the
Internet, a
collection of
computers
in a LAN,
and finally,
the LAN
connected
to the
Internet.

Setting Up a LAN

Remember, before you can share the Internet connection among your computers, your computers have to be able to talk to each other. This section describes how to set up a LAN using a 10Base-T Ethernet, which is the most common type of network used today in small and home offices.

To set up a LAN, you need the following hardware:

✔ **A Network Interface Card (NIC) for any computer that doesn't have a network port.** This can be a standard 10Base-T Ethernet port, a wireless Ethernet card, or a special home networking card that uses your phone lines or electrical outlets.

The home networking cards come as part of a kit (the most common standard comes from the Home Phoneline Networking Alliance, or HomePNA) and specifies which lines in your house are used. Be careful not to plug the network into the wrong connection, especially not into the electrical outlets, unless the instructions say to.

✔ **Network cables that work with your NIC.** For a standard Ethernet, this will usually be 10Base-T cables, which have modular connectors on each end that look like very wide telephone connectors. The Ethernet connectors are *RJ-45 connectors* (while telephones use a smaller standard, called *RJ-11*).

✔ **A central hub to which all of the computers will be connected.** This is required for the Ethernet connections, but may not be required for the HomePNA connections.

✔ **Networking software on your computers.** When you install a network, you generally install software to support the NIC (often called *drivers*) as well as networking software to let your computer talk to others (often called *networking protocols*) The drivers are usually included with your NIC hardware, along with instructions for installing them. The networking protocols are usually provided by your operating system (Mac OS, Windows, Linux, and so on) along with instructions for enabling them. For more information on setting up your networking protocols, see Configuring IP on your Windows 95 or 98 Computer, Windows NT or 2000 Computer, or Mac OS Computer, later in this chapter.

NICing Your Computers: The Joys of 10/100Base-T

As mentioned above, a Network Interface Card (NIC) is the hardware that lets your computer speak with a computer network. There are several options for connecting computers to a small LAN today, all of which are easier, simpler, and cheaper to use than most of the options available back in the prehistoric days of computing.

Today, many computers (all Apple Macintosh computers, most business PCs and even some home PCs) include a standard networking port built-in. That port is an Ethernet networking port, which is by far the most widely used standard for office and home networking today. The Ethernet on virtually all networkable computers uses an RJ-45 port (resembling a modular telephone jack, only wider) to connect the cables.

The standard method for connecting Ethernet networks is *10Base-T* or *100Base-T* wiring. Both of these are IEEE standards, and the names break down like this:

Part of Name	*Meaning*
10 or 100	The maximum communication speed of the standard, either 10 Mbps or 100 Mbps. Either of these speeds is far greater than you'll need for any affordable broadband Internet connection such as cable or DSL lines.
Base	Short for baseband, a signaling method that indicates only Ethernet will travel over the wires.
T	Short for twisted-pair, a type of cabling made up of two insulated copper wires, twisted around each other for the length of the cable to ensure a clean signal. Often these wires are further protected by a grounded covering, or a shield, so you'll see this wire referred to as shielded twisted pair, or STP. Twisted pair wiring without this covering is called unshielded twisted pair, or UTP.

Note that Ethernet cabling requires more than one of these twisted pairs of wires; an Ethernet cable is made up of four pairs, connected in a very specific way to an RJ-45 modular plug at each end. 10/100Base-T connections can connect two computers to each other with a special kind of cable called a *crossover cable*, which has one of the pairs crossed compared to a standard Ethernet cable. For connecting more than two computers, however, 10/100Base-T requires that each computer be connected to a central hub (more on that in the next section), which handles the communications between numerous computers without letting too much of the data collide.

Another type of cabling used to be very common for Ethernet networks called 10Base-2, also known as *thinnet*, run over coaxial cable rather than a twisted-pair. This was popular because it required no hub; all of the cables were connected *serially* (one computer after another, rather than all of them into a central point). This type of network was more expensive than 10Base-T, however, and was also more prone to errors; if one computer in the chain had trouble or lost its connection to the network, it was possible that the computers further down the chain would be cut off as well.

Use what you've got: phone lines and power lines

With the boom in home networking that goes hand-in-hand with the high-speed Internet connections, two new areas of networking have appeared on the market: networks based on your telephone lines, and networks based on your electrical lines.

The main providers of telephone line networking are an alliance of computer manufacturers called the Home Phoneline Networking Alliance, or HomePNA. HomePNA networks (or HPNA) use the standard telephone cables that already run through your house to provide a computer network, without interfering with your normal telephone use.

HPNA can run over your existing phone lines because it transmits the networking data at a higher frequency than your voice and much higher than your ears can detect. The advantage to this kind of network is that you don't have to add any wiring to your home, and your computer can be on the network as long as it can connect to a telephone jack.

HPNA originally ran at 1 Mbps, or 1/10th the speed of a standard Ethernet connection. However, in late 1999 the HomePNA organization released a new standard that transmits data at 10 Mbps, which is therefore capable of the same speeds as a 10Base-T network. As with 10Base-T, HPNA is now much faster than any of the affordable broadband Internet connections, and is therefore faster than you'll need for some time. Numerous products supporting the 1 Mbps standard are already on the market, and 10 Mbps products are slowly appearing now that the new standard has been released.

The disadvantage of HPNA is that it requires a special kind of NIC for each computer. If you already have an Ethernet card in your computer, you won't be able to use it and will have to install the additional card for HPNA. To set up a broadband Internet connection with HPNA, you'd need to buy an HPNA card or USB adapter for each computer, plus a more expensive device for connecting the broadband device's Ethernet port to the HPNA network.

Another disadvantage is that no Macintosh-compatible HPNA products are on the market yet, so you may be out of luck if you've chosen a Macintosh as your home computer. However, for pure flexibility, you can't beat using the wiring that's already installed, and HPNA provides that advantage.

There are other groups providing networking over home telephone wiring, such as a Microsoft/3Com alliance and others. Be sure you either buy all of your networking products from the same company, or that you're certain the different components you have all operate together without difficulty.

As for networking over electrical wiring, I won't go into it in any detail here because the technology has been promised for some time but isn't widely available. Currently, only one company, called Intelogis (`http://www.intelogis.com`), has products available, and while their product is slower than other networking solutions, that will no doubt improve over time. The networking principles are the same for electrical wiring as for telephone line wiring, however: You'll need a box with one cable going into your computer, and the other going into your household wiring. That box will handle the translation, and no hub should be necessary.

Wires? We don't need no stinking wires.

The most expensive but most flexible option available is to use wireless networking. Imagine being able to carry your laptop out to your porch, into your living room, or even out in your yard while staying connected to your computer network and the Internet. Such freedom!

The industry standard for wireless computer networking is IEEE 802.11, which operates at a fairly slow, but wireless, 1 Mbps. This is quickly being replaced by a draft (that is, not officially recognized) standard 802.11 HR (for High Rate), which operates at 11 Mbps, or roughly the same speed as a 10Base-T network.

Products that support 802.11 at 1 Mbps can interoperate, which basically means that you can put different brands of networking cards in each of your computers, and, if they all adhere to the standard, they'll be able to talk to each other.

If a wireless networking product says that it supports IEEE 802.11 and also claims a speed of 11 Mbps, the chances are good that it will operate with other wireless networking products making the same claim. That's not as certain as with the slower standard, because the faster version of 802.11 isn't ratified by the IEEE yet and may change before that happens. If you purchase the same brand of wireless networking hardware for each of your computers, of course, this isn't a concern, and they'll all talk to each other just fine.

A wireless network connection requires two basic components: a network card for the computer, and a base station to handle the communication between the wired network and the wireless network.

For our purposes, you would connect the base station to your high-speed Internet connection (or to a hub that is also connected to the high-speed Internet connection), and plug the wireless networking card into your computer. Figure 13-2 gives you an idea of how the network might be configured.

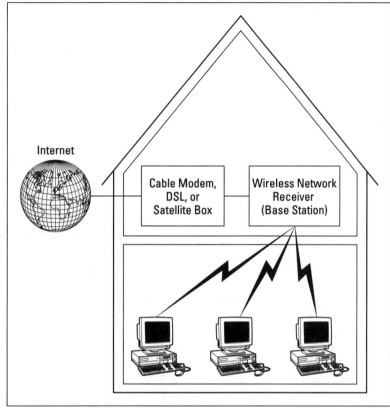

Figure 13-2:
A basic
wireless
computer
network
connected
to the
Internet.

Internet

Cable Modem,
DSL, or
Satellite Box

Wireless Network
Receiver
(Base Station)

Determining Your IP Addresses

The IP addresses you assign to the computers on your LAN depend entirely on how you'll be connecting them to the Internet.

If you're paying your Internet provider for each computer you connect to the high-speed Internet connection, your job in this section is done. Either the provider has given you an IP address and network settings for each computer, or the provider has given you a network configuration that includes using DHCP (Dynamic Host Configuration Protocol), which assigns your computers IP addresses automatically when they first start up. Skip ahead to *Buying Additional Addresses from your Provider* for the details on using the new addresses they give you.

For an internal, or *private*, network, whose IP addresses will never be seen by the Internet (until they've been translated by a NAT router, or by passing through a proxy server), you can number your network any way you want within the range of private addresses described earlier in this chapter. For your sanity, however, you should plan the address numbering for your network carefully before implementing it.

As described earlier in this chapter, there are several ranges of IP addresses you can use for a private network. The most common numbering scheme for small, internal networks is the 192.168.x.x range, so our examples will use that. Note that IP addresses ending in .0 or .255 are reserved, so don't plan to use those on your network. Stick with any numbers ending in .1 through .254.

To set up the IP addresses for your network, follow these steps:

1. **Choose an IP address range to use for your internal network.**

   Given that those address will never be seen outside of your LAN, you can use any of the numbers from the private address ranges shown earlier. For these steps, we'll use 192.168.0.x for our small LAN.

   When you set up an address for each computer, you'll be asked for a subnet mask for your network as well. The *subnet mask* is a way of dividing a network into smaller segments, for easier management, fewer conflicts, and so on. Essentially, the subnet mask determines how the computer's IP address is interpreted, although on a small home or office network, you don't have many worries there.

   For the purposes of sharing a high-speed Internet connection with a small LAN, a single subnet on your private network requires a subnet mask for 255 devices, or 255.255.255.0, so enter that wherever a subnet mask for your private network is required.

2. **Reserve the .1 address for your router or proxy server, depending on which you're using.**

   For our LAN, we'll set aside 192.168.0.1 for the router.

3. **For each computer you have on your LAN, assign addresses to each, incrementing the address by five for each computer.**

   For example, you might make your first computer 192.168.0.5, the next one 192.168.0.10, and so on. Remember, 192.168.0.0 and 192.168.0.255 are not available, but any number within those two is fair game.

   Keep an up-to-date list of the addresses you assign. It may also be helpful to attach a tag to each computer with that computer's IP address for future reference.

4. **Identify any other devices on your network that can operate over TCP/IP, and assign addresses to each of those as well.**

   For example, many networkable printers can use TCP/IP for printing, as can some networkable scanners. (As an aside, you can simplify your network, if all of your devices can use TCP/IP, by turning off all other network protocols that you aren't using, such as AppleTalk, NetBEUI, and others.)

5. **For each of your computers, follow the instructions below for entering the necessary configuration for that computer's operating system.**

Remember that TCP/IP is just about universal in the computer world, so your network can have computers running the Mac OS, any variety of Windows, UNIX, Linux, or other UNIX-like operating systems, OS/2, BeOS, and so on.

Configuring IP on your Windows 95 or 98 Computer

To configure your Windows 95 or 98 computer with the IP address you've assigned it, follow these steps:

1. **From the Start menu, or in the My Computer window, open the Control Panel, and open the Network control panel.**

A window similar to the one in Figure 13-3 appears.

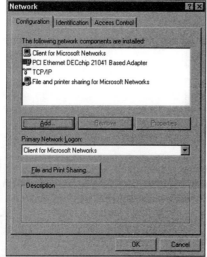

Figure 13-3:
Network
control
panel in
Windows 9x.

2. **If your NIC does not appear in this list, set it up first as described in the documentation included with the network card.**

3. **If TCP/IP does not appear in this list, add it by clicking the Add button.**

In the dialog box that appears, click Protocol and click Add. In the Select Network Protocol dialog box, select Microsoft in the left-hand list and TCP/IP in the right-hand list, then click OK.

4. **Back in the Network control panel, select TCP/IP in the list of components, then click the Properties button.**

   Note that if you have TCP/IP listed more than once, select the one that is bound to your NIC (indicated by an arrow and the name of your NIC following it), then click Properties.

   A dialog box similar to the one in Figure 13-4 appears.

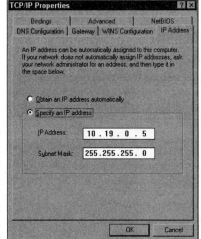

Figure 13-4:
IP Address
tab in the
TCP/IP
Properties
window.

5. **Choose Obtain an IP Address Automatically if you have a DHCP server running on your private LAN, or click Specify an IP Address to enter a predefined IP address.**

   If you choose to obtain an address automatically, skip to step 7. Otherwise continue with the next step.

6. **Enter the manual IP address in the IP Address field, and press Tab.**

7. **Enter the subnet mask (usually 255.255.255.0) in the Subnet Mask field.**

8. **Click the Gateway tab, enter your router's address, usually <your network numbering>.1, as in 10.19.0.1 or 192.168.0.1, in the New Gateway field, and then click the Add button.**

9. **Click the DNS Configuration tab, and select the Enable DNS button.**

10. **Enter a host if your Internet provider gave you one, and then enter your Internet provider's domain name into the Domain field.**

    The Internet provider may have given you this information, but if not, the domain name is usually the final part of your Internet provider's name, so for www.exampleprovider.com, the domain name would be exampleprovider.com.

11. **Enter the DNS server(s) given to you by your Internet provider into the DNS Server Search Order field, clicking the Add button after each one.**

    The DNS servers are the same whether you have a single computer using the Internet connection or a whole network of computers.

12. **Click OK to close the TCP/IP Properties when you're done, then click OK to close the Network control panel and, when you're prompted to do so, restart the computer.**

When your computer finishes restarting, your TCP/IP connection to your private LAN is installed and working.

Configuring IP on your Mac OS computer

These instructions assume that your computer is running Mac OS version 7.5 or higher, using Open Transport TCP/IP (rather than the older MacTCP). If you have a Mac OS computer that isn't using Open Transport, available since around 1995, I suggest you upgrade before adding that computer to your network.

To configure your Mac OS computer with the IP address you've assigned it, follow these steps.

1. **From the Apple menu, open the TCP/IP control panel.**

   A dialog box similar to the one in Figure 13-5 appears.

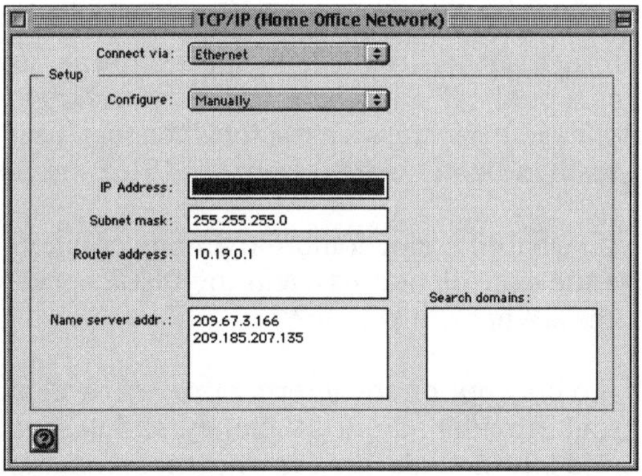

Figure 13-5:
TCP/IP
control
panel in the
Mac OS.

2. **Choose your NIC from the Connect Via pop-up menu, usually appearing as Ethernet.**

3. **Choose Manually from the Configure pop-up menu to enter a prede-fined IP address, or DHCP if you have a DHCP server running on your private LAN.**

   If you choose DHCP server, skip to step 7. Otherwise continue with the next step.

4. **Enter the manual IP address in the IP Address field, and press Tab.**

5. **Enter the subnet mask (usually 255.255.255.0) in the Subnet Mask field.**

6. **Enter your router's address, usually <your network numbering>.1, as in 10.19.0.1 or 192.168.0.1, in the Router Address field.**

7. **In the Name Server Addr field, enter the DNS server(s) given to you by your Internet provider, pressing Return between each one.**

   The DNS servers are the same whether you have a single computer using the Internet connection or a whole network of computers.

8. **Close the TCP/IP control panel, saving the changes you have made when prompted to do so.**

Your Mac OS computer is now configured to use your private LAN for TCP/IP.

Sharing by Buying Additional IP Addresses

When you purchase Internet service from a high-speed Internet provider, it usually issues you a single public IP address to use for your single computer, or it sets you up to get a valid IP address on the fly whenever your computer requests one (automatically, so don't worry) from the DHCP server.

Problems arise when you want to connect more than one computer to the Internet. They can't use the same IP address, and the DHCP server will give you only one valid address. What can you do?

One option (and often the only option the Internet provider will mention to you) is to give the Internet provider additional money, and in return you'll receive an additional valid Internet address for your second computer (or the DHCP server will be set up to provide you with an additional address for your second computer).

If you choose this option, your only requirement is to set up your networking hardware (network card if necessary, cables, and a hub if you are using 10 or 100Base-T). Don't worry about configuring your computers; your Internet provider will give you all of the necessary information you need to configure each computer, just as it did when you configured your first computer to use this connection.

Why this way is better

This is by far the easiest way to put multiple computers on your high-speed connection, because the steps involved are exactly the same as when you put your first computer on the connection, with the addition of a hub. If you want ease-of-installation, buying additional hookups from your provider is the way to go.

The other reason this method may be the best for you is if your provider forbids the use of NAT or proxy servers to share your connection. If your agreement says that you can use a single IP address for a single computer only, and for moral, ethical, or legal reasons you plan to adhere to that agreement, buying additional hookups from your provider is not only the best way to go, it's the *only* way.

Why this way is worse

If your Internet provider allows you to share a single connection among multiple computers, buying additional hookups can be a waste of money, as well as your time.

It's a waste of money because, if you don't mind setting up the hardware necessary to share the connection, it doesn't take long before the cumulative monthly fees exceed the cost of a NAT router or proxy server.

How to do it

To connect an additional computer to your Internet connection, follow these steps:

1. **Set up a LAN as described earlier in this chapter, but leave your active (Internet-connected) computer out of the loop for now.**

   You want your LAN to be in place, with all computers except for your active one connected to the hub, but you can't bring your active computer onto the LAN until you have the necessary configuration information from the Internet provider.

2. **Contact your Internet provider and purchase as many additional hookups as you need to connect the extra computers.**

   They'll provide you with the necessary networking information you need. Wait until you receive that information before you follow the rest of these steps.

   This information should look familiar, because it should be nearly identical to the configuration they provided for your first computer. It should include:

   • IP address or DHCP settings

   • Subnet mask settings

   • Domain Name Services (DNS) server addresses (usually two or three)

   • Gateway or router address

   • DHCP Client ID, if necessary

3. **On each computer on the LAN, open the TCP/IP settings and enter the information provided.**

   On a modern Mac OS you'll open the TCP/IP control panel. On Windows 95, Windows 98, and Windows NT 4.0, you'll open the Network control panel and open the TCP/IP properties. In Windows 2000, you'll open the Properties for the Local Area Connection, and open the TCP/IP properties from the window that appears,For other operating systems, look in your documentation under TCP/IP.

4. **Enter the information in the appropriately-labeled fields.**

   If you're assigning IP addresses to each computer, be sure not to enter the same address on more than one computer; each one must have a unique address. If you're using DHCP, the addresses are assigned automatically, so you don't have to worry about this.

5. **Close and activate the TCP/IP settings.**

   On a Mac, the settings take effect immediately when you save them and close the control panel. On a Windows computer, you'll need to reboot the computer to activate the changes.

6. **Once the settings are all correct and active, disconnect your Internet cable from your active computer and connect it to the hub.**

   Connect your Internet connector's cable to the Uplink port on your hub.

7. **Connect your active computer to the hub.**

   Connect a cable from the NIC in your computer to any empty port on the hub.

8. Browse the Web from any computer on your LAN.

If your Internet provider has instructed you to use *PPP over Ethernet* (PPPoE) software (MacPoET, WinPoET, and so on), be sure that software is running on each computer on your LAN that is communicating with the Internet. The PPPoE software is required on the computers on your LAN that have valid IP addresses to use the Internet.

You've now hooked your computers up to the broadband connection.

Sharing by Setting Up a NAT Router

One universal rule of connecting a computer to the Internet is that the computer must have a unique, valid IP address assigned to it. One computer, one IP address. However, while that rule can't be broken, it can be bent using *Network Address Translation*, or NAT. NAT is the process which can share a single public IP address among numerous computers, without any conflicts or lost data.

When you're using a NAT router, your small network of computers can talk to each other using a set of private IP addresses that aren't valid for Internet use. When any of your computers tries to connect to the outside world (the public Internet), the NAT router intercepts the packets of data, replaces the invalid internal IP address with the one public address you have, and sends the connection to its destination.

With a NAT router containing two network cards (NICs), all connections to and from the Internet pass through the router, as shown in Figure 13-6.

Figure 13-6: NAT router with two network cards.

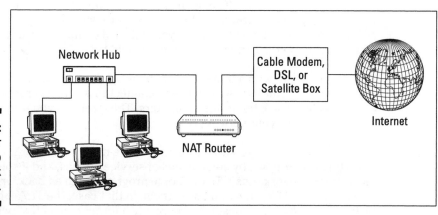

Network Hub

Cable Modem, DSL, or Satellite Box

Internet

NAT Router

This configuration is the same whether the NAT router is a commercial box or a computer with two NICs and some NAT software.

If a computer acting as a NAT router contains only one NIC, the structure of your network changes, as shown in Figure 13-7.

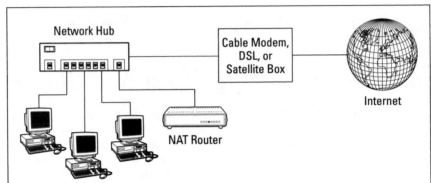

Figure 13-7:
NAT router
with only
one network
card.

NAT and security

Most NAT routers, by default, don't accept any incoming connections that haven't been requested from inside your LAN. You get this very powerful, automatic security feature as soon as you set up your NAT router.

Because a NAT router is sharing a single public IP address with a number of private computers, the router knows where only outgoing requests come from, and normally has no idea which computer should receive an incoming connection. For example, if someone tried to connect to your public IP address using a Web browser (which attempts to connect on port 80), the NAT router wouldn't know which of your internal computers was providing Web services, so the connection attempt would fail.

This provides you with a large measure of network security, because if someone outside of your network can't even connect to a computer inside, she can't possibly attack the inside computers. This protects you from random attempts to enter your network.

This does *not* protect you from attacks that are more insidious. Your network may still be shut down by some denial-of-service attacks, and if someone inside your network runs a Trojan horse program (such as Back Orifice or others), your NAT router won't stop them. In that case, the Trojan horse is inside your network requesting an outgoing Internet connection, which the NAT router is designed to provide.

One NIC or two?

If you're setting up a spare or underused computer as your NAT router, you need to decide whether the computer should contain one or two NICs.

A NAT router will function equally well for placing your computers on the Internet with one NIC or two.

However, there is a security drawback to using a computer as a NAT router that contains only one NIC. With two NICs, the computers on your network are physically blocked from the Internet by the NAT router; that is, all traffic to and from your LAN comes into the NAT router only, is passed from one NIC to the other, and from there into your LAN. When your NAT router contains only one network card, all of the computers on your LAN are physically connected to the Internet directly, and only *virtually* are they blocked from the Internet by the NAT router. With a single NIC, it's more likely, although still improbable, that a malicious person could compromise the connection and bypass the NAT router to get into your network.

I recommend that any computer connecting your LAN to the Internet contain two, rather than one network card.

See Chapters 15 and 16 for information on keeping your computers and your network secure, but be aware that, while a NAT router won't protect you completely, it's an excellent start towards staying safe on the Internet.

Sources of NAT routers

There are many sources for NAT services, both as standalone boxes you can plug into your network and as software you can install on a spare computer to turn that computer into a NAT router.

In practice, they operate in basically the same way. The standalone boxes, while they may be more expensive, are usually easier to set up and configure than software you can add to a computer. Which method you choose depends mainly on how much you want to spend, and whether you have a computer suitable for NAT routing.

Hardware-based NAT routers

Hardware-based NAT routers, which are essentially boxes with two network ports and a NAT router on a chip, are becoming more and more affordable (under US$100 in some cases, and dropping). These boxes are easier to install and configure than a computer running NAT software, and can be safer as well (given that a computer with only one network card is more of a security risk than a NAT router device with two network ports).

DHCP and NAT routers

If your Internet provider assigns you a public Internet address on the fly, instead of assigning you a permanent address, you've been using DHCP (Dynamic Host Configuration Protocol) to get your IP address every time you started up your computer. This means your NAT router, whichever brand or type you choose, *must* be a good DHCP client to receive its assigned public IP address. Not all NAT routers can act as a DHCP client. Check the feature list for your router before purchasing or downloading to be sure this service is available.

Note that even fewer NAT routers can act as DHCP *servers*, providing IP addresses on the fly to the computers inside your network. If you decide to use this optional feature, be sure your NAT router supports DHCP services before you purchase or download the router.

However, they are more expensive (even $100 is more than "free") and they don't help you use up spare hardware that may be lying around your home or office, so be sure to weigh all of the alternatives before deciding.

Most of the major networking companies and many minor ones make a NAT router, usually marketing it as a "DSL router," a "cable modem router," or even an "Internet connection sharing server," but the specifications for the device always mention NAT or IP Masquerading, so watch for that description. Some of the companies providing NAT routers include

- ✔ Netopia, www.netopia.com
- ✔ Sonic Systems, www.sonicsys.com
- ✔ NetGear, www.netgearinc.com
- ✔ MacSense, www.macsense.com
- ✔ Nortel Networks, www.nortelnetworks.com

There are many, many others, so check your computer catalogs for the latest information. Note that many high-end network routers can support NAT, although they're usually too expensive to use simply as a NAT router. However, if you already have a Cisco or other high-end router, check the documentation to see if NAT is an option.

PC-based NAT routers

PC-based NAT routers may run on PC-compatible hardware, but they don't necessarily run Windows. There are NAT routers that use Linux, DOS, and proprietary operating systems to operate on standard PC-compatible hardware, from the old and lowly 80286-based processors up to the latest Pentium processors available.

If you have some recent, or not-so-recent, PC hardware lying around your office or home, you may be able to add some networking cards and turn it into a NAT router. You may even want to buy, for US$50 or so, a computer just to use for this purpose.

Similarly, you may dedicate a Windows 98 computer to connect your network, or even have a Windows 98 computer that isn't very busy but is under a user's control (such as your receptionist's computer) to handle Internet connections in the background while the user is word processing or browsing the Internet in the foreground.

Here are some software-based solutions for turning a PC into a NAT router:

- **Internet Connection Sharing (ICS):** Built-in to Windows 98 and Windows 2000

- **WinRoute (www.winroute.com):** A good software solution that provides several levels of complexity and features for different prices.

- **FREESCO (www.freesco.org/):** This is a free software solution for NAT routing that creates a UNIX-like operating system on a floppy disk that sets up and runs a router. This may be more complicated than you bargained for, but you can't beat the price.

- **GNATbox Light (www.gnatbox.com):** Allowing up to 5 computers for free, supporting a paid upgrade to a professional version that supports additional users.

- **Internet Extender (www-acc.scu.edu/~jsarich/ieWeb/main.htm):** Another free solution, and this one runs from a single DOS floppy disk. Getting two NICs running for this product may be a challenge (involving installing a packet driver to pass information at the DOS level from one NIC to the other).

- **Linux Router Project (linuxrouter.org):** This is the ultimate in difficult-to-set up NAT routing products, but I include it here just to be thorough. This product is free, and can run from a single floppy disk, but requires some knowledge of Linux.

There are many others that are too numerous to list here, but entering NAT router into any Internet search engine, such as Yahoo, will provide a large collection of software and hardware solutions. Note that free NAT routing can be added easily to almost any Linux-based computer, so if you're comfortable with Linux and have a spare computer, this may be a good option for you.

Mac OS-based NAT software

Note that Mac OS computers can use any NAT software running on any other kind of computer. If you want the Mac OS computer to *be* the NAT router, however, you currently have two basic choices:

- ✔ VicomSoft, www.vicomsoft.com
- ✔ Sustainable, Softworks www.sustworks.com

Both of these companies make software to set up excellent NAT routers, so see their Web sites for details.

The nasty and nice things about NAT

Setting up a NAT router is better in some ways even than purchasing additional IP addresses from your Internet provider. For one thing, NAT is free after the cost of setting it up. If your Internet provider charges US$20 per month for two additional IP addresses, and a NAT router costs US$200 to set up, in just over 10 months your NAT router is a better bargain than the Internet provider.

Another reason NAT can be better is the added security you get for all of the computers on your private network that isn't available when you place each computer on an Internet connection with a public address.

A NAT router is transparent to many Internet protocols. If you use a proxy server, you can only connect to the Internet using protocols that the proxy server supports such as http (Web), FTP (file transfer), POP3 (e-mail), and so on. If the proxy server doesn't support it, you're out of luck. With a NAT router, many protocols just work without any effort. Some protocols (Microsoft NetMeeting's H.323 for video and audio conferencing, for example) work badly or not at all through a NAT router, but far more Internet services work through a NAT router than through a proxy server.

Any Internet service that your computer supports will work through a direct connection to the Internet, but some fail completely when operating through a NAT router. Be sure the services you *must* have operate through NAT before choosing this method. Also, buying additional connections from your Internet provider is much easier than setting up and maintaining a NAT router. This convenience can be significant, so consider how much your time is worth before choosing NAT.

Finally, running any kind of server from inside your private network (Web server, FTP, Napster, and so on) is more complicated when you're running a NAT router than with a direct connection. With most Internet services, you have to set up the service specifically in the NAT router so that *incoming* connections (say, to a Web site) are always forwarded to a particular machine (say, your Web server).

Sharing by Setting Up a Proxy Server

A *proxy server* handles Internet connections on behalf of the computers inside your network. The most common use of a proxy server is for Web browsing: instead of finding a Web server on the Internet to load a Web page, your computer asks the proxy server for a page, which goes out onto the Internet to get it, then hands it back to your computer. Unlike a connection through a NAT router, in which the router actually passes your computer's connection along to the Internet services you're trying to reach, your computer's connection stops at the proxy server. Only the proxy server communicates directly with the outside world; your computers speak only to each other, and to the proxy server.

Proxy pros and cons

The advantages to setting up your network this way are mainly that it's fairly safe, because no computers on your network speak to the Internet directly (and therefore only your proxy server can be attacked, which is relatively harmless).

Proxy services also provide you with a lot of control over how the Internet connection is used, letting you turn services on or off, or restrict the hours or computers that can use the connection. You can also exert some of the control over content and services that normally a firewall could provide, such as limiting access to certain sites, or blocking attachments or downloads. This can be important if you're setting the Internet access up for a small LAN with multiple users who can't necessarily be trusted, as in a public setting such as a library or club.

Finally, a proxy server can speed up your connection to some services. For example, a proxy server can be configured to save local copies (called a *cache*) of frequently-requested Web pages. When a user requests a cached page, the proxy server provided the locally-saved copy instead of waiting for a new copy to download over the Internet. Because your local network is faster than the Internet connection, this can save considerable time.

Unless you take caching Web pages into account, a proxy server is actually slower than other methods of sharing the connection, although not by very much. This may be a noticeable drawback, especially if you're using the connection for high-bandwidth applications, such as streaming video or audio, where even a small drop in performance can be noticeable.

Another drawback is the flipside of one of the advantages: None of the computers on your LAN are talking directly to the Internet. While that is good from a security standpoint, it also means that any Internet application that's not supported by the proxy server won't work at all. For example, if the proxy server doesn't support streaming QuickTime TV or radio, none of your computers can take advantage of this software. Many proxy servers are being updated regularly to support new technologies as they're released, so check with the developers of your product if you encounter software that won't work through your connection.

Sources of proxy services

There are many proxy service products available, both for small/home offices and networks as well as for large corporate networks. This section lists some of the more popular smaller products that should suit a small office or network well.

- ✔ **WinGate** (www.wingate.com): This is one of the first small network proxy servers, and at version 4.0 is still one of the leaders. They make several different levels of their product, depending on your needs, so read the product literature before buying.

- ✔ **WinProxy** (www.winproxy.com): Another inexpensive product that can share a connection with your small LAN. They charge different amounts for the number of users (that is, the number of computers on your network using the connection), but otherwise there's the single level of product that provides proxy services.

If you're in a do-it-yourself kind of mood, and happen to have a spare UNIX or Linux system running, you may want to look at Squid proxy server www.squid-cache.org. Squid is a free, open-source product that provides all of the features of the products listed above, but requires more research, time, and computing skills to set up and use.

Chapter 14

Hosting Your Own Web Site

· ·

· ·

*I*t seems like almost everyone has a Web site anymore. Perhaps you have one too. The benefits of carving out your own little homestead on the data frontier are numerous and significant. In this chapter, we examine a potentially new way to publish a Web site: hosting it directly from your own computer. In this model, people talk directly to your own computer whenever they want to visit your Web site. As you might imagine, the potential drawbacks to this approach are significant and deserve serious consideration, you may also find that for a growing business or your own personal use; setting up your own Web server has a strong appeal.

When you're ready to enter the big time, you need to set up a program (the Web server) to be in charge of responding to all the requests your computer receives from people who want to see your Web site. We also show you a simple page you can display to check that your Web server is working, and provide you with ways to drive more visitors to your site — and how you can find out lots of interesting information about them! Don't worry, you won't have to hire a private investigator — unless you want to find out some *really* juicy stuff!

Hosting or Hiring Out?

Anyone who decides to have a Web site, has two options for getting the pages onto the Web:

✔ Third-Party Web hosting (and what a party it is, let me tell you!)

✔ Setting up your Web server (and who would do this without a broadband connection?)

Third-party Web hosting

When you choose to have your Web site located anywhere other than on your own computer, you have a third-party hosting situation. In these cases, you hire another individual or company to make available to you a computer that is constantly attached to the Internet. From this computer you run your Web site.

Advantages

Some of the many potential advantages to farming out your Web hosting include these:

- ✔ **Expert administration:** Hopefully, the party you hire to host your Web site retains the services of people who are especially skilled in the administration of Web servers, even while you're asleep. This frees you from the continual burden of keeping your server running at peak efficiency.

- ✔ **Better Internet connection:** Most major Web-hosting organizations have connections to the Internet that make even broadband seem puny in comparison. Some of the better dedicated-circuit connections to the Internet are now capable, for instance, of transmitting the complete contents of the Library of Congress several times per second!

When you're in the market for a Web-hosting provider, remember to ask whether or not they have *redundant* connections to the Internet. This is just a fancy, techie way of making sure that they have more than one line going from their place out to the Internet. Multiple lines ensures that if one of them breaks, people can still get to your site via the other line or lines.

- ✔ **More horsepower:** Often, Web-hosting providers are able to afford much better computers than you would be able to purchase on your own. If the things you want to do on your Web site are particularly CPU-intensive, then there can be a definite advantage to going with a Web-hosting provider that can offer you the use of a really powerful computer.

Figure 14-1 shows how the buying power of multiple Web-hosting customers can be leveraged to purchase some truly kick butt computer hardware!

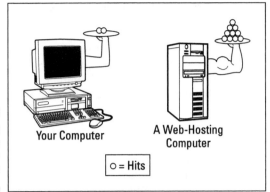

Figure 14-1:
Wimpy Web
server or
hefty host?

Your Computer

A Web-Hosting
Computer

○ = Hits

Disadvantages

Of course, it isn't all cookies and ice cream with Web-hosting providers. Indeed, farming out your site can have some disadvantages like these:

✔ **Limited access:** Perhaps the most obvious drawback to having your Web site hosted by a third party is that you will not have the same access to it as you would if you hosted it yourself. In physical terms, the computer that hosts your Web site will almost certainly be located at a different physical location, such as your ISPs office or data center. This may make it difficult or impossible to perform a task such as a server restart if your Web site should crash.

Many Web-hosting organizations offer remote access options so you can maintain some control over their Web sites. These range from simple command-prompt administration to full-blown simulations that look like you're actually sitting at the remote computer's console. PCAnywhere is one example.

✔ **Shared server space:** If you choose a professional Web-hosting organization to save some money, remember the savings you might reap are based on a number of factors, including your host's ability to share a server with other sites. Sure, *you* may have lower administration costs and lower your in-house bandwidth requirements, but your host's serving other Web sites can lead to significant problems.

Any hosting provider that allows multiple Web sites to co-exist on the same server will almost certainly restrict what any of these sites can do. This is a good thing from a security standpoint, but it can become troublesome when your site absolutely *must* do something that could be dangerous in order to do something nifty.

One of the greatest dangers with shared server space comes from the other Web sites running on the same computer as yours. These may include software applications written by people in completely different parts of the world — far beyond the jurisdiction of your local police. If any of these applications want to steal information (including credit card numbers) from your Web site, then they'll find no better place to attempt this than from the same computer as your own Web site!

✔ **Greater expense:** Ironically, after you have a broadband connection, the costs of having your Web site hosted elsewhere can easily become greater than they would be if you were running it on your own computer, especially if you got your broadband connection for reasons other than hosting your Web site! Because you have this connection anyhow, and because you (presumably) aren't using it 24 hours a day for its intended purpose — why not run your Web page in addition to whatever else you are doing?

Considerations for hosting at home

When you run a server of any kind on a computer, you need to keep a few things in mind: You are, essentially, sharing some of that computer's resources and information with the rest of the world. Keep these considerations in mind:

✔ **Disk space:** Running a Web server on your computer costs you some disk space. it requires space for both the server's program files and a lot space for all of the Web pages and files that you plan on publishing from your Web site.

✔ **CPU cycles:** If you do a lot of cool things on your Web site (such as serving-up streaming audio or hosting interactive video games), you may also have to sacrifice some of its speed. Of course, if you don't plan on doing anything cool on your Web site, then why even bother running one?

✔ **Bandwidth:** People need to talk to your computer to get Web pages from it. These little conversations take place along exactly the same Internet connection as the one you use to do your own Web surfing, e-mail, and so on. If you are lucky enough to wind up with a really popular Web site, you might find that your connection to the Internet becomes so bogged down with traffic that you can't use it for anything else!

✔ **Total control:** And what is the great reward for all of these sacrifices? At the end of each day, you are in complete, utter, and total control of your own Web site. You can offer pages that do anything you like. You can even let people reformat your hard disk if you are so inclined!

Responsibility comes along with the power of having total control. In this case, it's the heavy responsibility of making sure that your computer is secure against the maliciousness of crackers. Having a computer that is always connected to the Internet is a constant risk. Having a computer that you advertise to the public as being constantly connected to the Internet and then actually inviting people to visit it is an even greater risk. Make sure you read the chapters in Part IV very carefully and follow all of their suggestions.

Installing the Web Server Software

Web servers need to match the operating system of your machine. Fortunately, just about every OS has at least one program that should get you up and running, and many of these programs are free. This section lists our picks for the top operating systems.

Microsoft Windows

Right now the single most popular operating system in the world for home computer users is Microsoft Windows. Windows' unique combination of ease-of-use features coupled with widespread vendor support combine to make this operating system an excellent choice for a wide variety of computer users.

The Windows operating system comes in many different flavors:

- **Commercial:** Windows 95, 98, and Millenium Edition (Me)
- **Scientific and Business Desktop:** Windows Workstation (NT and 2000)
- **Server:** Windows Server (NT and 2000)

The most popular Web server for personal-use versions of Microsoft Windows is Microsoft Personal Web Server.

Personal Web Server

Personal Web Server (PWS) doesn't come as a part of every Windows operating systems. You may need to obtain and install it.

To install the Personal Web server check the ADD-ONS\PWS directory of the Windows CD or download the self-extracting executable and run it. A series of wizards will then guide you through installation.

Obeying usage rules

Usually, whenever you install a piece of software, you are implicitly agreeing with the manufacturer's license agreement. The license for the Windows operating system contains rules that limit the number of concurrent connections supported by the personal Windows operating systems. This is important because, when you run a Web server, every visitor to your site requires their own connection to see your pages. If you already have more visitors at your site than Windows allows (usually about 10), then Windows will typically refuse additional connections. This means that your new visitors will get an error message rather than your pages. If you discover that you have developed this problem, consider upgrading to Windows NT Server or 2000.

Internet Information Server

For Windows 2000 and NT Server, your best free choice for a Web server is Microsoft Internet Information Server (IIS). This comes bundled together with the Windows 2000 operating system but isn't always installed with NT Server.

If you're not sure if you have a Web server already running on your box, then a simple test allows you to find out. Select Start⇨Run and type **telnet localhost 80** in the box that pops up. Click OK. A Telnet window like the one in Figure 14-2 opens.

If, as soon as it pops up, the Telnet window says that the connection has been rejected, then you are not running a Web server. If, on the other hand, the Telnet window waits with a blank screen, then you are probably running a Web server.

Figure 14-2:
Looking for Web servers on all the right ports.

There are two ways to install IIS onto a Window NT/2000 machine:

- ✔ Directly off the Operating System CD
- ✔ From the Option Pack

Installing IIS from the same CD that originally contained your operating system is only useful for version of Windows 2000. Windows 2000 comes with either IIS 5 or Personal Web Server, depending on whether the personal or business products are being used.

For Windows NT, however, you will have to install IIS from the Option Pack. The Option Pack is smart enough to be able to detect which version of Windows you have installed and to install the Web server accordingly.

Linux

The single most popular Web server in the world is known as Apache, software created by a group of independent developers volunteering their time. These developers, scattered across the globe, coordinate their efforts primarily via the Internet.

Today, the most common way for a new Linux user to obtain the operating system is by purchasing it in boxed, shrink-wrapped form from a company known as Red Hat. Red Hat is the leading distributor of the Linux operating system at the time of writing. The main advantage to you in getting your copy of Linux from Red Hat is that the Apache Web server is included in that distribution! In this case, you can have your Web server installed right along with your OS.

If you need to download Apache for Linux, or any other version of UNIX, you get just the source code, which provides the actual instructions written by the programmers, rather than the machine language that your computer can directly understand. This method offers other developers a firsthand look at the code and a chance to give feedback on bugs.

You can visit the homepage for Apache on the World Wide Web at http://www.apache.org. From this page, you should navigate to the Downloads section . In general, you should download the most recent version that isn't an Alpha (relatively untested new version) or Beta (less buggy, but still not complete) version.

After you download the source code for Apache, you need to compile it before running it. Compilation on Linux typically involves running a program called Make, which runs through all of the files included in the software distribution and creates machine language versions of them that your computer can understand.

For complete instructions on using Make to compile the Apache Web server and then installing it to run as a part of Linux, consult the documentation that comes included with your download. Typically, this will be found in a file known as Readme.

iMac

The de facto standard for Web servers on Apple computers is also one of the oldest, most established packages out there — WebSTAR.

WebSTAR is a commercial product sold by StarNine Corporation. Currently, it is available for purchase as a part of their Server Suite product for the (rather high) price of US$600. Because this is a lot of money to spend just to get started, it's probably a wise idea to obtain a trial version of the software first to make sure that you really want to run your own Web site.

To get the trial version, you may download it from the company's Web site at

```
http://www.starnine.com
```

This site asks for a variety of information about you and what you intend to do with their product. When you finish completing the form, you see a variety of options for downloading, as shown in Figure 14-3.

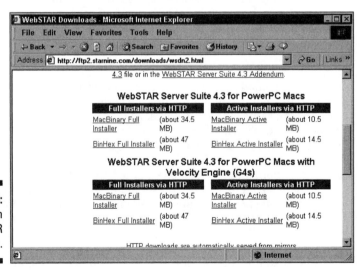

Figure 14-3:
Wishing on
a WebSTAR
option.

Choose the link for your machine: PowerPC Macintosh or a G4. After picking a download site, choose between the Full Installer (which puts all the installation files on your machine in one chunk) and the Active Installer (which starts the process and then pulls the files you or your machine selects).

When you finish downloading either of the installers, simply double-click on their icon to begin the process of setting up your new Web server.

We highly recommend that you use defaults for where to place your files on your hard disk. The Easy Install option makes a lot of good decisions for you regarding the specifics of how to initially set up and configure your Web server. If this is the first Web server that you have ever run, you probably wouldn't have any preferences among these options anyhow. And, if you find that something has been decided that you don't like later on, you can always change it.

At the end of installation, restart your computer, even if you aren't prompted to do so because it's probably a good idea — just to make sure that everything is given a chance to take effect.

To see whether or not your Web server is running, simply fire-up your Web browser. In the URL blank, enter the following:

```
http://localhost
```

A default WebSTAR page loads into your Web browser. This page was generated directly from the Web server running on your own computer. The word localhost literally means *this computer*.

Creating a Web Page for Your New Server

Regardless of which Web server you choose to install, you can publish a text or HTML document on it — after all, that's the beauty of the World Wide Web. If you already have a page, you can run in your new server, go ahead and test it. If you don't have a page or need a few points on working with these files, including where to store them so your server can access them, we show you how in this section.

Just the text, ma'am

You can create the simplest Web page just by sticking some text in a file and dropping it in the right place on your hard disk.

Be aware that the files you create with a word processors are *not* plain text. This is usually far from the case. Plain text files contain nothing other than letters, numbers, punctuation, spaces, and so on. Word processor files must contain a great many more symbols than just this in order to support all of the special formatting that you can place into a word processing file. This is true even if you don't use any of this special formatting.

The easiest way to create a plain text file on your computer depends on your choice of operating system, but these are the basic tools:

- ✔ **Windows:** Notepad
- ✔ **Linux:** ed, vi, pico, emacs
- ✔ **Macintosh:** Wordpad

After you've started up your trusty text editor, you can put some sample text in it. For example:

```
Hello Miss America,and all the ships at sea!
```

Putting your files where they belong

Text files, HTML files . . . where do you put all these files? (And if that isn't enough, you've got graphics and other files to consider, too.)

With the majority of Web servers, a special directory called htdocs holds all of the files served by a given Web site. You can begin by searching your local hard disks for a directory by this name. But, files under IIS on the Windows platform tend to be stored in various subdirectories under Inetpub, such as C:\INETPUB\WWWROOT. If you have just installed IIS on your computer and followed all the default choices during installation, you should begin by searching for a wwwroot directory.

When you have located the appropriate directory for your files, you should save text files there with a .TXT extension, which tells Web browsers to load your page without interpreting their content.

Now, try to load this page into a Web browser using the same localhost machine name that you saw above. For example, if you saved the file as hello.txt, you should be able to load it using:

```
http://localhost/hello.txt
```

The preceding line works only in Web browsers on the same machine as your Web server. In order to see your pages from other machines at this point, you must either replace localhost with the IP address of your machine, or set up a domain name for your machine. You find out all about domain names later on in this chapter.

Weaving a Web page for your server

Well, creating plain text files that the entire world can see is pretty exciting, but it isn't that much more impressive than e-mail at this point. The only difference is that with these kinds of Web pages, people have to come to you to see your creations. With e-mail, at least you can send your creations directly to your audience!

You can use the same text editor to create a simple Web page (or a very cool one) for publishing on your server. Type these lines:

```
<HTML>
<BODY>
    Hello,
        <a href="http://missamerica.com">
Miss America
 </a>
    and all the ships at sea!
</BODY>
</HTML>
```

Of course, if you're not familiar with HTML, this might look a little daunting, but HTML is really not too tough to figure out. The key is in the <TAGS>, which indicate the type of formatting or text style to display in the browser. For more information on HTML, check out *HTML 4 For Dummies*, by Ed Tittel (published by IDG Books Worldwide, Inc.).

To get this page working on your own computer, save it to the same directory described in the text file section. Only, this time, save it with an .HTML extension. To see your page as it would look on the World Wide Web now, simply load it into a browser using the http://localhost/*filename*.html format. Figure 14-4 shows the result.

Microsoft tends to use the .HTM extensions, rather than the .HTML standard used by the rest of the world. However, you can usually get away with saving your files as .HTML without anything bad happening.

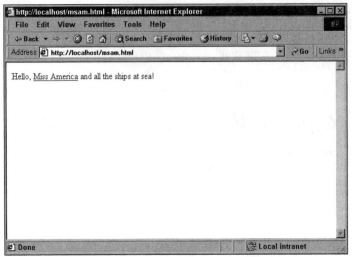

Figure 14-4:
Gee, your
first Web
page!

Becoming the Master of Your Own Domain

As we demonstrate in the preceding section, if you want to access your Web site from your own computer, you can use the name `localhost`. You probably didn't set up your own Web server just to look at it yourself, however, . . . unless you are really extremely narcissistic, extremely shy, or still testing a megasite. Eventually, you want people all over the world to be able to visit the Web site running on your computer.

For this to happen, you must first be connected to the Internet. If you have DSL or most kinds of cable modems, this won't represent a problem for you — you are always on. On the other hand, those of us with satellite Internet access have to dial in every time we want to use the Internet.

If DSL is your broadband of choice, you should seriously consider using a third-party Web hosting service because you must still use the slower upload.

When you have addressed the issue of connectivity, people all over the world already should be able to access the Web server running on your computer. The only catch is that they need your machine's IP in order to do so.

> ## Internet disservice providers
>
> Some ISPs take it on themselves to shield their users' computers from outside access. There are a couple of reasons why they may do this:
>
> - To help keep your computer safe from crackers
>
> - To force you to buy a business account for Web hosting, rather than using a personal account
>
> If your ISP is preventing outside access for the first reason, you may be able to talk them into turning off their assistance. On the other hand, if they are out to up-sell you a more expensive product, you may have no alternative other than finding a different provider.

In order to access your computer remotely, a user would enter a line such as:

```
http://63.22.141.87/test.htm
```

In this example, your IP would be `63.22.141.87`, and the requested page, `test.htm`.

Most users would find it very difficult to remember a string of digits like this for every time that they wanted to visit your Web site. For these people (nearly all of us), the Domain Name System (DNS) of the modern Internet was invented. Using DNS, a Web site can register its IP to be associated with an easily remembered name, such as `eviloscar.com`. Then, whenever surfers enter this easily remembered name into their Web browser, they are referred to the appropriate IP.

You can register a domain name at either of two levels:

- Registration-only
- Registration and hosting

Registration-only

Registering your domain name really doesn't do anything for you other than reserve the name for your exclusive use. This option is useful if you should ever happen to think of a really clever name that isn't already in use. By now, most of the really clever names ending in `.com` have already been thought of and registered.

If you think of a domain name that you really like, but it's already taken, then check to find out whether you can get the same domain name with a different ending. For example, `eviloscar.com` is taken, but maybe `eviloscar.net` or `eviloscar.org` is still available. Provided eviloscar.com isn't an official trademark owned by someone else, then it is perfectly legal for you to register the other names.

To register a domain name and check on domain name availability, you can go through a number of sources:

✔ `http://www.nsi.com`

✔ `http://www.interaccess.com`

✔ `http://www.register.com`

Registration and hosting

To really use your domain name with your Web site, then it must be registered and hosted. Having a domain name hosted means that, besides simply owning a domain, you have designated one or more computers on the Internet to be responsible for answering requests for information about this domain. These computers must run DNS servers, which are completely different from Web servers.

Showing you how to set up and run a DNS server is well outside the scope of this book, so we assume that you have your DNS hosted elsewhere. A practical advantage to this means you've got one less burden for your own computer to endure, which allows it to devote more of its resources to serving your Web pages quickly when requested.

Most ISPs are capable of hosting your domain names as well as registering them for you. If your current ISP cannot, then don't hesitate to ask another. The ISP that hosts your domain name *does not have to be the same ISP that provides your broadband Internet connection!* It can be any ISP, anywhere in the world. They just need three things from you:

✔ Your domain name

✔ Your IP address

✔ Your money

Most broadband Internet uses a static IP that never changes. Some, however, use *dynamic* IP, which constantly assigns new numbers to the same computers. If you have such a system, then how can you give your IP address to the service that will host your DNS? In these cases, you need to use a service that is specifically designed to host DNS for dynamic IPs. One example of such a service is TZO.com (`http://www.tzo.com`).

You're Up and Running . . . Now What?

You'll never feel quite as good about your computer as the day when you first have your Web server up and running and waiting for visitors. Now, you have just two little points remaining:

✔ How do you get visitors?

✔ How do you find out about them?

Publicizing your site

You can use a number of ways to promote your site and increase traffic.

✔ **Search sites:** When most people want to find out something on the Internet, they head for one of the Internet's big search sites. Some of the more popular ones include Yahoo!, Alta Vista, and Lycos. All of these sites accept submissions for inclusion in their lists of Web sites. This can be an excellent way to get people to visit your site who are specifically interested in whatever topics your Web site covers.

  If you can afford to spend a little money on your publicity efforts, you can get your site listed on a lot more search engines with a lot less effort. In exchange for about US$60 per year, a service named SubmitIt (http://www.submitit.com) makes sure that your site gets listed on about 400 search engines and directories. You can visit them on the Web.

✔ **Web rings and link exchanges:** Multiple Web sites covering a single topic area, the English rock group Marillion, for example, will often band together and place links to each other on their Web sites. When these efforts are organized and intended to increase traffic to the sites of all participants, they are often known as Web rings or link exchanges. To find out more about joining such a scheme, visit http://www.webring.com.

✔ **Blatant self-promotion:** You can put links to your Web site at the bottom of all the e-mails that you write or put links to your Web site in every message you post to Internet newsgroups. You can even use your Web site, such as www.eviloscar.com, as an example in any book that you might happen to write!

Finding out about your visitors

When visitors come to your site, you would probably like to know a little about them. This kind of information is stored in the log files maintained by your Web server. To get at this information, you must first find these log files. Then, you must figure out how to interpret them.

Where do you keep your logs, old server?

The location of your log files depends on your choice of operating system and Web server. Table 14-1 summarizes the basic differences.

Table 14-1	How Logs Differ by Server
Platform	**Location**
Windows IIS	\WINNT\SYSTEM32\LOGFILES\W3SVC1
Windows PWS	\WINDOWS\SYSTEM\LOGFILES
UNIX Apache	\WEB\LOGS
Macintosh WebSTAR	:LOGS:

Now, what language is this?!

When you find the logs, open them up in your favorite text editor and take a look at their contents. Each line represents a single request from one visitor to your Web site. Various pieces of information are strung together from left to right on each line, so you can find out a lot about your visitors from the data contained in this file.

The exact organization of this data leaves a lot to be desired, however. If you are looking for charts and graphs that show you trends and interesting facts about your visitors, rather than just a big dump of data, then you should look into one of the many off-the-shelf tools available to help you process and digest these files. One of the most popular of these is known as WebTrends, which you can purchase or download for evaluation at `http://www.webtrends.com`.

Part IV
Protecting the Wealth of Broadband

The 5th Wave   By Rich Tennant

"THIS IS YOUR GROUPWARE?! THIS IS WHAT YOU'RE RUNNING?!
WELL HECK – I THINK THIS COULD BE YOUR PROBLEM!"

In this part . . .

Security on the Internet is a very hot topic indeed. It seems like every day brings a new news story about some company losing money when one of their vital systems is broken into, or *cracked*. You might think that, as a private citizen, your computer is in no danger of being targeted by crackers. You would be wrong!

With broadband access you can enjoy many cool features and expand your small or home office, but that also means you can outgrow the security measures you've taken for granted to this point.

Keeping your system safe begins by restricting access to it via the Internet. This prevents unwanted access to your computers by ill-intentioned individuals all over the planet. In this part, we also discuss software that can help to keep your children safe — or your employees out of trouble — on the Internet.

Chapter 15

Preventing High-Speed Vandalism and Theft

*I*n a perfect world, you could leave your wallet on the front step of your house to make sure you remembered to take it with you every morning. Sadly, in the real world, your wallet would be a distant memory before you even shut the door. In the same way, you *should* be able to connect your computer to a network that leaves you exposed to virtually every other computer user in the entire world and not worry that they'll attack, play tricks, or sneak things out of your computer when you're not looking.

Unfortunately, crackers try to do all of these things and worse. It seems that setting up an always-on Internet connection somehow puts up a big neon sign reading, "We're Open, Come On In! Free Data Here!"

This chapter discusses how people will try to get to your computer, how to find out who's checking out your computer, and how to stop them from getting in or from even finding out you're there.

How Others Can Attack You

Back when you used a dialup Internet connection, you weren't much of a security target. You logged on, did what you needed to do, and logged off after a while. Chances are that your IP address (the unique Internet address assigned to your computer) changed each time you logged on, so to everyone else on the Internet, you were never in the same place twice.

Hackers good, crackers bad

When you read about computer security, you'll see two terms used: *hacker* and *cracker*. *Hacker* is used pretty casually, especially in the mass media, to refer to anyone who tinkers under the hood of computers, whether for good or evil purposes. In most Internet circles, we distinguish between two terms:

✔ *Hackers* are the ones who know how to make their computers do everything short

of sit up and dance. They can often re-write parts of any program to perform better than before and can offer helpful solutions to others.

✔ *Cracker* was created to avoid confusing the good hackers with those with criminal intent: stealing information, using your machine to invade other sites, and so on.

Now, however, your Internet connection is always on, or at least it's on whenever your computer is on. Your computer either has the same IP address all of the time (known as a *static* IP address), or it keeps its address for a long time, if the address is assigned *dynamically*, using DHCP (or *Dynamic Host Configuration Protocol*). Keeping the same address means that anyone who finds you has a while to figure out your weaknesses before your address changes again, if it ever does.

Stealing the sacred data

The first risk that most people think of is data theft. If someone can gain access to your computer over the Internet, that person may find valuable information on your computer, such as your bank account information, credit card data, your passwords to other services, and so on. Unlike having a wallet stolen (you're bound to notice right away), if someone steals a copy of data from your computer, you may not even know it's gone. That's why you need to prevent the theft before it can happen.

It's NOT nice to share

The easiest way to gain access to your computer is if you leave the door open. Many computers come with a built-in feature called *file sharing*, which turns your computer into a small file server. The idea behind this feature is good; it lets you publish a folder or an entire disk of information for others on your network to use and then leave for you.

Unfortunately, when you have an always-on connection, your network is the entire Internet community, and you probably don't want millions of people you don't know to have any access to your computer.

When I first hooked up my computer to a cable modem, I looked into the network neighborhood and saw a bunch of my neighbors' computers, ready to be shared. All I needed was a password, and a lot of software on the Internet could help you crack Windows networking passwords. Fortunately, most cable modem companies and other high-speed Internet access companies are taking steps to filter out Windows networking and other Internet traffic that is often used accidentally. However, you shouldn't trust your Internet provider to protect your computer. Be sure to turn off file sharing, personal web sharing, and other services that may be handing out your data over the Internet.

Beware of geeks bearing gifts

Another way crackers steal your data or otherwise take control of your system is to send you a Trojan horse. A Trojan horse is a program that appears to be one thing (such as a new game or a great utility) but is actually something more dangerous (such as a password-stealer or a remote-control program). You may get a Trojan horse if, for example, you run an attached program in an e-mail message from someone you don't know or from whom you weren't expecting attachments.

One Trojan horse that has been very popular among crackers is called Back Orifice. Back Orifice (and its successor, Back Orifice 2000, or BO2K), a program that lets you control another computer over a network or the Internet. Some legitimate commercial products can perform the same task (PCAnywhere, Timbuktu, and so on), but Back Orifice would come unannounced and eventually provide its programmer with remote control without necessarily letting the computer's owner know. Back Orifice was also very difficult to remove, as it kept hiding itself around the target computer's system. See the section on viruses later in this chapter for other examples and ways to combat them.

Entering an open port

Port scanning may or may not be an attack, depending on the experts you talk to. It's definitely a warning, however, so it may help to think of it as a kind of pre-attack.

If your computer has networking software installed, it may be listening for connections whenever it's turned on. That listening, and any connections that someone can make to your computer, happen over ports. A port in the real world might refer to a socket into which you plug a cable; in the computer world, a port is a virtual socket into which network services can connect. There are 65,535 possible ports, and each kind of network connection on the computer has its own port number; for example, Web servers use port 80 by default. If your computer is running any servers (Web servers, peer-to-peer file sharing, and so on), it is listening on one or more network ports.

Any port in a storm

Computers listen for other computers on partic-ular ports. A port is like a numbered channel on which your computer can set up a particular kind of network connection. For example, World Wide Web connections generally travel on port 80. AOL Instant Messenger uses port 5190 to connect by default. If your Web browser were to try to connect to a Web site on port 5190, that connection would fail, even though the Web address was correct.

As a real-world analogy, think of different kinds of plugs and sockets. You normally wouldn't, for example, insert an electrical plug into a tele-phone socket, or a headphone plug into a com-puter monitor socket. In the same way, you wouldn't connect an e-mail client to a Web port or a Web browser to a file sharing port. They have different numbers, and those port numbers are expecting different kinds of data.

Most of the time, Web servers, browsers, and other Internet software handle the port numbers automatically, but when you're talking about security, it helps to know that they exist.

Before a cracker can break into your system, he or she has to know whether your computer already has any openings. If your computer is listening for connections on one or more ports, the cracker may be able to enter your system by pretending to be whatever the port is listening for. For example, if your computer is running a personal Web server, the cracker can enter your computer on port 80 just as a Web browser would but take different actions when connected.

What does all that have to do with port scanning? Port scanning is the process of checking your computer out over a network (in this case, the Internet) to see which ports are open on your computer. The cracker who is port scanning you doesn't try to set up a connection yet; instead, he or she is collecting information on the vulnerabilities you may have for future use. When a port is listening for connections, that port is considered to be open. The following code example shows the results of a port scan using a popular UNIX-based utility called nmap.

```
Starting nmap V. 2.53 by fyodor@insecure.org
         ( www.insecure.org/nmap/ )
Interesting ports on powerbook (10.19.0.6):
(The 3069 ports scanned but not shown below are in state:
         closed)
Port       State       Service
7/tcp      open        echo
7/udp      open        echo
13/tcp     open        daytime
21/tcp     open        ftp
23/tcp     open        telnet
37/tcp     open        time
43/tcp     open        whois
79/tcp     open        finger
```

```
137/udp      open          netbios-ns
138/udp      open          netbios-dgm
139/tcp      open          netbios-ssn
445/tcp      open          microsoft-ds
7648/udp     open          cucme-1
Nmap run completed -- 1 IP address (1 host up) scanned in 12
             seconds
```

This computer has a large number of services open, including Microsoft file sharing (ports 137 through 139), and could be at risk from crackers.

You can find out which port numbers carry many kinds of connections by visiting www.isi.edu/in-notes/iana/assignments/port-numbers, among other sites, or by using an Internet search engine to search for port numbers. For example, if your computer is running a personal Web server, the cracker can enter your computer on port 80 just as a Web browser would but take different actions when connected. If your computer is set up for Windows file sharing, it's listening for file sharing connections all the time, on ports 137 through 139.

Port scanning isn't exactly an attack. It's not like breaking into your house; it's more like checking to see whether your doors and windows are locked. Most likely, the only people interested in whether your doors and windows are locked are criminals, but you might also have friends and neighbors checking so they can warn you of your vulnerabilities.

Many firewall packages can warn you if someone port scans your computer, and often they can even tell you the Internet address of the person scanning you. The firewall also protects you from unauthorized connections, so you can treat the port scan as proof that you need the firewall, and relax knowing that you're protected.

You might also notify the Internet provider of the port scanner's account, if you can find out the right person to contact, but that's a lot of work for little benefit. Our recommendation is to treat a port scan as a warning that you should be on your guard, and the only action you should take is to make sure you take the precautions we list in the firewall section later in this chapter.

Denying service

An unpleasant but usually not fatal kind of Internet attack is known as a denial of service, or DoS attack. In a DoS attack, the perpetrator stops your computer's access to the Internet altogether, perhaps by flooding your computer with so many connections it simply has no capacity for anything else, or by remotely exploiting a bug in your computer's OS that causes a crash.

For example, one of the ways to see if a computer is available on the Internet is to send small network packets and listen for a response, using a handy feature called *ping*. Unfortunately, it used to be possible to crash a target computer by sending a bad ping, in what was called the Ping of Death denial of service attack (a crash that has been fixed in most operating systems in use today). Chapter 16 goes into detail on how pings work and how you can prevent them.

Another kind of DoS attack is to flood a computer with so many bogus connection requests that none of the legitimate attempts to connect can get through. Crackers have brought down entire Web sites using various DoS attacks, and they can possibly bring down your computer as well, temporarily. An attack that is a disaster for an e-commerce company is only an inconvenience to you because all you have to do after a DoS attack usually is to restart your computer. However, it's best to avoid these attacks altogether.

A good personal firewall can usually protect you from DoS attacks. The publisher of your OS (Apple, Microsoft, Red Hat, and so on) usually releases updates or patches to fix the flaw that allowed the DoS attack, so stay up-to-date on the latest OS releases as well.

Invasion of the identity snatchers

Perhaps the most disturbing kind of Internet attack is when the attacker pretends to be you, either by intercepting a connection or by stealing passwords and account information. Intercepting a connection happens, for example, if the cracker captures your attempt to connect to a service (say, a secure Web site), collects your sensitive information, and passes the connection along so you think you connected without any problems. This isn't very common, but it is a real danger.

Another more common attack is when a cracker gains access to your password for an account, either by collecting the password as you enter it or by figuring it out. You can prevent crackers from stealing your passwords or otherwise gaining access to your accounts by setting up hard-to-guess passwords and changing them frequently or by simply protecting your privacy more carefully, as we show you Chapter 17.

To set up strong passwords, follow as many of these rules as you can:

- ✔ Avoid real words, names, or dates that mean something in your life, because a cracker who knows you may guess them.
- ✔ Make passwords harder to guess by adding punctuation or numbers, as in `brain*scan` or `gue55thi5pa55word`.

✔ Combine the first letters of a common phrase to make your password. For example, you might take the phrase "If elected I promise to lower taxes for all" and turn it into the password "ieip2ltfa". Notice how we've turned the word "to" into the number 2, to foil crackers.

✔ Change your passwords regularly. That doesn't mean once a year whether you've been cracked or not; it means changing passwords every two weeks, or every month at the outside. It's not as convenient, but convenience and security don't always go together.

By following these instructions, especially the last one, you can strengthen your passwords and close that entry door to crackers.

Being used and discarded

One of the more insidious attacks doesn't involve any damage to you at all. When a cracker's program finds a weakness in your computer or network, their programs can use your computer as launching points to attack others. In this kind of attack, the crackers actually take control of part of your computer and use it to hide their tracks. If the victim traces the attack back across the Internet to its source, the trail leads directly to you, because it appears to be coming from you or your network.

What Security Products Can't Prevent

You can install all of the security software and hardware on the market, configure it perfectly, choose complicated passwords, but a cracker may still be able to get your data, steal an account, or take over your computer. How? Here's an example: A co-worker of mine once gained access to my computer at work by calling the computer department, pretending to be me, and asking them to change the password on my account, which they happily did.

That co-worker didn't have to crack anything in my computer — he cracked a person in the computer department instead through lying and trickery. In computer circles, that technique is called *social engineering*. You don't need to know much about computers to use social engineering. Knowledge of people, and how to make them believe you, is all you need.

People on some popular Internet services, such as America Online, encounter social engineering often. Someone sends an instant message to you, claiming to be an AOL representative, and telling you that due to a system error, the sender needs you to confirm your billing information, including your credit card of course and may also ask for your AOL password, just to prove your identity.

Here are two rules that will help protect you from some kinds of social engineering:

- **Never give out information to people if *they* contacted *you*.** Be suspicious of anyone who shows up at your door, calls you on the telephone, or contacts you online and asks for personal information. Ask for a way to contact their organization, then get back to them when you're sure it's legitimate.

- **Never, ever give out your password to anyone, even if they own the service where your account is.** Even your network administrator at work doesn't need to ask for your password. The people who maintain your accounts at Internet providers, Web sites, and other places can just delete your password without ever knowing what it is if necessary. Nobody will ever have a legitimate need for your password, and if you are somehow convinced to give it to someone, change it immediately.

Other than these rules, you can avoid social engineering attempts by taking basic precautions. Ask for proof of ID from any company representatives you're dealing with, keep the information you provide to a minimum, and feel free to ask why they need anything suspicious.

Hiding from Unwelcome Guests

In the section on port scanning, we tell you how others test your computer connections with a potential intrusion on mind. An essential step for protecting your computer on the Internet is for your computer to seem as though it isn't there. When a cracker scans randomly for open ports, you should make sure your computer doesn't answer if anyone knocks.

If a cracker scanning for open ports finds that a computer at your address has port 137 open, for example, the cracker may attempt to connect to your computer using a Windows file-sharing client. The same could be true if your computer answers as a Web server (port 80), an FTP server (port 21), and so on. To safeguard your computer from these attacks, teach your computer to ignore the knock at the door.

Batten down the hatches

The first step in making your computer disappear from the Internet is to close all of the open ports on your computer. This is easier than it sounds; you basically have to turn off any network services you're not using on your computer. If you don't need to use personal file sharing, turn it off. If you don't want your computer to act as a Web server, turn off that feature.

When your computer is acting as a server (that is, listening for connections) its listening methods vary from one OS to another and from one configuration to another. For example, a Mac OS computer by default has no Internet ports open, but as soon as you turn on Web Sharing to set up a mini-Web site, your computer is open on port 80. Because the open ports vary so much, you need a way to find out the ports on which your computer is listening.

Using Netstat to see open ports

If you're using any version of Microsoft Windows or a UNIX-like OS (such as Solaris or any variation of Linux) you can type a command, called Netstat, at any console or MS-DOS window. This command reports the status of your network connections, including which ports are open for connections. The following example shows Netstat's response in a Windows MS-DOS console:

```
Active Connections
   Proto  Local Address            Foreign Address       State
   TCP    an.example.com:137       an.example.com:0
             LISTENING
   TCP    an.example.com:138       an.example.com:0
             LISTENING
   TCP    an.example.com:nbsession an.example.com:0
             LISTENING
   UDP    an.example.com:nbname    *:*
   UDP    an.example.com:nbdatagram *:*
```

The Proto column shows which protocol your computer is listening to (usually TCP or UDP, both of which are Internet protocols). The Local Address column shows your computer's public IP address or name, a colon, and the port number where the computer is listening (such as ports 137 and 138 in the above example). The number following the colon may also contain the name of the service instead of its port number, as in nbsession above instead of 139.

The actual numbers and names don't matter very much, except to tell you which services to turn off. All of the entries shown above refer to Windows file sharing, indicating that this computer should have all file sharing services turned off to make that computer as invisible as possible to the Internet. If you don't know what the entries mean or the port numbers refer to, don't worry. Turn off the services you can identify and that you don't need, and we'll take other precautions in this chapter to help prevent the remaining services from being a problem.

In Windows, you can turn off file sharing in the Network control panel. In the Mac OS, use the File Sharing control panel, or leave file sharing on but turn off any option that enables connecting over TCP/IP. To turn off personal web sharing open the Personal Web Sharing control panel on the Mac, or use the Network control panel in Windows. For details, consult the online help or other documentation for your OS.

Note that Mac OS computers don't have Netstat, but you can find other utilities that can scan your computer for open ports. A program called MacTCP Watcher (later folded into Anarchie, which is now Interarchy) from Stairways Software (www.stairways.com or www.interarchy.com) can show you the open ports where your computer is listening, or you can scan your Macintosh using utilities such as Internet Helper (tectonicdesigns.com/mac/files.html).

Scanning your computer from the Internet

Several Web sites can scan your computer (at your request) and report back to you on any security flaws they find. Many of these sites also sell security products, so they're hoping that a security scan convinces you to buy their products. That may not be a bad idea, but for now, let's just use their sites to discover the weak points in your security setup.

Numerous sites offer similar features, but to start, visit one of the following sites:

✔ www.secure-me.net

✔ grc.com (follow the links to Shields Up)

✔ www.webtrends.net/tools/security/scan.asp

When you visit these sites, they'll probably already have the IP address you're connecting from (your computer's address, or your NAT router's public IP address if you're using one), and they usually ask for some additional information, including your name and where to send the security report. The scan may take a while, especially if there is a large number of people ahead of you, but the results should be useful for telling you how open or visible your computer is to the world.

Turn off any services on your computer that the scan identifies and you don't need. The security-scanning site may offer some advice on how to do this, or you can check with your computer's documentation for more information.

Setting Up Personal Firewalls

One of the best new technologies to come along in a while is the category of product known as personal firewalls. You may already know that a firewall is a device that acts as a traffic cop between you and the world, monitoring the Internet traffic going in and out, and stopping dangerous traffic based on a set of rules. If you have a network, a firewall is usually a separate device, possibly running on a dedicated computer or on a network router that handles your Internet connection (see Chapter 16). A personal firewall, on the other hand, runs in the background on *your* computer, watching the Internet data that is coming and going, and warning you or stopping the connection cold if any suspicious data comes through.

A personal firewall installed on your computer isn't quite as safe as a standalone firewall that is on the network between you and the public networks. Because a personal firewall is on your computer, by the time the personal firewall software identifies an attack or other cracking attempt, the dangerous network traffic is already on your computer. Although the personal firewall software keeps the attack from having any effect, it's possible that an attack could bypass the software and reach the rest of your computer. That scenario is unlikely, however, and personal firewall software still provides a lot of protection. It's certainly better than having no protection at all. More personal firewall packages are available every month, but these lists should provide you with a good start.

For users of Microsoft Windows, here are some personal firewall options:

- Black Ice Defender from Network ICE (www.networkice.com)
- McAfee.com Personal Firewall (www.mcafee.com)
- Zone Labs' ZoneAlarm (currently free for personal use, at www.zonelabs.com/zonealarm.htm)
- eSafe, from Aladdin Knowledge Systems (www.eAladdin.com/esafe/)
- Norton Personal Firewall and Norton Internet Security from Symantec Corporation (www.symantec.com)

These are some of the options for Mac OS users:

- Intego's Net Barrier (www.intego.com/netbarrier)
- DoorStop, from OpenDoor Networks (www.opendoor.com)

As a multi-user environment, UNIX-like operating systems (such as BSD and Linux) can use firewall software as a personal firewall or to protect an entire network. These products include ipchains (built into many Linux distributions), Phoenix Adaptive Firewall from Progressive Systems (www.progressive-systems.com), and many others.

Setting your firewall rules

Most personal firewalls, as with most network firewalls, are designed to refuse incoming connections by default. That's the safest option, and it lets you turn on services one by one only when you are sure you need them.

Personal firewalls operate using rules. When network traffic approaches the firewall, the firewall software performs a quick comparison of the network traffic to its set of rules. If the network traffic matches a rule, the firewall handles it as instructed, including these two ways:

✔ Stop the traffic from passing through, as shown in Figure 15-1.

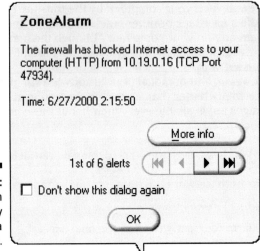

Figure 15-1:
Zone Alarm automatically blocking a connection.

✔ Ask you what to do with this kind of network traffic, as shown in Figure 15-2.

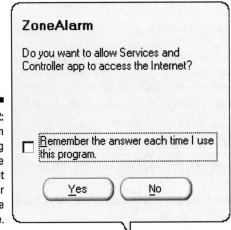

Figure 15-2:
Zone Alarm asking about some Internet traffic for future reference.

Most personal firewall software can ask you for a decision whenever some Internet traffic occurs for which it doesn't yet have a rule set up. Your answer to the question can apply just this once, or it can determine the rule for all future traffic of this kind. For example, if your firewall detects an incoming Web connection (someone points a browser at your computer's IP address), the firewall could either ignore the connection, let the connection through, or check the connection for certain criteria. Some firewall packages can let the connection through, for example, only if it's coming from an approved list of IP addresses. You could set up your friends and family to see your Web site, but nobody else would even know you have a site.

Logging and monitoring activity

One of the key features of personal firewalls, after the obvious benefit of preventing unauthorized access, is their ability to identify attacks and suspicious activity. Most personal firewall software can keep a running log of this information, including the source of the activity (usually the IP address or domain name of the attack or scanning), the time and date, and the nature of the suspicious behavior.

The activity logs are useful for several reasons. For one thing, they let you know the firewall is working. After you have the personal firewall configured, it may operate completely in the background without bothering you at all, so quietly that you may wonder whether it's doing anything at all. One look at the log file will tell you how many connection attempts, port scans, or denial of service attacks were thwarted, and you can bask in the glow of a tool doing its job well.

Another use for the log files is to provide evidence of wrongdoing. This isn't important so much for legal battles (although it could be) but for stopping crackers at their source: their Internet providers. If your personal firewall identifies a cracking attempt or other attack, most Internet providers will shut down a perpetrator's account without delay. Often an Internet provider won't even know its members are misbehaving until someone like you provides a log showing the exact time the attacks took place, and the nature of those attacks.

Don't let the log files alarm you, however. You may see frequent port scans and connection attempts in your logs, mostly automated and performed by people with more time on their hands than common sense. Those people have nothing personal against you, and probably don't even know you're there (especially if your personal firewall is hiding your presence effectively). As long as the firewall stopped the suspicious behavior, your log file is simply interesting and nothing to panic about.

Responding to an Attack

When you have a personal firewall in place, you should start watching for the signs of an invasion: port scans or mysterious connection attempts (and thank your firewall for stopping them). You need a plan for handling these situations. I recommend that you contact someone's Internet provider and take some action in any of these circumstances:

- ✔ **If you receive an intentional Trojan horse or other malicious file.** Report anyone who tries this approach on you, whether it's a simple instant message or a phone call asking for private information.

- ✔ **If you see repeated attempts from the same site.** Many times, port scans are harmless, but if you see multiple port scans from the same Internet site or at least three failed attempts to log in to your computer from the same IP address, consider that a genuine attempt to breach your defenses. If you ignore it, the cracker may find a hole in your firewall or a weakness in your OS. Your best bet is to notify the cracker's Internet provider and get that person shut down.

- ✔ **Any attempt at social engineering.** Anyone who tries this approach on you, whether it's as simple as sending you an instant message claiming to be from technical support or as elaborate as calling you on the phone requesting confirmation of your billing information, is committing fraud and should be reported.

For other situations, use your best judgment, but the criteria should be genuine possibility of damage, rather than just innocent attempts to rattle your doorknobs or unlatch a window. When you decide to report a cracking attempt, whom should you notify? That largely depends on the source of the attempt, but the first line of defense should usually be the perpetrator's Internet provider.

If you received e-mail or an instant message from the cracker, the Internet provider should be part of the sender's address or the service they're on. For example, if someone sends you an e-mail containing a Trojan horse from hotlink.com, you can report the problem to the owners of Hotlink (abuse@hotlink.com). If you receive an attempt at social engineering from an AOL Instant Messenger user, you can complain to abuse@aol.com.

If your e-mail program supports this option, you can view the headers (hidden routing and delivery information) in a mail message to learn more about the sender. The following example (with completely fake names and addresses) shows a sample e-mail header:

```
Return-Path: <qhelp@bogusname.net>
Received: from public5.example.com
        (public5.example.com[192.168.12.1])    by
        your.email.com (8.9.3/acct-2.6) with ESMTP id
        CAA14130    for <stockman@your.email.com>; Tue, 27
        Jun 2000 02:46:46 -0400 (EDT)
Received: from workstation (next.step.example.com
        [192.168.12.80])    by public5.example.com
        (8.9.3/8.9.3) with ESMTP id OAA01885;    Tue, 27
        Jun 2000 14:16:20 +0800 (CST)
Message-Id: <200006270616.OAA01885@public5.example.com>
From: "Qschool" <qhelp@bogusname.net>
Reply-To: qhelp@devnull.net
Subject: Make Money Fast!
To: Techie@public5.example.com
X-Mailer: Cheap and Easy Mail 1.0
Mime-Version: 1.0
Date: Mon, 26 Jun 2000 11:43:56 +0800
Content-Type: multipart/mixed; boundary="----
        =_NextPart_000_007F_01BDF6C7.FABAC1B0"
Content-Transfer-Encoding: 7bit
X-UIDL: bf942c8d567667ca8d7490ddf7c42b54
```

In this example of an e-mail header, the sender has obscured her true account in the From and Reply To lines. However, she couldn't hide the path the message took to reach you, and so the true mail servers that were used are shown (public5.example.com and next.step.example.com). You can therefore report the problem to the abuse or root account at example.com to try to stop this e-mail sender from striking again.

Many of the larger Internet providers, such as AOL, Earthlink, MSN, and so on, have special accounts set up to receive complaints about their users. Check their Web sites for the exact address, but usually the e-mail address is abuse@example.com, replacing example.com with the Internet service in question (aol.com, earthlink.com, and so on). For smaller Internet providers, you can try the abuse account, but also try to send mail to root@example.com, replacing example.com with tinyisp.com or whatever the actual domain name is. Again, you should check the Internet provider's Web site for details, because they may have a special account for reporting members who are misbehaving.

Protecting Yourself from Viruses

Viruses are dangers that have been with us almost as long as the personal computer revolution itself. A virus is a malicious program that hides in other programs (such as a Trojan horse) or attaches itself to documents, spreading from computer to computer. Sometimes the viruses are destructive, but more often they simply display a message or steal data when the conditions are right.

Here's a list of the risky behavior that can lead to virus infestations on anyone's computer:

- **Downloading, downloading, downloading.** The more files you collect from the Internet, the greater your risk of infection from viruses. The greatest risk is from applications (executables), which can spread infection when you launch them, but you also face a risk from documents that contain macros (such as Microsoft Office documents) that execute when you simply open the document.

- **Running suspicious or unsolicited programs.** Even if someone sends you an e-mail with a flowery message (remember the "Love bug" virus?), you could end up with a mess if you open files you weren't expecting or aren't sure about.

- **Swapping disks willy-nilly.** If you constantly pass floppy disks from co-worker to co-worker, or bring Zip disks back and forth to school and among your fellow students, the chances are good that one day those disks will bring something unintended home. Some viruses can infect your computer just by inserting an infected disk into the drive.

If you follow those practices regularly, will you get a virus on your computer? Chances are yes, but it's not guaranteed. Mac OS computers, aren't subject to many viruses at all, and the ones that do exist haven't proven to be destructive yet. There are no known UNIX viruses, so if you're running Linux, BSD, or other UNIX-like operating systems, you're probably safe from this threat.

The vast majority of viruses affect Microsoft Windows users. Some of these viruses take advantage of Visual Basic and affect any Microsoft Office users, which can include Mac OS users as well; but the bottom line is that if you use Microsoft Windows, the virus authors really are out to get you. Fortunately, you can take precautions to protect yourself from viruses:

- **Don't download so much.** Use more commercial software installed from a CD-ROM instead of pirated programs from your favorite warez site.

- **Don't open or run anything you don't understand.** Although virus-scanning software can find and disable most known Trojan horses, the best way to avoid them is to delete any files or e-mail attachments from people you don't trust implicitly (without opening them). Find out everything you can about the file before you double-click it. Be sure the document is from someone you trust to be cautious, and that it's a document you were expecting. Unexpected documents may have been sent by a macro virus, not by the person whose name is on the message.

✔ **Follow the Web sites of the virus experts.** If you visit the Web sites operated by some of the virus watchdog organizations (`www.cert.org`, US Department of Energy's `www.ciac.net`, and so on), you'll stay informed about current threats. You may also want to visit the Web sites of the anti-virus software manufacturers, such as Symantec (`www.symantec.com/avcenter`) and McAfee (`www.mcafee.com/anti-virus`), but be aware they may be more hysterical than the sites with nothing to sell.

✔ **Install an anti-virus package.** If you take reasonable precautions, your anti-virus software may never raise a warning flag, but it still may be a good idea to install some software. After it's installed, however, visit the manufacturer's site at least once a month to keep the virus definitions up to date.

✔ **Turn off dangerous features.** If your news and mail reading software allows JavaScript, ActiveX, or other extensions to operate in your e-mail or news messages, turn those features off. If you can turn off the startup macro features of any software that supports macros in documents, turn it off. Many operating systems, including Mac OS and Windows, auto-play CD-ROMs when you insert them, but that's also a feature you can turn off (on the Mac, use the QuickTime control panel, and on Windows, use a third-party utility such as TweakUI to disable this feature).

✔ **Make sure your personal firewall blocks Trojan horses from connecting to their controllers.** Many of the remote-control or remote-connection Trojan horses have identifiable habits that your personal firewall software can block and can prevent a password-collecting program from sending those passwords back to its parent, or for a remote-control package such as Back Orifice from announcing its presence for someone to connect to it.

Following these precautions should help protect you from viruses and make your Internet browsing more relaxed.

Chapter 16

Circling the Wagons: Keeping Your Network Secure

In This Chapter

▶ Bolstering security for the network level

▶ Building a firewall around your network

▶ Leveraging NAT routers for traffic control

▶ Blocking the wrong kinds of access and tracking crackers

*I*n Chapter 15, we show how to protect each computer on your Internet connection by using personal firewalls and monitoring logs. If you use a network, you have an added level of security you need to worry about: Keeping people off your network entirely. Once they've wormed their way into your network, they can cause all kinds of havoc that you would rather not deal with.

This chapter builds on the same basic concepts in Chapter 15, but adapts these to the special considerations of a network. Because one method of network security is to use both individual and network measures, we recommend that you also follow Chapter 15 for setting up individual firewalls. Here, we explain how to create a safe network — circling the wagons against outside attack — so your computers can talk to each other, and to the Internet, without fear.

Knowing the Networking Risks

The computers on your network are at risk for many of the same attacks as any individual computer that is always on and always connected to the Internet. But, being networked means you're at risk of attack on more computers at the same time as well as a few additional risks that you should consider.

Understanding internal and external protocols

When you connect your computers to a network and connect that network to the Internet, each computer on the network is running a network protocol called *TCP/IP*. That's the universal networking language (or *protocol*) computers use to speak to the Internet, so it has to be installed and active. No problem so far, right?

If you let your computers talk to each other on your local network, however, TCP/IP may not be the only network protocol that's active. For example, whether you're using Windows computers or Macintoshes, they're probably using their proprietary, built-in file sharing features (Windows uses a networking protocol called NETBIOS).

In their default configurations, the personal file sharing used on Mac OS and Windows computers isn't much of a security risk, because they use the AppleTalk and NetBEUI protocols, respectively, and most Internet routers don't carry those protocols. Because the Internet isn't configured to handle AppleTalk or NetBEUI, nobody can connect to your computers over the Internet. Usually.

The problem with these features is that they may *not* be limited to your private network. Both Mac and Windows file sharing can be configured to accept connections over TCP/IP, which means that your connection to the Internet may be broadcasting to the world that your computers are available for connections. Even if you have password protection on your computers, the basic security built-in to the Mac OS and Windows can be cracked.

This risk isn't a reason to turn off personal file sharing if you need it. If you *don't* need it, turn it off at once; the first rule of network security is to turn off unnecessary networking. If you do need to use file sharing, however, you need to make sure that it's protected from the outside world by a firewall of some kind, as described later in this chapter.

Avoiding the weak link

In Chapter 15, we discussed keeping your data safe by protecting the computer it's stored on. When you connect your computers to a network, however, you may be using that network to create backup copies of your data. (For example, you might copy your My Documents folder from one computer to another every night as a safety precaution.) Backing up files this way is a good idea, and it's one of the strengths of having a network in the first place. The computers can share each other's data, and you're less likely to lose something important if a disk crashes or a computer goes down.

On a network that's connected to the outside world, however, you also want to be sure your data is safe wherever it's kept. If it takes seventeen passwords to get to your valuable data on Computer A, but you back it up to good ol' friendly Computer B which doesn't have a password anywhere, your data is an open book.

Remember that computer security is a tradeoff between convenience and safety. You can make your data (stored on wide-open Computer B) safer by adding levels of security onto it, which is probably a good idea but may be less convenient than the way you're doing it now. Another option would be to make sure nobody can reach Computer B from the Internet, which would be more convenient because you wouldn't have to change the way you back up your data.

The ideal solution would be to do both: strengthen Computer B's security, *and* make sure that Computer B (and any other computer on your network) is inaccessible from the Internet. Any weaknesses like these on your network can lead to an attack. Using a firewall can help, as can monitoring who is connecting to your network regularly.

Adapting Security Strategies to Your Network

The best way to protect your network is for it to be invisible. Gone. Hidden away where nobody can see it. Because networks differ from individual computers in the way they communicate and connect to the Internet, you need to understand their workings and bolster your individual security measures. But, many of the principles, such as using a firewall, monitoring traffic, and tracking villains all work in a similar way for networks.

Same bricks, bigger firewall

Virtually all protected networks on the Internet are behind some kind of firewall. In networks, these devices sit *between* the Internet connection and your network rather than on your single machine, but they still determine what kind of traffic enters and leaves your network. Network firewalls follow similar sets of rules for dealing with this traffic:

> ✔ If an attacker tries to connect to your network using one of the remote control cracking tools, such as Back Orifice, the firewall sees that network traffic, recognizes it as an attempt to crack your network, and stops it from getting in.

✔ Firewalls can follow specific rules for suspicious connection attempts, which show up in your firewall or router log. After you identify where an attacker is coming from, you can use the firewall to block all connection attempts from that address, or from a range of addresses (say, to block an entire Internet provider's customers from reaching you).

✔ More typically, network administrators set up firewalls to block all incoming connections, or restrict them to certain kinds of connections. For example, you might set up your firewall to reject all incoming connections except to your public Web server, which you want people to see.

Setting up a network firewall works

The difference between a network firewall and an personal file is usually in its location and the virtual guard who sits on this wall watching out for your interests.

A firewall can be a piece of software running on a regular computer, or it can be a dedicated box that plugs into your network. You should also know that the system running the firewall (whether it's a computer or a standalone box) may also be performing some other tasks on your network, such as acting as a *router* (a kind of network traffic cop) or some kinds of servers.

The important thing to remember about a firewall is that it has to sit on your network *between* your computers and the Internet, as shown in Figure 16-1. Here, a firewall sits in relation to your computer network (referred to as *internal computers,* or *inside the firewall*) and the Internet (*external computers,* or *outside the firewall*).

The key to network security is remembering that any access to your network is a risk. Therefore, you should shut off any access to your network that you don't need. Firewalls are one way to do that, and they shut off access by following a set of rules you define.

Making your traffic follow the rules

The set of rules that a firewall uses to allow or block data is something you create and modify as your networking needs change. However, there's one simple firewall rule that should help you create all of the other rules:

Block everything, then make exceptions as needed.

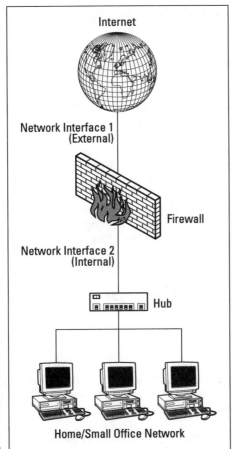

Internet

Network Interface 1
(External)

Firewall

Network Interface 2
(Internal)

Hub

Figure 16-1:
Protecting
your
network
with
firewall.

Home/Small Office Network

In other words, your firewall should initially be configured to stop all network traffic, especially from the Internet side of the connection. However, because that's not a very useful configuration (blocking the Internet entirely), you can then open each service you need to use.

For example, you know you'll be browsing the Web, so you could immediately open up Web access from the internal side of the firewall. You could also open up e-mail access, because you can be pretty sure you'll be needing that. As you need to use different network services, you can open up additional access in the firewall.

Many firewall products come with a set of rules defined for the most common network services, but you may want to go through that set of rules turning off the access you know you don't need.

Deciding on a model: Firewall or router?

A regular firewall, running on its own computer or as part of a network router, is the best way to protect an entire network.

Most network routers have firewalls built-in that you can turn on at any time to begin protecting your network. Because the router is handling traffic in and out of your network anyway, it's a logical place to put a firewall.

You can also set up a dedicated computer that is running some firewall software, in this case, a spare computer running a UNIX-kind of operating system, Windows NT, or similar high-level system.

A NAT router also provides a lot of the same features as a firewall, in that all traffic passes through the NAT router, and incoming connections only reach your computers if the router is configured to allow them.

NAT, Your Hero — A Router to the Rescue

If you followed our advice in Chapter 13 and set up a NAT router to share your high-speed Internet connection, you already have a great deal of protection in place, keeping the crackers out of your network. That's because of the way NAT works, and you get added security as a bonus.

You may recall that NAT uses the one public Internet address your Internet provider gave you, and shares that among all of the privately addressed computers on your network. Your computers may all have IP addresses such as 192.168.0.1 or 10.0.0.2, which are invalid for the public Internet connection, but the NAT router is translating those addresses into the valid ones assigned to you by your Internet provider.

One of the security side effects of this is that by default, only connections that your computers request can get through the NAT router. For example, Computer A on your network may click a download link on a Web page to begin downloading a file. Because Computer A requested that file, the NAT router lets it through. If some Web site on the Internet started sending an unrequested file to your network, the NAT router would see that no computer on your network was downloading, and would stop the incoming file cold.

The advantage to this is that many kinds of cracking attempts involve connecting to a computer on your network from the outside. But when the cracker tries to connect to your network through the NAT router, the router says to itself "Nobody inside the network asked for that connection, and I don't have any rules set up to handle that connection, so I'm going to drop that connection."

TIP

What to watch for with routers and network cards

If you've been shopping for a NAT router based on our advice, you may have trouble finding a commercial product because the feature called Network Address Translation, or NAT, in the computing world is often called Internet Sharing in the retail world. They avoid the term NAT as being too techy, and sell Internet Sharing servers instead of NAT routers. Don't be fooled, but read the specifications on any commercial device before buying it to make sure NAT, sometimes called IP Masquerading, is supported.

The only requirement that the router needs to be secure, whether you're using a firewall or a NAT router, is to have two network cards installed, instead of the single network card most computers have. See Chapter 13 for more details on networking.

Using one network card leaves your network vulnerable, because the network traffic from the Internet could possibly get to other computers on your network without ever passing through the firewall. The firewall's protection would be strong, but if the attack bypasses the firewall its strength doesn't matter.

With two network cards, no traffic gets to your network without passing through the firewall first. That's the safest way to operate network protection.

All commercial NAT routers include two network interfaces, as do all commercial routers with firewall capabilities. This precaution only applies if you choose to put a spare computer into service protecting your network.

That's why you gain a great deal of safety from the NAT router. With some NAT routers, not even a ping can get through, so your network may not even appear to exist to the casual observer.

The upshot is that, for most networks, if you're using a NAT router to share a single Internet address with your internal network, you probably don't need a firewall. (Note to security fanatics: Yes, I know that a NAT router isn't a true firewall, and that some attackers can get through NAT who would be stopped by a well-configured firewall. I also know that for the vast majority of users, NAT is sufficient. If you're looking for an ultra-secure network, set up a true firewall on the network and personal firewall software (such as ZoneAlarm) on each computer, plus encryption and checksums on every hard drive.)

Blocking Pings

As we mention in Chapter 15, using pings is one way crackers try to infiltrate or clog your system. A ping is a packet of information someone sends, telling it to come back when it finds its destination.

Here's an example of using the ping command included with Microsoft Windows to ping www.idgbooks.com:

```
Pinging www.idgbooks.com [38.170.216.15] with 32 bytes of
        data:

Reply from 38.170.216.15: bytes=32 time=117ms TTL=114
Reply from 38.170.216.15: bytes=32 time=115ms TTL=114
Reply from 38.170.216.15: bytes=32 time=114ms TTL=114
Reply from 38.170.216.15: bytes=32 time=114ms TTL=114
```

The reply is similar to the sound or sonar bouncing back to a bat's ears, indicating that something's actually there. The time= line indicates how long the ping took to come back. The higher that number (shown here in milliseconds, or thousandths of a second), the slower your connection to that server will be.

Here's an example of the results of the ping command included with Windows, pinging the computer at www.apple.com:

```
Pinging www.apple.com [17.254.0.91] with 32 bytes of data:

Request timed out.
Request timed out.
Request timed out.
Request timed out.
```

Apple's Web site didn't disappear, as you might think from the "Request timed out" messages. Instead, Apple may have configured its Web server not to respond to pings, because responding to pings can provide a security risk. (Pings have been used to shut down Web sites, either by crashing the computer with a corrupted ping message or by sending so many pings that the computer can't handle any real connections.)

One of the ways you can hide your network is by doing what Apple has done. Your firewall (described later in this chapter) or NAT router may be able to avoid responding to pings.

Tracking traffic with logs

As with individual machines, your network is prone to vulnerability due to bugs or other weaknesses. For this reason, many firewalls and NAT routers can keep a log of the network traffic that they handle. Regular traffic that passes through (your browsing the Web, for example, or checking your e-mail) wouldn't be logged, but an attempt from someone outside of your network to connect to your hard drive would certainly be mentioned in the log.

The following example shows a log entry collected on a NAT router:

```
10/19/00  11:15:08   uplink - NAT in drop: TCP, no SYN, no
              conn
10/19/00  11:15:08   tcp 192.168.0.15:21 192.168.123.44:4560
              (75)
```

The first line of this entry from the router indicates that a packet (incoming on NAT) was dropped, and no connection was established. The second line indicates that the connection attempt (from fictional IP address 192.168.0.15) came in on TCP port 21, which happens to carry FTP (or file transfer) connections.

You can find out which port numbers carry many kinds of connections by visiting www.isi.edu/in-notes/iana/assignments/port-numbers, among other sites, or by using an Internet search engine to search for port numbers.

In other words, someone outside of my network tried to connect for the purpose of transferring files, presumably without my permission (since I'm not running a file transfer server). Is this an attack? No, not when it's the only line in the log coming from this address and aimed at this port. If there were a series of 20, 30, 50, or more connection attempts from the same IP address, I'd be suspicious, whether I knew what the port number meant or not.

Chapter 15 walks you through the process of reporting anything you think may be cause for concern. One additional resource you have in using a router is that your router's technical support group may offer interpretation of your log's contents, so consider exporting the log for a translation.

Staying Up-to-Date

Network security isn't like building a wall, it's more like weeding a garden. You can clear out the weeds, put some mulch down to prevent new ones, but you'll still find that a new weed will pop-up where you least expected it. With network security, the crackers are discovering new weaknesses in firewalls, browsers, networking software, and other software that you're using every day.

When you want to observe animals in the wilderness, you need to go to the places where they congregate, and look around. When you want to find out the latest security information for your network, you need to go where the security experts hang out on the Web. Fortunately, although they mainly come out at night, you can find their tracks at any time of day.

A good starting point is to visit any of the following sites:

- **Microsoft** (`www.microsoft.com/security`). Although Microsoft isn't always as forthcoming about security issues that affect its own products, it has a good section on security that explains concepts, discusses newly-discovered security holes, and (here's the important part) makes patches and updates available to fix the security holes in its own products. If you use any Microsoft products on your network, this site should be a regular stop on your security errands. The Microsoft site has some good sections for beginners, too, so this may be a good starting place in general.

- **Firewall, Router, and Operating System Sites.** Whoever makes your firewall or NAT router and your computer's operating system (Microsoft, Apple, RedHat, and so on) probably has a section on security issues that involve their products. Bookmark those sites, and visit them regularly, downloading and installing the updates they make available.

- **SecureMac** (`www.securemac.com`). If you have Mac OS computers on your network, be sure to visit this site occasionally for the latest Mac security news. It also has links to utilities for testing, protecting, and fixing your Mac's security issues.

- **Lycos and other search engines.** Lycos (`dir.lycos.com/Computers/Security`) has an excellent summary of many of the network security sites on the Web. Look for the ones that apply to your network, and visit one or two of the ones you like best once a week or so.

- **L0pht Heavy Industries** (`www.10pht.com`). The L0pht (that's a zero instead of the letter "O") has been a combination hacker site and security site (not too unusual a combination, really) for years, and they're often the site where new security information first appears. Unlike the computer companies such as Microsoft, which has something at stake, the folks at L0pht don't stand to gain anything by protecting security information. For that reason, they tend to be brutally frank about security issues, and that makes them a good site for any of us to visit. This site can feel kind of heavy, so don't get too bogged down in the details. I generally scan the headlines, skip most of it, and pay attention only to the issues that directly affect my networks.

- **CERT Coordination Center** (`www.cert.org/advisories/`). Carnegie-Mellon's computer emergency response team provides regular information, updates, and explanations on a wide range of computer security and virus issues.

These sites and the host of others track computer security issues so you don't have to. Checking with your favorite couple of sites each week or so can help you stay on top of security issues that concern you so you can keep your software up-to-date, your network locked-down, and your computers safe.

Testing the Fortress

Just as you would test an individual machine's strength against attack, we recommend that you check your network security using one of the Web's own security sites.

Most of these security sites keep a running log of everyone who uses them to scan a network. If you scan a network that you aren't personally in charge of, you may find yourself facing complaints and even disconnection by your Internet provider for trying to crack someone else's network, even if that weren't your true intention. To be safe, scan only your own computers, and let others scan theirs if that's what they want.

For example, you might visit www.secure-me.net (available from the excellent DSLReports.com site), which can provide an in-depth security scan or a quick probe of your network to make sure no obvious ports are open. Another site to use is AntiOnline, (www.antionline.com).

For example, a scan of my network at secure-me.net resulted in the report shown in Figure 16-2.

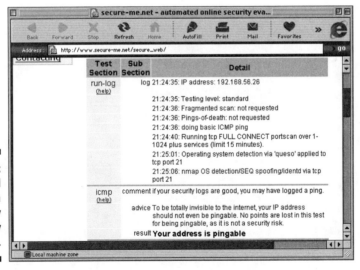

Figure 16-2: A partial result of a security scan on my network.

The security scan should have two major results:

✔ **Information from the scan:** You'll see in the report provided by the security scan whether your network has open ports, what kind of risk that entails, and why they might be open for a reason. You can then visit your computer's documentation for information on closing those holes.

✔ **Information from your logs:** Your router's log files should show the results of the scan as well, indicating that an attempt to ping happened here . . . an attempt to connect to your FTP server (if one exists) happened there, and so on. This check can both assure you that your log feature is working, and provide examples of log entries you'll know about, so you'll be more likely to recognize troubling log entries later on.

Test your security regularly (once a week, once a month, whatever feels comfortable) to be sure no new weaknesses have developed. (Already I'm losing points because my NAT router responded to a ping, which many routers can be configured to ignore.) Also remember that, over time, those scanner Web sites will be enhanced, possibly to find weaknesses they couldn't before. Regular scanning can help you keep your network tightly under wraps, and your computers safely hidden from the world.

Chapter 17

Protecting Your Privacy

· ·

In This Chapter

▶ Why it's risky to share too much about yourself

▶ Avoiding leaving tracks

▶ Omitting information or lying to those too nosy for your own good

▶ Hiding your information

· ·

Although security and privacy often go hand-in-hand, they're very different concepts. Security is protecting your equipment and data from damage or unauthorized access. That's a very good thing, and it's discussed thoroughly in chapters 15 and 16. While a breach in security can also violate your privacy, however, they're not the same thing.

When you protect your privacy, you're protecting your personal information from damage or unauthorized access. Someone who tricks you into revealing your social security number, for example, has breached your privacy without damaging the security of your computer or network. Protecting your privacy takes a different approach than protecting your security, but it's no less important.

Your biggest foes in the battle for your privacy aren't breaking any laws. They're just doing their job, which is selling stuff. The job of most merchants who use the Internet is to collect information about you so they can sell it to others or use it to hawk their wares. There are also people who try to collect information from you for other reasons, such as credit card fraud or identity theft. All of these privacy-invaders offer you things in exchange for your information, such as enticing Web sites, online games, contests with exciting prizes, and other brightly-colored trinkets. Don't be fooled.

Because you use a high-speed Internet connection and stay connected to the Internet 24 hours a day, you encounter more privacy issues than someone using a dial-up connection, if for no other reason than because you're using the Internet so darned much.

This chapter describes some of the privacy pitfalls involved in high-speed, always-on Internet access, and how to protect yourself from your nosy neighbors all over the world.

What, Me Worry?

Before you start to hide your identity and cloud the Internet waters to travel in secret, you need to know what the risks are. After all, why bother to take precautions unless you know something bad can happen?

There are several reasons to protect your privacy that range from minor annoyances to danger from others. To be fair, the minor annoyances category is huge and affects most Internet users, while the danger from others category is small and happens rarely. However, if you can take precautions against all of these situations, you probably should.

I want to be alone

The biggest reason to protect your privacy is to be left alone. Many people want to avoid being bothered, whether by junk e-mail, intrusive advertising, chain letters, or pyramid schemes.

Posting a message in a newsgroup or on a public bulletin board Web site may result in your e-mail address being picked up by spammers, who send unsolicited commercial e-mail to everybody they can. Some people configure their browsers and newsreaders to post under an assumed name, or fake e-mail address, to avoid this problem. Merely revealing your presence can result in unwanted attention.

The price of privacy

Each time you browse the Web, you're engaging in a sales transaction whether you know it or not. Almost every site you visit asks you to give up your privacy, and they always offer something in exchange. Your job is to decide how much your privacy is worth.

Try this test: On one Web site you want to enter a contest to win a car. The site, naturally, asks you for your address, telephone number, average yearly income, gender, and blood type. Do you enter?

If you answered "yes," you're willing to sell your most personal information for a one-in-two-million (or other unlikely odds) chance of winning a prize. That's a pretty low price for your privacy. If the site said you'd actually receive a car in return for your information, that would be a much higher price for your privacy. It might even be worth it.

Web sites that ask for your personal information just to use the site are asking something for nothing. Don't give them the information they want. Web sites ask for your private information because it's worth something to them. Decide how much your personal privacy is worth to you, and then make sure you sell it for at least that price.

It takes time to delete junk e-mail, and to wade through a Web page's banner ads, and to close or prevent unwanted instant messages from people you don't know. Protecting your privacy (your e-mail address, your instant message address, and avoiding intrusive Web sites) can help avoid these situations.

Making you a better target

The more a company knows about you, the more plausible their sales pitches aimed in your direction can be. The process of targeting sales and marketing information based on information companies discover about you is called profiling. For example, when you have a new baby in the household, your regular mail suddenly becomes inundated with baby-related sales pitches. That's because those companies have invaded your privacy just enough to find out you have a new child, and they're using that to target their advertising.

The same tricks work online. Bookseller Amazon.com, for example, keeps track of what you purchase so they can recommend similar books to you. Tracking your purchases appears to be convenient, with the company helpfully offering books you'll like and not bothering you with books you won't like.

On the other, more suspicious hand, however, you have a big corporation tracking your purchases so they can get you to buy things more effectively.

If a company knew you were browsing a lingerie site and started to send you advertising for other risqué products, would you be pleased or embarrassed? There's a fine line between helpful and intrusive, and you can control much of what companies find out about you and your product preferences.

A company reading your requests for retirement planning may target you for ads that play on your fears of going broke as you get older. As another hypothetical situation, another firm may see that you've bought a book about hypochondria, and may target you for quack medical cures.

We're from the government and we're here to help you

Many people are leery of letting the government (in any country) find out too much information about them, not because they're necessarily doing anything wrong, but because the government may not always be the helpful, friendly, benign entity it is today. If the government begins abusing its power, it will be too late to un-send the information the government may have about you.

Stories throughout the media tell about governmental organizations collecting e-mail and other postings based on subject, whether they contain certain keywords, and/or based on the sender's or recipient's name. If you're concerned about such collections, you may need to encrypt your communications.

In some countries, having the government pay attention to your Internet-based activities can be genuinely dangerous. Residents of those countries will do well to protect their online privacy and identities in every way possible.

Granted, that's not a likely scenario in many democratic countries today, but if you're concerned that your discussions on the "How to throw pies at officials" bulletin board may be monitored, it's best to hide your identity and protect your privacy in other ways.

You may not be you

Identity theft doesn't require the use of the Internet at all. With some choice information about you, such as your social security number, date of birth, mother's maiden name, and several of your recent addresses, an unscrupulous person can apply for official documents and credit cards in your name, pretending to be you, but at a new address. If the identity thief is clever enough, you won't know it's even happening until your credit history is trashed and you're on the hook for bills you never authorized.

The Internet comes into the picture when your personal information is compromised while you're surfing the Net, such as when you enter contests, answer surveys, or attempt to make purchases at fake or insecure Web sites. Thieves will try all kinds of tricks, including masquerading as official Web sites, to get you to enter your personal data for them to use.

This doesn't happen very often, in the physical world or on the Internet, but it's a genuine risk that you should avoid by keeping your data private.

Credit card theft is a related risk, rare but still dangerous, that you can prevent by keeping your personal information private unless you are sure you're giving it to genuine merchants who take reasonable precautions with your data. Precautions will be discussed later in this chapter.

Browsing the Web without Leaving Tracks

More and more Internet software is designed to track what you're doing. Web browsers contain all kinds of information that can identify you to the sites you visit, and in many cases you don't even know it's being provided. It's kind of like having people sifting through your wallet and briefcase and taking notes while you're in line to buy doughnuts and coffee. Even though nothing's missing from your pockets, you've still been robbed.

Fortunately, there are ways to reduce, if not eliminate, the information about you floating around e-commerce and other Web sites. You can't eliminate the information completely if you're buying things, entering contests, subscribing to mailing lists, and so on. Once you ask a Web site for something, you're in their records forever. You can, however, block some of the privacy-invading habits of the sites you visit.

No, not that kind of cookie

A lot has been said in the media in recent years about cookies. Although there is a world-wide obsession with baked goods, this kind of cookie has a more nerd-like definition. A cookie (in the Internet sense of the word) is a piece of data that a Web site places on your computer so it can recognize you when you come back.

For example, when you log on My AOL.com (at my.aol.com, where they customize the Web page for your account, according to your preferences), the My AOL.com Web site can place a cookie on your computer. The next time you visit that site, it logs you in automatically, using the ID and password saved in your cookie file. Cookies can also contain a list of items in your shopping cart, your preferences for a site, or just anonymous information that identifies your computer if you visit the site again.

This sounds convenient, and it is. Web sites can welcome you by name, display pages that match your interests, and let you know about the results of your past visits (order status, and so on).

However, many sites add a cookie to your computer for their own benefit, not yours. Doubleclick, a well-known Web-based advertising company, places a cookie on your computer whenever you visit a Web page that has a Doubleclick-placed ad. As you go from site to site, Doubleclick can track your progress and customize the ads you see to be the most effective.

Currently, most sites can't identify you personally from your cookies. A Web site may know that you're on the computer with cookie ID 123456789, but they don't know who the person is behind that cookie. However, there was a recent uproar when a company that places and tracks cookie information that includes people's Internet addresses was going to merge with a company that had personal information that also included people's Internet addresses. The result could have been one big database that showed which cookies belonged to which real people, and that company could know your browsing habits and the sites you have visited.

You can avoid collecting cookies by following these steps:

1. **In your Web browser, open your browser's preferences.**

   Usually, you'll find the preferences using the Preferences command on the Edit menu or the Options command on the Tools menu.

2. **In the Preferences window that appears, click the category containing your cookie options.**

   The location of the cookies settings vary from browser to browser. Figures 17-1, 17-2, and 17-3 show some examples.

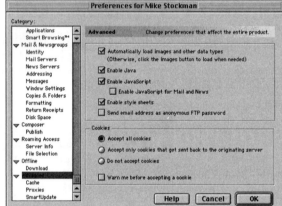

Figure 17-1:
Cookie preferences in Netscape 4.x for Mac OS, Windows, or UNIX.

3. **To prevent all cookies from being stored on your computer, select the option that prevents all cookies (such as Never Accept, Do Not Accept Cookies, and so on).**

4. **If you want your browser to ask you whether to save each cookie, select Prompt, Ask for Each Cookie, or similar option.**

   Selecting this option may result in a lot of prompting from your browser. Opening a page on the My Netscape news page, for example, may place four or more cookies on your computer, and you'll be asked about each one.

5. **Click OK when you're done to save your changes.**

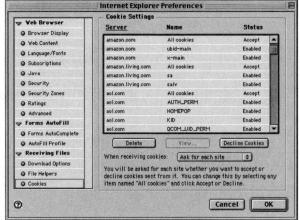

Figure 17-2:
Cookie
preferences
in Internet
Explorer 4 or
5 for Mac
OS.

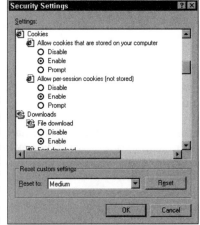

Figure 17-3:
Cookie
preferences
in Internet
Explorer 4 or
5 for
Windows.

Note that some browsers are adding more selective options for blocking cookies. Internet Explorer for Macintosh, for example, can remember your preferences for each site, and never ask you again. (For example, you might block all cookies for doubleclick.net, an advertising site, and Internet Explorer forever after blocks cookies for that site.)

Microsoft is also adding features to Internet Explorer for Windows to block cookies more selectively. Netscape 6 also contains preferences for blocking cookies for each site, or each company, and so on.

Cookie cutters

As with any other Internet issue, people have written all kinds of utilities to deal with cookies. Until Web browsers provide more control over cookies (expected in Netscape 6 and IE 5.5 with some add-ons), here's a short list of some of the more popular tools for Windows and Mac:

✔ **Window Washer and MacWasher from www.webroot.com.** The large collection of freeware and shareware utilities from Webroot can help clear out and control cookies for Netscape and Internet Explorer.

✔ **MagicCookie Monster for Mac, from download.at/drjsoftware.** This utility is freeware and helps you control cookies in Netscape for Macintosh.

✔ **Cookie Cutter for Mac.** This utility also helps control cookies for Netscape for Mac but currently has no Web site for downloading. You can find it at any Tucows archive (www.tucows.com) by searching for it by name.

Traveling incognito

When you browse the Internet, companies can identify which IP address you're using, as well as which OS your computer has, how your computer monitor is configured, which browser you're using, and other information that you may or may not want to reveal.

Several sites have been set up to show you exactly what information a Web site can see about you, your computer, and your browser. For example, if you visit www.privacy.net/analyze/, you might see information about your computer similar to that shown in Figure 17-4.

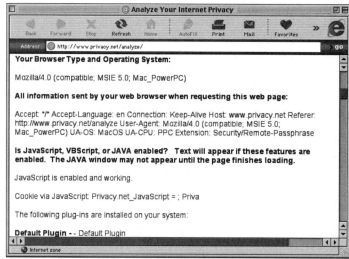

Figure 17-4: Privacy.net's analysis of the information my Web browser is freely telling every Tom, Dick, and Harry who comes along.

Web sites can often even tell which site you came from when you browsed to their pages, so if you visit your parent's Web site directly from viewing the Children of Bad Upbringing support group's Web site, you may have some explaining to do.

For this reason, there are services available that let you mask all information about your computer while you're browsing the Internet. Some of these services are free, and some cost a regular service fee.

The way these anonymous browsing services work is by capturing all of the Internet addresses you enter into your browser or click on a page. Instead of sending your browser directly to those pages, the anonymous service loads the page on their own computers and has your browser open the pre-opened pages. The Web site you're visiting sees only the anonymous service's computer, while you still see the page you wanted. (This all happens automatically and almost as quickly as browsing normally takes.)

Figure 17-5 shows a page at one anonymous browsing service that lets you enter a URL (Web address) to browse without compromising your privacy.

Once you enter a Web address into an anonymous browsing service, you can continue browsing the Web knowing that none of the sites you visit will see any details about you or your computer.

Figure 17-5: Anonymizer.com's Web site, offering both free and commercial services to let you browse in private.

Sites that offer anonymous Web browsing include

- ✔ Anonymizer, at `www.anonymizer.com`, providing free and paid services

- ✔ Junkbusters, at `www.junkbusters.com`, providing good advice and techniques, as well as some assistance, for eliminating the junk mail and privacy invasions

- ✔ SilentSurf, at `www.silentsurf.com`, free and paid

- ✔ Aixs.net, a free service (although swimming with advertising, as are most of the free services)

- ✔ C.O.T.S.E., at `www.cotse.com/anonimizer` (note the misspelling of anonymizer); totally free and surprisingly few ads as of this writing

Numerous other sites offer anonymous browsing. Go to your favorite Internet search site and search for anonymous browsing or similar terms. As with the rest of the Web, sites will disappear, and others will arise, so check for new services regularly if you can't find what you want.

Using Your Secret Decoder Ring

It's often been said that using e-mail is like sending a postcard. Internet mail travels by hopping from computer to computer around the world until it reaches its destination, and it could potentially be read by anyone intercepting it along the way, just as a postcard could. Unlike regular mail, e-mail has no envelope to protect it from prying eyes.

There is so much e-mail hopping around the Internet, of course, that the chances of anyone actually seeing yours is very, very slim. However, if anyone took an interest in you and your e-mail personally, it wouldn't be too hard for that person to see at least some of the messages you're sending to friends, business associates, and loved ones. That's probably fine most of the time (do you really care if someone intercepts that collection of light bulb jokes you're forwarding to fifty of your closest friends?), but you may not want someone else reading, say, your innermost feelings about teddy bears that you're sending to a childhood friend.

As always, paranoid users of the Internet became alarmed by this long before you or I, and so there is a way to place a wrapper around your e-mail to prevent anyone other than the recipient from seeing it. On the Internet, envelopes are called encryption.

Quick summary of encryption

Encryption is the process of altering a message so that its meaning is no longer clear except to people who know the code. For example, take the following sentence:

Hey, Tommy, meet me at the clubhouse at noon.

If you replace each letter with the letter of the alphabet 13 places following (wrapping to the beginning when you get to the end), you get a sentence that looks like this:

Url, Gbzzl, zrrg zr ng gur pyhoubhfr ng abba.

The letter H from the first sentence is converted to the letter U in the encrypted example, because U is exactly 13 places in the alphabet after H. This is not a robust method of encrypting text, but it's provided here as an example.

(A quick aside: this method of encryption is called ROT-13, and is a common but simple way to hide text from casual readers in e-mail or newsgroups. Because it's so simple, it's not a useful method of encryption, but it provides a decent example anyway.)

Fortunately, there are real methods of encrypting text that are, so far, immune to any known methods of decoding. These methods are available for you to use to protect your e-mail and other information. (Many of these methods were available only in the United States until recently, and now are available all over the world except for some hostile nations.)

Most Web browsers use a form of encryption (called SSL) to protect your transactions while you're connected to secure Web sites. For e-mail, however, you'll be using another kind of encryption called public key encryption to protect your messages.

Some e-mail programs, such as the one built-in to Lotus Notes and some versions of Microsoft Outlook, have some encryption and signature features built-in. For the rest of us, the most popular encryption package is free, and is called PGP (which modestly stands for Pretty Good Privacy), available at www.pgp.com/products/freeware. A commercial version of this product is available at www.pgp.com.

The next section gives some examples of how you'd use PGP or similar products to encrypt and sign e-mail.

How to use encryption and signatures

This section provides a brief summary of how to use encryption and signatures to protect yourself in Internet communications. It's a brief summary because this is too large and complex an area to be covered here, but you should get an idea from these examples.

There are two concerns with sending documents (e-mail, contracts, proposals, and so on) over the Internet:

- ✔ Secrecy, which prevents anyone other than the intended recipient from seeing its contents

- ✔ Validation, which guarantees that the message is really from you, and hasn't been tampered with along the way.

The leader in the field of software that does both of these things is called PGP (mentioned in the previous section). PGP exists in two forms: a commercial product, available from Network Associates at `www.pgp.com`, and a free product, available at `www.pgp.com/products/freeware`. Both provide excellent ways to protect your privacy on the Internet (and the commercial version adds more features, a better interface, and technical support).

To protect the secrecy of a document, PGP requires that you have the public key of the person to whom you're sending the document. This key is useless for cracking the encryption, because it's a one-way key: all it can do is encode the document, not decode it. Once you have the person's public key loaded into PGP, you'll encrypt the message. Fortunately, PGP adds itself to most e-mail programs as a plug-in, so encrypting the message usually takes a single command. For example, in Figure 17-6, a private message is ready to be sent.

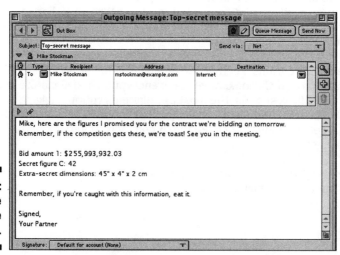

Figure 17-6: A message ready to be encrypted.

After you choose Encrypt from the PGP menu and choose the person who will be receiving the message, you end up with something like the window shown in Figure 17-7.

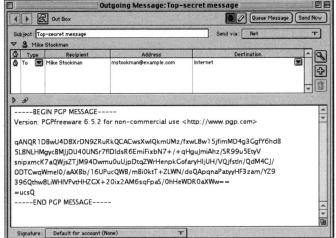

Figure 17-7:
A message
that has
been
encrypted
using PGP.

As shown here, the encrypted message bears no resemblance at all to the original. Nobody except for the intended recipient can decode the message without a bank of supercomputers pounding away for hundreds of years. And because it's one-way encryption, even you, the original author, can't decrypt the message. Only the recipient can, using her private key and a secret password or phrase.

Adding a digital signature to a document serves two purposes: It verifies that the document comes from a particular person and nobody else, and it verifies that the document hasn't changed at all since it was signed. It's kind of a technological notary public, but without the cool embossing.

Here's how it works: You create the document, and when you're ready to sign it, you choose a command in PGP. PGP applies your private key to the document (say, the e-mail message) and attaches the signature to the bottom. Anybody receiving the document can use your public key (which you've given to just about everyone you know) to verify that the signature is valid, and that it matches the exact document that the recipient is reading.

If even one character is altered in the document, even something as simple as a missing carriage return or space, the signature will not match the document, and the verification fails. This guarantees that when you receive a signed document, it's exactly the same as when it was sent.

For example, in Figure 17-8, a message is ready to be signed.

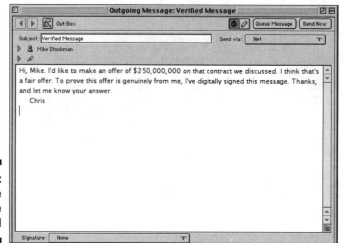

After you choose Sign from the PGP menu, you end up with something like the window shown in Figure 17-9.

As you can see, the original message is unchanged, except for the signature appended to the bottom. Anybody receiving this message who has the sender's public key can now verify the signature. (Note that you can sign *and* encrypt the same message, for all levels of protection that are available.)

Recent federal legislation has given digital signatures the same legal weight as the kind you sign with a pen on paper (even though digital signatures are actually more reliable), so it's worth your while to look into using PGP or something similar to validate your messages.

How useful is this to protect yourself? One reason to sign your messages, Web postings, or newsgroup messages is so that nobody can change them and claim you wrote something. If you sign everything that goes out, you can prove at any point that altered copies aren't what you said.

If you're concerned about business messages traveling the Internet, talk to your legal representatives about whether signatures (or even encryption) would be prudent measures to take.

Posting Messages without Posting Your Identity

When you post messages in newsgroups, chat rooms, and other public forums, you're probably entering your actual e-mail address, the IP address of your computer, and probably even your real name, and that information is attached to each message you send. That's fine if you like junk e-mail, because spammers are notorious for harvesting e-mail addresses from newsgroups, Web bulletin boards, and other public forums. The rest of us, however, would like to cut down on the junk mail, and would prefer not to announce our identities to the world.

You might also want to protect your real identity to avoid harassment when posting on sensitive or unpopular subjects (such as brussel sprouts, taxes, or Macintosh vs. Windows).

Your children may even want to use some of these techniques to avoid having their true identities known. (See Chapter 18 for more information on protecting your children online.)

As always, there are methods that let you avoid posting messages as yourself or let you post as yourself without revealing too much information about yourself.

Lying for a good cause

The best way to protect your personal information online doesn't even involve technology or any computer tricks. Set up a false identity for yourself, then use that for any sensitive Internet communications. Remember, computers are very gullible and will accept anything you tell them, passing that information on to anyone who asks for it.

Here's how to take advantage of your computer's gullibility: when you visit a Web site that has a message board, chat room, or other public forum, enter a false name, false e-mail address, and any other information they're looking for. This lets you carry on in conversations with people, using an identity you can re-use each time you visit the newsgroup or Web site and still protect your actual identity, e-mail address, and other information.

It doesn't matter if you use an obvious choice, such as a historical figure or cartoon character. People will know it's an assumed identity, but that's fine as long as your true identity is hidden.

Note that even if you set up a false identity for use in a Web site-based discussion, the Web site's operator and possibly others can still see the IP address currently assigned to your computer. That information could be traced, by contacting your Internet provider, to you and your computer, so setting up a false identity won't let you get away with everything.

A false identity in chat groups, newsgroups, and bulletin boards is like wearing a mask to a party. The casual observer won't know who you are, but someone determined may be able to find out your identity anyway, especially if you do something illegal or threatening that gives them incentive to find you.

Here's how you might set up your false identity using the Microsoft Outlook Express 5 newsreader:

1. **In Outlook Express, choose Accounts from the Tools menu.**

2. **In the dialog box that appears, click the Add button, then choose News from the menu that appears.**

   A dialog box similar to Figure 17-10 appears.

3. **Enter the name under which you want your newsgroup messages to appear, such as Anonymous, Just This Guy, and so on, then click Next.**

   This name is used only for display purposes (to show people who wrote the message), so enter anything you'd like here, within reason. Just remember that people will partly judge you on what you enter here, so anything offensive or obscene is likely to get you ignored, flamed, or (if it's a moderated list) bounced from the group.

   A dialog box similar to Figure 17-11 appears.

4. **Enter the e-mail address you'd like attached to messages you post from this account, then click Next.**

   This could be a real anonymous account you've set up, such as those created through www.cotse.com or a free account under an obscured name on a service like hotmail.com or yahoo.com. You might use your real e-mail address here, but that would defeat the purpose of this anonymous news account.

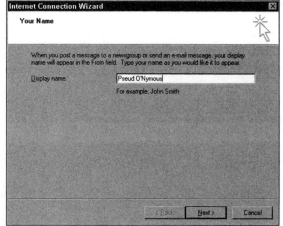

Figure 17-10:
Entering
your
pseudonym
for a new
News
account.

Figure 17-11:
Entering an
e-mail
address for
a new News
account.

You may also want to put in a completely bogus e-mail account here, such as junk@nomailserver.com, or nothing@example.com. Just be sure you're not using anyone's real account here who might get e-mail directed at you.

Any time you need to enter a fake Internet address, anything ending in example.com, example.org, or example.net is safe to use without any chance that it's real. That's because the example names have been set aside as sample names and will never be used for real sites.

When you click Next, a dialog box similar to Figure 17-12 appears.

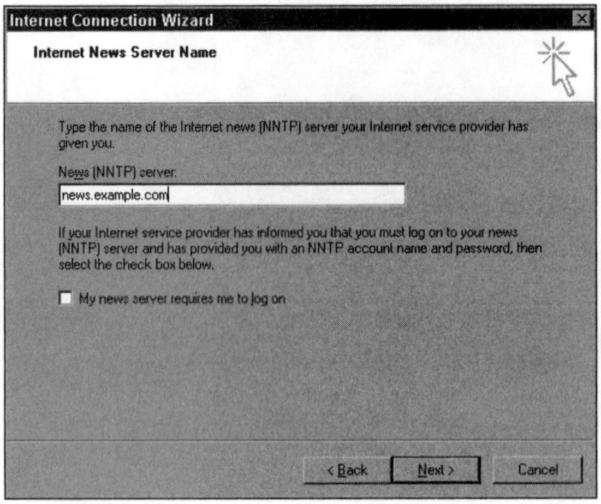

Figure 17-12:
Entering the
real server
name for the
new News
account.

5. **Enter the real news server address your Internet provider has given you, then click Next.**

   This part of the process has to be genuine, or you'll never be able to read or post messages from the account you're setting up. If your Internet provider has told you to log on to this news server, you'll have to select the appropriate checkbox and enter your real name and password here. Don't worry, they won't be displayed with messages you post.

6. **Click Finish in the final dialog box of the setup process.**

To use your new anonymous account, select it in Outlook Express the same as you would your regular news account, and read and post messages as usual.

You might try posting a test message to the alt.test newsgroup, which has been set up as a place where you can test your configuration without cluttering up the real newsgroups. Nobody reads the messages in alt.test, so it's safe to post anything to see the results.

As a test of my own anonymous configuration, I posted a message to alt.test, then opened it in Outlook Express to see the results. They appear in Figure 17-13.

So far, there's no way to tell the message is really from me. Just to be safe, let's view the headers, which are the hidden Internet routing information that every message contains. Most newsreaders hide this information, but you can see it if you want to. In Outlook Express, you can see the headers by opening the message, choosing Properties from the File menu, clicking the Details tab. To see all of the information, we'll also click the Message Source button to open the headers in a new window, as shown in Figure 17-14.

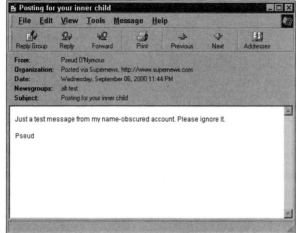

Figure 17-13:
My
anonymous
newsgroup
message as
viewed in
Outlook
Express.

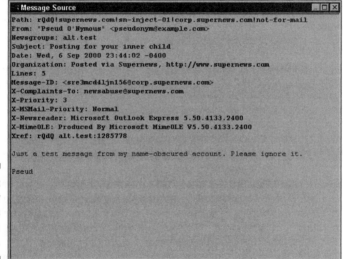

Figure 17-14:
My
anonymous
message
headers.

These headers don't show any of my accurate personal information, so my test posting was a success.

However, some of the information shown here (the Message-ID field, in particular) could be used to find me if someone convinced the operator of the news server (in this case, Supernews) to look up the message and provide my real Internet address. This method protects your identity from the casual observer, but you shouldn't go trying to overthrow governments this way, thinking your identity is secure.

Tracks you can't avoid leaving

As shown in the previous section, there are some tracks you can't avoid leaving on the Internet. Your Internet address (the IP address, something like 192.168.2.5) is unique to your computer at the time you're posting these messages or visiting these Web sites, and it could be traced to you at any time. Armed with your IP address and the time the message was posted, your Internet provider could, if faced with a court order (for example), cough up your full name and address to whomever was asking.

Every time you visit a Web page without going through an anonymous service, your IP address is probably recorded. It's not attached to every e-mail or newsgroup message, but a unique message ID is generated and is linked with your IP address in the records.

Because the contents of many Web pages and newsgroups are archived on a regular basis (DejaNews has done this for many years, at `www.deja.com/usenet`), your messages can be stored, complete with whatever name you were using and your message IDs or IP addresses, forever if anyone wanted to find them.

The next section adds a few more quick tips for hiding your identity on the Internet, but remember that you're almost never completely anonymous, and if you're worried enough about someone finding you, the safest thing is to avoid posting messages completely.

Traveling even more incognito

Here are a few final tips that can provide more obscurity to your use of the most common Internet services, including Web browsing, e-mail, and newsgroups. These methods are not foolproof, but each one you use hides the trail further.

- ✔ **X-noarchive: Yes.** Including the header X-noarchive: Yes in your newsgroup messages may keep them from being stored in the Deja and other archives on the Internet, but this isn't foolproof. If your news program doesn't let you enter customized headers, you can try including X-noarchive: Yes as the first line of your message, although this is even less certain to work.

- ✔ **Use anonymizers**. Anonymous Web browsing services may also provide anonymous news or e-mail services as well, and these can all obscure the identifying information from your posts. However, those services might also be faced with a court order or something otherwise compelling, and in that case you're just adding one more step between other people and your identity, not eliminating the trail altogether.

✔ **Use an anonymous computer.** Many public libraries have Internet-capable computers available for you to use, as do many colleges and universities. If you use one of these public computers, and browse the Web through anonymizing Web services, and send e-mail only from free, anonymous, Web-based accounts, the chances of someone discovering your real identity are limited to a librarian's ability to remember you were there at the time in question. It might work, but only if you don't make a habit of it.

Ultimately, you can bury your true identity ever-deeper as you use the Internet, but you sacrifice convenience and, often, most of your free time in the process. At some point, paranoia must give way to having a normal life, and the services provided in this chapter should give you some peace of mind. Good luck.

Don't Trust Anyone over 30Kbps

One of the most common ways to gain access to private information doesn't involve very much technology at all. This method, called social engineering, involves tricking the victim into revealing information by pretending to be a trusted or authoritative body.

For example, in the real world, someone might call you on the phone claiming to be the telephone company, and asking for your account number and a credit card to verify that you're really the account holder. You would (I hope) be suspicious of this call because no legitimate group ever uses a credit card to verify who you are and because, if they're the telephone company, they already know this information.

The same scams are everywhere on the Internet. America Online and AOL Instant Messenger users are frequently bothered by instant messages, claiming to be from technical support or billing, asking for financial data, passwords, and other sensitive information that America Online's actual representatives either already know or would never need to know.

The scam artists trying to steal your personal and private information are counting on you to be uninformed and easy to fool. To avoid that condition, read this chapter (of course) and visit the following Web sites often:

✔ The U.S. Department of Energy's Computer Incident Advisory Capability (CIAC) at `ciac.llnl.gov/ciac/CIACHoaxes.html`

✔ Scambusters, at `www.scambusters.org`, which provides current information on the scams and ripoffs that are going around, and how to avoid them

> ✔ The Official Internet Blacklist, a site dedicated to publicizing sites and scams you should avoid, at `www.blacklist.com`

Check with these sites occasionally, just to stay up-to-date on what to avoid. In the meantime, the following sections should give you the edge in avoiding privacy-invading scams on the Internet.

Surfing with suspicion

Nobody who initiates contact with you (they start instant messaging you, they e-mail you out of the blue, they post something to you on a Web page, and so on) can be trusted. Period.

Beware of sites that ask for more information than seems reasonable. Does a company need to know your name, address, telephone number, or income for you to read their articles? Probably not, except that their advertisers would like to know that, and they'd like to sell your name to direct marketing firms. Unless they plan on giving you a cut of what they get for selling your name (and if you can make that deal, let us all know), don't give it to them.

The risk to your privacy isn't very bad when a single site collects your name, or places a cookie on your computer. The problem arises when sites merge, or share information, and can take your cookie from one site, your address from another site, and match them up to track your browsing.

Imagine if you went to your local MegaMart Store and they wanted you to fill out a complete profile before you could buy milk, eggs, or office supplies. You wouldn't provide the information, and nor should you online.

Don't assume that because a site seems legitimate, it is. If you've never dealt with a company before, find out something about them before doing anything wild and crazy (like giving them your money or personal information).

Here's a true story that happened while I was researching this book. I saw a message posted in a parenting newsgroup about a cool service for getting your baby's name and picture on a memento. I visited the site, and couldn't find out anything about the company running the site in any of the usual places (usually found under About Us or Contact Us links of some kind). On the page where you order the product, there was only a company name and a post office box, in case you wanted to send a money order.

To find out more about the company, I visited a domain name registry service, which is one of the organizations that can set up domain names (such as yournamehere.com). These sites, such as `www.registry.com`, not only set up sites, but they can show you the public information about who owns an existing site.

I visited www.registry.com, entered the parenting souvenir site I had visited, and found that a company in Chicago with a different company name
had registered it. Fair enough, I thought, because sometimes a site is registered by the Internet provider on behalf of their client. So I decided to visit
the Web site of the company whose name had popped up.

It turned out that the company registering the name was an advertising
agency who mainly represented pharmaceutical companies. The result of my
investigations was that this site for parents to buy sentimental products with
their baby's pictures was actually a front for a drug company that was, most
likely, assembling a mass-marketing list of new parents for advertising purposes.

There's nothing illegal about that, but the company went to great lengths to
appear innocent of any ulterior motives, while hiding all traces of the parent
company. If I hadn't checked them out, I could have been suckered onto their
mailing lists and been bombarded with junk mail for the rest of my life.

Remember: Trust only the companies you know, and check out the companies you don't know. Ask your friends if they've done business with a particular Web site or organization, and if the companies won't tell you about
themselves, don't tell them anything about yourself, either. Assume they're
hiding their information for reasons you wouldn't like.

Knowing whom to trust

One way to improve the chances of protecting your privacy and avoiding
junk e-mail, marketing stalkers, and other unpleasantness is to look on the
Web site for a *privacy policy*. Most sites now include a summary of how they
plan to use your information, and, more importantly, what they promises *not*
to do with it. ("eMegaMarketingCorp.com promises never to provide your
name or address to any college alumni association, even if they promise us a
cut of the donations.")

The problem, of course, is knowing whether the site will adhere to its
promises or not. That's where privacy organizations jump in to help. There
are some privacy authorities that have formed to help assure you, the consumer, that a company will keep its privacy promises.

For example, many Web sites have a TRUSTe logo next to their privacy policy.
The TRUSTe organization awards this logo to any Web site that promises to
follow a set of privacy rules. If the site breaks those rules (say, by selling its
entire customer list to those people who call you at dinnertime to sell you
stuff), TRUSTe is supposed to discipline the site, or even revoke the logo.

The example in Figure 17-15 shows the TRUSTe logo on the Microsoft Web
site. To find it, we clicked the teeny-weeny Privacy Policy link at the
bottom of Microsoft's home page.

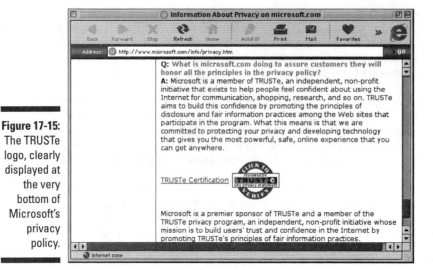

Figure 17-15:
The TRUSTe logo, clearly displayed at the very bottom of Microsoft's privacy policy.

Clicking the TRUSTe logo shows you their page assuring us of Microsoft's good intentions regarding privacy, as shown in Figure 17-16.

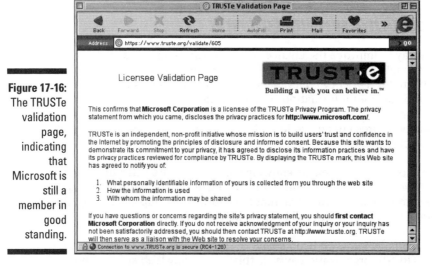

Figure 17-16:
The TRUSTe validation page, indicating that Microsoft is still a member in good standing.

The lesson from all this is to check for a privacy policy, and decide how much you believe the company before giving them any information about yourself or your online habits.

Chapter 18

Keeping Your Children Safe

. . . .

. . . .

*T*he Internet has now grown to encompass just about every topic and interest that you can name. In doing so, it has become a kind of microcosm, reflecting the strengths and weaknesses of our own real-world societies and cultures. Or, to put it another way: It ain't all good out there, baby!

If you have children, you have probably already worried about them using your new connection to the Internet to get into all kinds of trouble. If you have employees, then you probably know that they can act even less responsibly than children sometimes. In this chapter, we show you how to limit the mischief that could affect anyone who uses your Internet access.

Protecting the Sheep from the Wolves

With so many potential threats on the Internet, you may find it hard to even know where to begin to protect vulnerable children. None of us can stop *all* these problems before they happen — unless we completely stop using the Internet — and with all the great information available, who wants to do that? Here's a quick look at some of the specific dangers that are out there.

Avoiding equal opportunity dangers

A large number of dangers associated with the Internet represent an equal threat to you, indirectly from your children or your employee's use. Some of these may attack you directly. Others will only become a problem for you if your kids or workers get caught in the act of being themselves — then it will be your responsibility to answer for their actions.

A few of the most common Internet dangers include

- Legal violations from downloading copyrighted materials
- Files lost or damaged by Internet viruses
- Damage from people breaking into your systems
- Legal problems from your people breaking into other systems

Copyright infringements

Probably the most common illegal activity on the Internet today is the trading of copyrighted materials. For some reason, when people participate in the Internet, they seem to believe that the normal laws of society no longer apply. Perhaps it's the "cover" of anonymity that some people use on the Internet — you can steal 1,000 files without anyone ever even knowing who you are!

Probably the best example of this illegal trading is the popularity of exchanging MP3s of popular songs. These songs are the property of the recording companies that paid for their creation. If they catch anyone using your Internet connection to illegally traffic in them, they will hold you legally accountable! Of course, if you already own the CD, you can get legal MP3 versions of those songs.

If your Internet connection is being used by anyone that you think will find it impossible to give up their free copies, you might try pointing them in the direction of the many truly free sources for their materials that are out there on the Internet. The online CD store CDNow (www.cdnow.com), for example, offers many free samples of the songs on the CDs that they sell, which are perfectly legal.

Viruses

Viruses are small computer programs that embed themselves surreptitiously inside of other computer media. Because the media that they hide in may be completely harmless, or even entertaining, viruses can get into a computer completely undetected. Just a few of the ways that computer viruses have been distributed lately include

- E-mails
- Programs
- Short video clips

One of the worst things about many computer viruses is that extremely long periods of time may elapse before they ever begin wreaking havoc on your computer to the point where you would notice. While they go undetected, they are capable of transferring themselves to any other computer that your computer contacts, which might take the form of a computer diskette or an e-mail. A single computer virus can easily wipe out an entire company's computers without appropriate safeguards!

The least offensive computer viruses will simply give you a notification that you have been affected and then go away — kind of like a practical joke. These programs are written by programmers who just want to prove they can do it.

The worst brand of computer virus attacks the data on your system. These viruses may delete important files. Or, in the case of particularly intelligent viruses, they may transmit sensitive information — such as your bank account data — from your computer to the author of the virus while you are connected to the Internet! This is a particularly great danger for people with broadband Internet connections, because they are *always* on the Internet! For more information on viruses, see Chapter 15.

Cracking

Cracking goes in two directions. If you allow your Internet connection to be used by other people, then you must worry about it in both cases. First, you obviously don't want people getting into your systems and stealing your private information. Additionally, you also don't want your kids or employees to mess with other peoples' computers, even for more harmless hacking. Besides not being very nice, cracking is a serious, illegal activity that carries significant penalties (including jail time) in most parts of the world.

In recent years, law enforcement agencies have gotten much better at tracking down the sources of these activities. So, even when a cracker is lucky enough to break into a system, they usually get tracked down to their source and arrested. For this reason, it has become more popular nowadays to break into an easy system first — like *yours* — and then use that as a base for breaking into something more difficult . . . like the U.S. Department of Defense, for example. Imagine your surprise if the FBI shows up on your doorstep because they had traced a break-in attempt by someone across the country to your home or office!

Protecting your most precious possessions

Chances are, you wouldn't even dream of letting your kids travel to the seedy side of town without a chaperone — if at all! You can think of the Internet kind of like this, except that for every bad thing on the Internet, there are a million others that would be wonderful for your kids to have, including everything from information for schoolwork to tons of free entertainment to interaction with people from other countries and cultures.

Clearly, with all of these potential benefits, it wouldn't make much sense just to simply forbid your kids from using the Internet. But you should know about some potential dangers that specifically affect children.

Objectionable content

As you know, there are numerous things to see and hear on the Internet. Many of these things would be considered objectionable by many parents. Some of the more common of these things include:

- ✔ Sexually explicit materials
- ✔ Political extremism
- ✔ Cults

If you've surfed much at all, you may think to yourself, "Why doesn't someone clean up all this garbage?" Two main issues prevent this: determining who's to say what the garbage is and who has authority to do the cleaning. One person's political extremism is another's deeply held conviction. Remember, the Internet is a global phenomenon, and many sites exist beyond the boundaries of any political entity — such as on ships at sea!

Dangerous people

The fear that a stranger may harm their children in some way chills most parents to the bone. The Internet can make this fear very well founded indeed by bringing your children into closer contact with people who are even stranger than whatever strangers you may already have imagined!

We mention above that anonymity is a key factor in the apparent lawlessness of the Internet. The ability to actually *seem* like a completely different person from who you really are is another factor to take into account when evaluating the dangers of the Internet. Not only can your children pretend to be much older on the Internet than they really are, but older people with questionable intentions can also pretend to be much younger and less obviously threatening.

The main vehicle by which most contact between potentially threatening people and your children is likely to occur is in chat rooms. You can use many different ways to chat on the Internet, and we discussed several of them in Chapter 10. In this chapter, we show you how you can use special monitoring software to limit the kinds of topics that your kids can talk about on the Internet.

Who bought the private island?!

In the good old days, parents only had to worry about their kids ordering stuff from the latest TV infomercial. Usually, these items would arrive at the house COD and were easily returned. At worst, you would be out the customary $19.95 for which all such merchandise retails.

In the Internet age, kids can wreak far more havoc if they have access to your credit card number. Literally thousands of dollars of merchandise can be ordered off the Internet without any proof that the legitimate holder of the credit card is the one making the purchases. You could conceivably wind up owning hundreds of acres in Alaska, for example, if your kids have the skills and the inclination!

One of the quickest, simplest, and most cost-effective ways to safeguard your credit card is to request that your company only honor purchases that are accompanied by your signature. Not all companies support this practice, but it's worth checking to see if yours will. Mind you, this also makes it impossible for you to use your credit card for legitimate purchases over the phone or Internet. So, consider carefully.

Safe-guarding your most valuable resources

Any human-resources person will tell you that it isn't your equipment or your patents or even your business partnerships that make your company what it is — it's your people! Used correctly, the Internet can empower your staff to increase their productivity in ways that were scarcely imaginable just a decade ago. Used incorrectly, it can help them all find better jobs, so they can leave you like rats deserting a sinking ship!

A little bad information is worse than none at all

The dream of the World Wide Web is free access to all kinds of information for everyone on the planet. Everyone contributes information about whatever they know about; for example, we might contribute data about the speeds of various DSL connections. In return, everyone is able to surf for things that they need to know.

Used correctly, your company can benefit from both sides of this equation. By posting information to the Web, your people and your organization can become more recognized as authorities within your field. By having access to the data posted by others, your team can often find answers to questions that would otherwise have taken them forever to solve by themselves.

Free advice is worth what you pay for it! The problem with answers off the Internet is the complete lack of accountability associated with sites other than a direct manufacture's FAQ or monitored support forum. Contrast this with the situation if you were given an answer by the Technical Support staff of your Internet Service Provider. If that information turns out to be incorrect, you simply phone them and tell them exactly why their suggestion was incorrect (and what they could do with it, if you were so inclined!) But, to whom do you complain about inaccurate information randomly located on the Internet? If you are lucky, you will know where the data came from — but why should they care? After all, you aren't putting any money directly in their pocket, are you?

The thief of time

Of course, it isn't all business solutions and productivity pointers out there on the Internet. If you really believe that your employees are going to spend every second of their days looking for new ways to be better workers out on the Internet, then you may be living in denial. Or, perhaps you're still living in a pre-Internet 1950s sitcom, in which case the assumed work ethic makes sense.

Anyhow, the reasons why your employees might use the Internet for non-business-related purposes while still at the office vary. In some cases, they may legitimately be looking for business data, but wind up somewhere else through inaccurate search results. In other cases, they may not have Internet connections at home, so they want to surf while they can. And then, of course, there are those who are just plain lazy!

Fortunately, technology is quickly devising ever newer and better solutions to the problem of inaccurate searches. Most of these solutions revolve around the construction of increasingly intelligent search engines that target specific audiences. These are often referred to as portals, because they are intended to serve as doorways to information.

The thief of personnel

Another way in which the blessing of the Internet can be turned into a curse is through the spiriting away of your employees by other corporations in a number of ways:

- ✔ Other employers seeing your technical people's postings on the Internet
- ✔ Your people using your Internet connection to research other employers
- ✔ Recruiters spamming your domain to find possible job candidates

People with nothing to hide seldom fear investigation. Before you make a sweeping pronouncement threatening anyone found looking for jobs using your Internet connection, pause for a moment and reflect on how this sounds to your employees. In general, employers who are doing as much for their employees as their competitors have no reason to fear turnover. After all, what incentive would your people have for leaving? On the other hand, by showing that you fear this, many of your employees may interpret this as a signal that you must not be doing as much for them as they might get elsewhere!

Letting "Big Brother" Keep Watch

Along with enormous access to data have come some fairly significant dangers. We show you most of these in the previous section. Fortunately, the information age has also brought with it a number of technological means for increasing your control over the flow of data in and out of your computer (or office). Some of the more popular methods of data control include

- ✔ Filters to watch for unacceptable words and images
- ✔ Blockers that restrict access to questionable sites
- ✔ Jammers to prevent inappropriate software from running
- ✔ Snoopers that allow you to see what your connection is doing
- ✔ Recorders for keeping logs of everything your connection does

Filters

An Internet filter is a program that sits between the software on your computer and its connection to the Internet. The main purpose of a filter is to listen for anything traveling across your Internet connection that you might deem objectionable. This might be as simple as a list of dirty words (which can also be pretty fun to put together!) Or, it may be as complicated as concepts usually associated with job seeking — such as searching e-mails for attachments named resume. Figure 18-1 shows a filter in a system's configuration.

Okay, so you can stop people from using so-called swear words. But, of course, most people know at least a few sound-alike spellings that they can substitute to still get their point across. If tracking this sort of thing really keeps you up at night, make sure that whatever software you purchase accounts for this possibility.

Blockers

A blocking application is intended to completely prevent a computer from accessing entire portions of the Internet. These portions are determined as unacceptable either by the manufacturer of the blocking program or your preferences.

If your blocking software allows you to participate in the selection of sites to block, please try to keep as open a mind as possible. Consider that hundreds of years ago, if the Internet had existed, many people would have chosen to block the sites of Charles Darwin and his fellow evolutionists. On the other hand, perhaps you still dismiss evolution as merely a theory, in which case — go ahead and block to your heart's content!

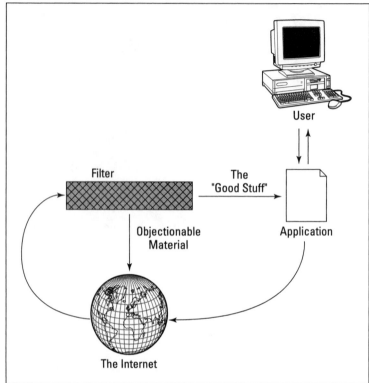

Figure 18-1:
A filter's
place in the
grand
scheme of
things.

Blockers may either sit on each and every computer with access to the Internet, or on a separate computer through which all of your other computers' Internet traffic must pass. Figure 18-2 illustrates the latter of these two arrangements, known as a proxy server arrangement, and we cover that in more detail in this chapter.

Jammers

A jammer program specializes in preventing other programs from being able to run properly. Of course, it only attacks the kinds of programs that you specify when you install it. A jammer must be installed on every computer where you intend to prevent other programs from operating. The most common targets for jamming programs are

- Video games
- Chatting software
- Newsreaders
- MP3 collectors

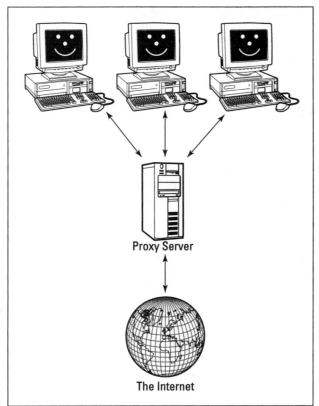

Figure 18-2:
Using Proxy
servers to
block the
"bad" stuff.

Proxy Server

The Internet

You might wonder to yourself, "How can these programs possibly tell a video game from any other kind of program?" One way is that jammers connect to the Internet frequently to download updated listings of all the current games. They also look for the distinctive changes in graphics and sound that typically accompany video games.

Snoopers

Snooping software allows you to see what your Internet connection is being used for on a real-time basis. For example, you could sit in your office but instantly see that an employee in a completely different room has just visited a pornographic Web site. Whether or not this kind of spying is ethical is left up to the reader's conscience — but it sure is fun!

Snooping works in a couple of different ways. In its simplest form, you can usually snoop on your children or employees by setting up a proxy server or firewall. See the section on proxy servers later in this chapter. For details on firewalls, see Chapters 15 and 16.

In a more complicated scenario, you can use a packet sniffer to intercept messages as they travel from one computer to another. You can then examine the contents of these packets. The two disadvantages to packet sniffers are cost and difficulty of use.

Recorders

A recorder works similarly to a snooper, except that a recorder allows you to look at events after they have already happened. The disadvantage to this is that it makes it impossible to catch anyone red-handed. Even if you find that a certain computer was used for a certain, unacceptable activity at a certain time, it is not always easy to prove who was using that computer at that point in time!

You're being watched! If you already know that your emphasis on appropriate Internet use is going to be a case of "do as I say, not as I do," then you might want to think twice about installing recorder software. If you will be the only one reviewing the logs, then you have nothing to worry about. If, on the other hand, you will be delegating this task to another individual, then you might be setting yourself up for some real embarrassment!

One clear advantage to using recorder software is that you don't need to glue yourself to your monitor 24-hours-a-day in order to stop users who are up to no good with your Internet connection. You can simply let the logs keep rolling and review them for problems at your leisure.

Another advantage to recorder software is that you can install it on individual computers, rather than having to install it on an intermediate firewall or proxy. This may or may not represent a monetary savings, depending on how many computers you must buy software for. It always, however, represents a savings in difficulty — proxy servers and firewalls tend to be among the hardest software applications to run properly!

Filtering Out Those Gosh-Darned Nasty Words

Filtering software is one of the most popular ways to keep children safe and employees out of mischief on the Internet. By carefully listening to everything that comes and goes across a computer's Internet connection, a filter can intercept and prevent the transmission or receipt of questionable materials.

These materials may include

- ✔ Profane words
- ✔ Provocative images
- ✔ Politically incorrect language

Finding a good filter

In this section, we show you some of the more popular filtering packages currently on the market. We then briefly discuss a typical installation of one of these packages. We conclude by talking about how to use filtering software to your best advantage and troubleshoot some of its more common problems.

Your choice of products

Several filtering programs are available on the Internet and these are all (at least) fairly good at what they do. Here, we describe some of the more popular packages.

Cyber Patrol

One of the oldest and most respected names in content control is Cyber Patrol. It offers a variety of packages targeted at different markets:

- ✔ Home
- ✔ Business
- ✔ Education

One key feature of Cyber Patrol is that it blocks access to certain Internet sites based on lists which are compiled by Cyber Patrol themselves and updated *daily*. The advantage to this is that Cyber Patrol is able to block offensive sites almost as quickly as they pop up. The disadvantage is that you have to pay extra for a subscription to their list service. Check the site for more details on costs.

Cyber Patrol also allows you to limit the hours during which Internet use is permitted on a given computer. So, if you don't want your kids on the Internet when you aren't home, or if you don't want your employees on the Internet outside of business hours, then this is a good choice for you. You can also limit the total number of hours allowed on the Internet per day, to make sure that Junior has enough time to do all his homework!

You can visit Cyber Patrol's site on the World Wide Web at

```
http://www.cyberpatrol.com
```

ChatNANNY

ChatNANNY is very easy-to-use, inexpensive software that monitors all of the chatting and Web usage that occurs on a given computer. Anything offensive that occurs in any of these contexts is logged for later viewing. Although having the word chat in its name would certainly lead you to that conclusion, ChatNANNY is capable of monitoring much more than Internet chat.

ChatNANNY allows you to pull up reports on Internet activity long after it has occurred. For every chat that has taken place, ChatNANNY lists the person with whom the chat was held. For every chat or Web site, it categorizes content according to a few hot topics, such as sex or violence.

One topic it uses, "Personal," is of particular interest. As a parent, you may find it is not enough to prevent your kids from discussing illicit activities on the Internet. You would also like to make sure that they aren't giving out their address or telephone number to complete strangers. This category allows you to monitor exactly this kind of activity. You can visit ChatNANNY's site on the World Wide Web at

```
http://www.chatnanny.com
```

CYBERsitter

CYBERsitter is excellent filtering software, and even won *PC Magazine* Editors' Choice Award for 2000. Like CyberPatrol, it features up-to-the-minute blocking lists available and maintained over the Internet. Unlike CyberPatrol, however, it requires no subscription fees.

CYBERsitter extends the filtering offered by many of the other packages described here by blocking certain information from newsgroups. Newsgroups offer bulletin-board style postings for almost every conceivable topic, many of which you might find quite objectionable.

Unfortunately, CYBERsitter is available only for the Windows operating system. So, if you are using Linux or iMac, you have to look elsewhere for a filtering solution. You can get this version at CYBERsitter's site on the World Wide Web:

```
http://www.cybersitter.com
```

If you are a Linux fanatic, you should still be able to use your favorite OS without having to sacrifice any of your filtering needs. Simply configure your OS with a password that only you know. Then, setup another partition on your hard disk with the Windows operating system. You can install whatever filtering software you like on this partition and reserve it for the use of your kids.

Net Nanny

Net Nanny offers a couple of different flavors of its software. For home and personal use, their flagship product is simply called Net Nanny. Like the other software we describe here, it encompasses the standard array of filtering and blocking functions.

However, Net Nanny also offers a product for business and other professional uses called NNPro. This product installs on a separate computer that monitors the activities of several other computers and prevents them from getting up to any mischief. For this reason, it's an excellent choice in multiple-computer situations, such as corporations.

You can visit NetNanny's site on the World Wide Web at

```
http://www.netnanny.com
```

SafetyNet KoolBar

Unlike any of the other products on our list, SafetyNet Koolbar is 100 percent free. You simply download it from the Web site and, after installation, it attaches itself to your Web browser's toolbar. Then, it blocks whatever materials you deem inappropriate: violence, pornography, and so on. The only real downside to the KoolBar is that it consumes a portion of your screen with advertising. If you have a particularly small monitor, or one with limited graphics abilities, then this can be a bit of a sacrifice. After all, it doesn't make much sense to save $30 on filtering software if it costs you $200 to upgrade your computer in order to use it, does it?

You can visit KoolBar's site on the World Wide Web at

```
http://www.koolbar.com
```

Installing filters

The act of installing filter or proxy software should be no different from installing any other kind of software on your system. The main issue involves whether the software is to be installed directly onto the computer(s) that will be monitored, or whether it requires a separate, dedicated computer for that purpose.

Individual filters

If you intend to use software that blocks or filters Internet traffic from multiple computers, then you need to obtain a separate copy of the software for each computer. If you would prefer, many companies sell multiple licenses without requiring you to actually take shipment on several copies of the software. This can be useful if you want to avoid having stacks of software boxes piled up in your office!

Proxy servers

With a proxy server, you need to install the software on only one computer. This computer acts as the gate through which all of the other computers in your home or office access the Internet. For more information on setting up a computer to share Internet access among multiple computers, see Chapter 13.

Common usage

After you install the software, you will find yourself repeating a typical pattern for as long as you continue using your software:

1. **Checking the logs for violations.**

   You should frequently examine the output of your software for reports that indicate violations in the policies you have set forth. The exact output varies from one software package to the next, and you should consult your documentation for exact details. Nevertheless, almost all of the programs we mention in the preceding section give you at least *some* indication as to the nature of the violation; meaning was it sexual, violent, and so on. Also, all of the software packages also tell you the exact time and date of the violation — if not the precise identity of the offender!

2. **Releasing caught transmissions.**

   Many proxy software packages actually detain e-mail messages and similar transmissions that they think may contain inappropriate content. In some cases, these e-mails may not be genuinely harmful and will need to be released so that they may continue the journey on to the intended recipient.

   Many filtering packages utilize lists of keywords to govern what they block. So, for example, if you want to prevent your employees from receiving humorous e-mails at the office, you might add the word "joke" to your keyword list. Then, any e-mail containing the word joke would be blocked at the gate. Unfortunately, this stoppage would hold true in the case of legitimate uses of this word, such as "This new sales proposal is a joke!"

3. **Updating block lists.**

   If your software blocks access to certain Web sites, then you should keep the list of blocked sites as up-to-date as possible. Many packages automatically download a list of recommended blocks every time they are started, plus scheduled refreshes. Other programs require that you specifically connect to the Internet, download the newest list, and then install it. Consult your software's documentation for specifics.

4. **Upgrading the software.**

Minor bug fixes and patches are typically included for free with the purchase of a given filter's license. Larger, more significant upgrades may
require the purchase of a new license and additional actions on your
part. Be sure to check for new versions of your software on a regular
basis, because new Web sites will figure out new ways to circumvent old
programs!

Troubleshooting monitoring software

All software programs have their tips, tricks, and "gotchas." The advanced
security utilized by many filtering programs makes resolving some of their
issues even more difficult. The two activities that cause headaches for the
most users are de-installation and inappropriate sites that seem to always get
let through.

De-installation

Trying to uninstall filtering and blocking software via the standard mecha-
nisms provided by your operating system usually is guaranteed to end in failure. Typically, in order to be of any use, filtering software cannot be as easy
to remove as regular applications. Think about it, if you could take the software off a system easily, what would be to prevent your kids and employees
from doing exactly the same thing?

Every filtering package has its own routine for de-installation when you no
longer wish to use the product. What almost all of these programs share in
common is the need for your unique administrator's password in order to
proceed with the de-installation. You will be asked to create such a password
when you first install the software. If you don't write it down and carefully
keep track of it, you risk having to completely re-install your operating
system whenever you decide that it's time to stop filtering the Internet!

Flaws in the armor

Occasionally, you may discover that you can access a site that is blatantly
violent, obscene, or whatever — and without any interference from your
blocking software at all. Now, this may be a cause for celebration in some
quarters, but it is probably not compatible with the reasons you installed
blocking software in the first place.

To resolve this problem, you should first obtain the most recent copy of your
software's blocking list and see if this helps. If not, you either have to add the
site manually to your software's list, or report it to your software's manufacturer for addition to the list that it distributes.

You might wonder how the software manufacturers compile their lists in the first place. Well, they use two main sources: consumer complaints or suggestions and corporate research. The complaints and suggestions usually come via their corporate Web sites, which provide special forms that you can fill out to report offensive material you want them to add. The research they do involves retaining numerous censors who are specially trained to find and report offensive material out there on the Internet.

Teach Your Children (And Employees) Well

Someone once said that there is no substitute for good people. In a similar vein, all of the blocking and filtering software in the world won't help you if you foster a culture in your home or office that encourages the kind of behavior that you are hoping to prevent. In other words, it isn't enough to try to make bad behavior technically impossible. You should try to discourage it through positive examples and discussion.

For tomorrow's generation . . . and the next

In the case of your kids and the Internet, you should bear in mind a few points that you've doubtless encountered in other aspects of parenting. One parent to another, here are our suggestions:

- ✔ **Tell them *why* they shouldn't see everything.** Most people, not just kids, are less likely to follow rules that they don't understand. Think of how you would react, for example, if your employer suddenly started requiring that all employees use the stairs instead of the elevators for a day. It would make a difference to know that the elevators had become dangerous and needed repairs.

- ✔ **Explain why the bad stuff is out there.** What a great opportunity to discuss freedom of speech! It is important to help your children determine the difference between self-regulation (which is what filtering and blocking software enable) and censorship. One of these is a technical marvel for keeping yourself and your children safe. The other is a dangerous threat to any free society. You might even consider dressing up like Thomas Jefferson if you think it would help you make your point.

✔ **Discuss whether or not their friends have access.** As with any other form of peer pressure, you need to address the usual objections based on what "so and so" gets to do versus what your household rules are. If your child goes to a neighbor who doesn't use an Internet filter, you stand a better chance of your rules riding along if you discuss the issue beforehand.

Setting up employee guidelines

It may be helpful to establish a specific company policy that regulates the use of company computers for non-business purposes. A few variations on these policies have been tried over the years, to varying degrees of success:

✔ **Absolutely no personal use:** At one extreme of the business policy spectrum is the rule that completely forbids employees from using their computers and Internet connections for anything other than business. A statement that computers may be monitored and examined at any time without notification usually accompanies this position. Many employees perceive this as an extremely totalitarian approach to the problem that can make it difficult to retain some of the better technical talent — who tend to object to strong arm tactics.

✔ **No personal use during business hours:** A less restrictive approach to reducing productivity decline from Internet access is to establish a policy that limits non-business use to non-business hours. If your people work a wide variety of hours, then you may have to stretch a bit to make this work in your situation.

✔ **General use within reason:** Rather than trying to enforce the concept of business hours and business use, many corporations have just decided to establish a set of basic guidelines for what constitutes acceptable use of company property at any point in time. Typically, these guidelines forbid pornography of any sort. They may also frown on games, chain e-mails, and other obvious wastes of time.

✔ **Freewheeling:** At the far left of the Internet use policy spectrum are the companies that say, "Party hearty, dude!" If you feel comfortable with this approach, then more power to you. It is important to take into consideration, however, some of the legal dangers presented by this position. For example, even if you are not personally offended by pornography, allowing it in the workplace may present a sexual harassment danger if some of your employees are offended or use it to intimidate others. For further information, always consult a lawyer!

Part V
The Part of Tens

The 5th Wave   By Rich Tennant

"I don't mean to hinder your quest for knowledge, however it's not generally a good idea to try and download the entire Internet."

In this part . . .

At this point, we've almost finished our discussion of broadband Internet access. Sad, isn't it? Well, don't worry — we saved the best for last! In this part, we show you some of the most fun things about getting broadband Internet access.

We start by showing you various tools that you can get for free on the Internet to make your broadband experience even more enjoyable than usual. Then, we tell you a bunch of places out on the Internet that you can visit to find fun things to do. Finally, since we all have at least a little bit of a "show off" in us, we conclude by telling you ten things you can do with your broadband connection to impress your friends. So, gather in the crowd and start the show!

Chapter 19

More Than Ten Internet Tools You Need

In This Chapter

▶ Communicating instantly around the world

▶ Finding e-mail and newsgroup tools

▶ Using file-sharing software and intelligent agents

▶ Keeping track of your time, your file transfers, and your URLs

▶ Blocking spies and trash

*T*he Internet offers a wealth of information and entertainment just waiting for hungry users to harvest it. But, before you go out in the fields, you should make sure you're taking the right tools with you for the job. In this chapter, we show you some of the tools we find most exciting.

Getting Your Messages and Getting Them NOW!

Instant messaging is all the rage nowadays. Unlike conventional Internet chat rooms, instant messaging software can be available all the time — just like your fancy, new broadband Internet connection. This way, as soon as your friend on the other side of the planet types a little message for you, you can have it pop up on your screen in a matter of seconds! (Check out Chapter 14 for more details.)

The Web currently has several competing standards for instant messaging (IM) standards. Here is a list of the ones that currently lead the pack:

✔ AOL Instant Messenger (http://www.aol.com/aim)

✔ ICQ (http://www.icq.com)

- MSN Messenger Service (http://messenger.msn.com)
- Yahoo! Messenger (http://messenger.yahoo.com)

The software that AOL gives you on CD isn't compatible with most kinds of broadband Internet access. AOL Instant Messenger is a separate and *completely different* piece of software.

Demanding Your Inalienable Right to Junk Mail

Where would the Internet be without e-mail? After all, using e-mail is probably the main reason why many of us got started a-whoompin' and a-whompin' down the Information Superhighway in the first place! For those of you who haven't decided what software to use for e-mail with your new broadband connection, though, here are our thoughts on your options.

Microsoft Windows

It's no secret that one of the best things about using Microsoft Windows is all the software you can find for it. E-mail packages are no exception. The traditional choice for serious e-mail users (such as salespeople who rely on it for their income) is Eudora. In more recent years, Microsoft's Outlook and Outlook Express (the version that is included free with Internet Explorer) have come to dominate — surprise, surprise!

Outlook has become such a popular email package in recent years that it is now the target of choice for many of the viruses currently circulating on the Internet. In particular, Outlook's address book format allows viruses to replicate themselves easily by mailing themselves to all of the people on your address book. If you are going to use this software package, make sure to install an anti-virus program and keep it up-to-date, as we show you in Chapter 15.

For those with a desire to stand apart from the pack, Pegasus Mail also makes an e-mail program that is worth investigating. Although not quite as full of features as the other two entries, Pegasus is a quality piece of software that functions well and is, well, just different.

- Eudora (http://www.eudora.com)
- Outlook Express (http://www.microsoft.com/windows/oe)
- Pegasus Mail (http://www.pmail.com)

Macintosh

The best choice for Macintosh e-mail is currently the Outlook Express software that comes bundled with Internet Explorer. Since Internet Explorer now comes pre-installed on iMacs, it would be hard to imagine things getting any easier than this.

If you find the idea of using a Microsoft product on an iMac too horrible to contemplate, you might consider installing Netscape Communicator and using the Messenger product that comes bundled with that, instead.

UNIX

The first e-mail software, Sendmail, was conceived and implemented on the UNIX platform. Since then, UNIX hackers have created a veritable slough of alternatives for both client and server programs. Needless to say, almost all of them operate in text-only mode and require the memorization of a long dictionary of cryptic commands to fully use them.

The two most popular e-mail clients for UNIX are called Pine and Elm. Apparently, the people doing e-mail software for UNIX like trees.

- ✔ Elm (`http://www.myxa.com/elm.html`)
- ✔ Pine (`http://www.washington.edu/pine`)
- ✔ Sendmail (`http://www.sendmail.org`)

Pssst . . . Here's the File, Pass It On!

Unless you've been living in Outer Mongolia for the past year, you have probably heard about the controversy regarding the sharing of music over the Internet. In brief, many people are using the software packages listed in this section to trade materials for which they do *not* hold the copyright. Well, duh!

If you own the copyright on some materials or have access to things you're sure are in the public domain and would like to share them, then the file-sharing programs described here are a good way to get started. Perhaps these are songs that you have written and recorded or pictures that you have taken.

What sets this file-sharing system apart from regular file-download sites is that it has no one, central point on the Internet that holds all of the files being shared. Instead, the central site merely maintains a registry of all the users currently logged into the system. These users are the ones storing the files being shared. When you decide you want to download or send something, the central site will patch you through to the other users' computers *directly*.

Here are some of the most popular applications for this kind of file swapping:

- Napster (`http://www.napster.com`)
- Gnutella (`http://gnutella.wego.com`)
- Hotline (`http://www.bigredh.com`)

Comparison-Shopping without Boring Your Husband

Some of the neatest tools being developed for the Internet today are called *intelligent agents*. These programs collect information of a certain type from the Internet, then organize it for you in a way that is easier to understand and compare.

The most popular application for this technology currently is the cross-referencing of prices for comparison-shopping over the Internet. If you are interested in buying ten more copies of this book, for example, you can use one of these tools to figure out which online book retailer can give you the absolute best price. (We get paid the same, regardless, so it's no skin off our noses!)

- Click-the-Button: `http://www.clickthebutton.com`
- iChoose: `http://www.ichoose.com`
- E-Boodle: `http://www.eboodle.com`

Reading All the News That's Fit to Encode

Sometimes you want to post a message to be seen by the general public. Bomb threats, scandalous revelations, and desperate pleas for attention are the three instances that immediately come to mind, but then, everyone has their own purposes. Whatever your purposes are, the tool to assist you in your quest is a newsreader for the Usenet.

The term Usenet is just a system run over the Internet that allows large groups of public messages to be shared among multiple computers, but you're likely to see it referred to as Abusenet, Excusenet, or Obtusenet. These messages are organized into specific categories, because they appeal to very specific and/or marginal interests, like indoor organic gardening. Before entering the newsgroups, especially ones that aren't so constructive, be prepared for free speech on a scale as you have never experienced it before. 'Nuff said?

Windows and Macintosh

Outlook Express contains a newsgroup reader in addition to its e-mail functionality (see the previous section). At present, Outlook Express is easily the best package available for either of the above platforms.

UNIX

You can get Outlook Express for Solaris, if you are so inclined. But, if you prefer a package with a more traditional UNIX feel to it, your best bet is called TIN. This newreader is available for download directly from the organization that develops and supports it at

```
http://www.tin.org.
```

Seeing Archie without Jughead

If you are using a UNIX computer to communicate with the Internet, then the graphics-intensive software downloading Web sites that are available to the rest of us might not be quite your cup of tea. If you still want to see what free software is out there for the taking, however, you can use Archie. Archie is one of the first attempts at compiling extensive cross-references for the many public FTP sites on the Internet.

Free UNIX clients for the Archie system can be downloaded from this site:

```
http://www.kristall.ethz.ch/LFK/software/ftp/pub/mirror/
            archie-client.
```

If you're using a non-UNIX operating system, then you are much better off using any of the big, "free software" Web sites that are targeted at your specific platform.

Avoiding the Billionth Billing Hour

If you're stuck paying for your broadband service on a timed account (by the hour rather than a flat rate), it's a good idea to keep track of exactly how many hours you're spending online each month, so you can avoid those nasty surcharges. Although many tracking packages are freely available, Cost Check Pro is one of the best. Besides tracking your time, it also calculates telephone charges for several long-distance carriers (although you have to live in Great Britain to get this particular benefit). Download Check Pro from

```
http://members.xoom.com/AdamGreen.
```

Blocking Nasty Snoopers

Many companies want to find out as much as they can about their customers. Some software companies accomplish this by asking you for data about yourself so that they can send it back to their main computers over the Internet. A smaller percentage of these companies either don't ask for this information or don't tell you that they will be sending it back across the Internet. Instead, they gather the data secretly or transmit it secretly back the next time you connect to the Internet.

In the United States, at least, there are currently no laws on the books to say that this kind of behavior is illegal. Obviously, much of this is unethical, but not illegal! Of course, if these programs help themselves to data on your system that is *really* none of their business (like your accounting records), then you may have a case for litigation. When in doubt, consult an attorney!

If you want to make sure that your system is never victimized by this kind of software, you might want to check out a piece of software called Opt Out. The commercial version works the best, but you can also get a free version from this site:

```
http://grc.com/optout.htm
```

Following the File Trail

On Windows and UNIX systems, one of the most valuable tools for trouble-shooting your Internet connection is freely available as a part of the operating system itself. This tool is called *traceroute,* and it allows you to see the exact path traveled by your data as it moves back and forth from your computer to any other point out on the Internet.

To use it, simply type `traceroute` for UNIX or `tracert` for Windows at the MS-DOS command prompt, followed by the name of the machine to which you would like to see your path. For example:

```
traceroute www.eviloscar.com
```

The primary usefulness of this tool is if it shows a particularly long delay (or if the path completely stops) at a machine owned by your own Internet Service Provider. You will generally be able to tell this, because the output will have a name that includes your ISP's name. Imagine the surprise in Tech Support's voice when you can specifically tell them the name of the machine that is broken on their end and causing your Internet connection to suffer!

Keeping Secrets Strictly to Ourselves

Speaking of paths on the Internet, keep in mind that most messages on the Internet travel across multiple computers to reach their destinations. Such transferring means that any computer along this path can intercept, decode, and examine your messages if they care to do so.

Fortunately, programs exist that allow you to encrypt your messages so strongly that even the government can't decode them. Unfortunately, this software can be pretty difficult to use. So, if you want to use it with your e-mail client, it is best to get a front-end that connects the two easily for you.

This one's definitely worse than tearing the tag off your mattress! Because governments can't crack the strongest encryptions, the transfer of these technologies between countries is a very serious matter. In the United States, you can go to jail for many, many years if you give a copy of some encryption software to a friend in, for example, Iran. You will see warnings about this and might be tempted to consider them technicalities. They are not. Be careful.

Here are a few different packages that you might consider to assist you in keeping your e-mails private:

- ✔ For Windows, KeyView: `http://www.keyview.com`
- ✔ For Macintosh, PGP: `http://www.math.ohio-state.edu/~fiedorow/PGP`
- ✔ For UNIX, mailcrypt: `http://www.nb.net/~lbudney/linux/mailcrypt.html`

Tearing Down the Banner Ads!

Banner advertising is the term applied to those obnoxious little graphics that you find plastered on most Web sites that urge you to click them to go to another Web site that will attempt to sell you something that you probably don't want (yes, that's a long trail to follow). As you might be able to tell, we find this practice as annoying as you do, if not more so. Fortunately, technology has provided a means for suppressing this kind of trash once and for all. You can download software that prevents any of these banners from loading into your Web browser from this site:

```
http://math-www.uni-paderborn.de/~axel
```

Recalling That Site You Visited One Night Last Year at 3:00 A.M.

How many sites have you visited in the last year — 10, 100, 1,000, more? Many of us visit at least ten different sites per day for our work or entertainment. We see a lot of interesting content, but typically don't have the time to record our observations for later review. We're too busy getting the job done.

This blur of sites can be a problem if and when you vaguely recall having seen something somewhere out on the Net that would solve your problem. You can't remember where to find it, but you know that it's out there. For these instances, check out a URL organizer! These packages keep a careful eye on the sites that you visit and help you to record and categorize these sites so that you can easily find them later on.

A good example is the URL Organizer package at `http://www.urlorg.com`. You can download an evaluation copy of this software and begin experimenting. After you see what it is like to actually be able to remember all of the places on the Internet that you have been, chances are good you won't go back!

Chapter 20

More Than Ten Web Sites a High-Speed Internet User Can't Live Without

*T*hroughout this book, we've raved about all the many features and technologies you can use with broadband as you explore the Internet. Some of the sites that offer these cool features are cool sites; some are pure garbage. In this chapter, we help you find some of the best places first. And then, for those times you feel in the mood to sniff at the hog trough, we show you a sure fire way to get to some of the weirdest, poorest sites around!

Viewing Internet Video without the Hassle

Now that you're convinced that you can *really* send and receive video via broadband without the hassle, it's time to send the kids' school play to Grandma or publish your first venture into filmmaking.

Just sign up for a free account with ClipShow (`http://www.clipshow.com`). You can then send them videotapes, and they will digitize them *for you* and post them on *their* Web site. If you don't want the whole world to see them, don't worry — *you can make them completely private!*

Game Over Man, Game Over!

So, you've finally decided that your real reason for owning a computer and a high-speed Internet connection is to enhance your game playing. Well, good for you — now what?

Whatever you're looking for, the chances are good that ZDNet's Game Center (`http://www.gamecenter.com`) has it. Categories include

- ✔ Games you can play online
- ✔ Ways to cheat at games
- ✔ Tips on playing games better (legitimately)
- ✔ Purchasing games

Playing "Find That Tune"

The only reason that this chapter is being written on time is that the following site happens to be down at the moment. We discovered it while researching this book and have been addicted ever since!

Do this: Think of a song you heard a long time ago and really liked, but never got the chance to buy before it went out of print. Now, visit Scour (`http://www.scour.com`) and put that song's name into its search engine. Voilà — you should get a list of at least a few places where you can download this song and hear it again.

In the United States, this kind of song-trading is currently illegal. So, be warned — you are on dangerous ground if you get caught doing this!

Many places on the Internet specialize in exchanging MP3s and such, but this site is the only place we've found that does such a good job at *finding* them!

Wrangling from the Videoranch Collection

You have to like Michael Nesmith, if only for the interesting elements of his biography. His mom invented Liquid Paper. He was in the Monkees. After that, he essentially invented music videos, laying the foundation for MTV. Now, he's at the forefront of the Internet explosion — getting ready to pioneer yet another genre (all the while, continuing to write books, music, and movies — jeesh!).

His site on the Web is the Videoranch (`http://www.videoranch.com`), and it has just about everything you could imagine under one roof:

✔ Virtual reality chatting

✔ A Web cam (of Nesmith's real New Mexico ranch)

✔ Live audio feed from the KPIG radio station

✔ Online store for Nesmith's merchandise

Oh yeah, and once a year they host a think tank at the ranch with some of the greatest living thinkers who try to figure out how to solve the world's problems. They broadcast their answers over this Web site when all is said and done.

Sharing Your Peculiar Tastes with an Unready World

With all of the music that's available out on the Internet, wouldn't it be nice if at least some of it were legal? Funny you should mention it — that's exactly what we were going to talk about next. Almost as if we put those words in your mouth, isn't it?

You may already have seen the commercials for SonicNet. They typically feature some famous musical artists to catch your eye. The concept behind the site is quite deserving of a quick visit, actually: You create your own radio station.

Essentially, you go to SonicNet's site (`http://www.sonicnet.com`) and search for all the artists that you enjoy. When you find ones that they actually have in stock, you can add them to your station and specify how often to play them.

You don't have to be the only one listening. If you like, you can e-mail the URL of your radio station to friends, family, or anyone else you think might be interested. This way, they can all listen to the music you like and think either how cool or how weird you are.

Now, of course, the more popular and mainstream the music you like, the better your chances of building a radio station you like. If you happen to be a fan of hardcore polka, for example, the options available to you aren't as good as to the rest of us.

George Is More Furious Than Curious Nowadays

Let's begin with a disclaimer that the following is not the nicest and most polite one around. Some of the behaviors it asks you to imagine are immoral, illegal, and — if you're into the whole *ethics* thing — just downright wrong. Still, it's all just a game and *supposed to make you laugh*!

Furious George and the Cross-Country Crime Spree (`http://www.snowplow.org/furiousgeorge`) is a game that begins with the head of Curious George smiling at you from a map of the United States. You might remember Curious George from those delightful children's tales where his charming curiosity invariably leads him into misadventure. Well, in this game, he also gets into misadventure.

The difference is that George seems to have gotten a significantly embittered attitude as he has grown up. And, the misadventures he gets himself into as he travels from state to state in this game are the direct result of committing "atrocities" in each of those states. If you are concerned about violent content, this is probably not the site for you (though it is otherwise unobjectionable).

Getting the Most from Your Insomniac Nights

If the ultra-violence of Furious George isn't the sort of thing that makes you chuckle, then here's an even more amusing site. We're not exactly sure what it's supposed to be — but you can waste a lot of hours playing around with it:

`http://sodaplay.com/constructor/index.htm`

It's called SodaPlay, and the idea seems to be that by clicking on the dots and moving them, you change the behavior of the little robots. If you add, remove, or modify the dots enough, you can create completely new inventions. The whole thing is a little like Frankenstein creating artificial life, really.

You might wonder how anything this interactive could possibly happen in your own Web browser. After all, most Web pages just kind of sit there. The magic for this site is provided by Java, a Sun Microsystems invention that allows completely different kinds of computers (UNIX, Mac, or Windows) to run exactly the same code. Imagine the difference that this could make in software stores if everything started being written in Java!

Viewing "Stinky Finger" and Other Flicks

At the time of writing, you can see a particular commercial on American TV that shows an animated character standing in front of a brick wall. The character smells his finger and goes "Yuck!" He does this a couple more times, then finally pronounces: "Stinky!"

If this is the sort of sophisticated humor that tickles your funny bone, then you should check out the Angry Kid series of short films at Atom Films (`http://www.atomfilms.com`). If not, then you should still visit this site, because they have lots of other videos that you might find much more entertaining.

Of course, all of this video over the Internet is made practical (if not possible) by the fact at you have a broadband Internet connection. You can imagine how painful it would be to download even a relatively minor video segment if we were stuck back in the days of 28.8 Kbps modems!

Don't Let the World Burn Down without Your Noticing

Computer types can get very wrapped up in technology sometimes. Legend has it that one programmer actually let his office completely burn to the ground around him because he was too involved in his latest coding project to notice.

Taking this kind of an attitude towards the world in general can be dangerous to yourself and to others. Remember, for every one person like you that is too busy working to take an interest, three more have nothing better to do than go out and vote!

Still, just because you need to stay informed doesn't mean that you have to completely abandon technology all together. One great, and highly technical, site for staying abreast of the world situation is CNN (`http://www.cnn.com`). CNN is, of course, Ted Turner's extremely successful Cable News Network.

Using this site, you can download video streams of all the latest news stories, or get all of your information just by reading regular articles.

If They're Free, I'll Take Several

There's a card-carrying cheapskate in each and every one of us. All it takes sometimes are the right tools to set that frugal fiend loose. You can find many items on the Internet that help you maintain your miserliness, such as:

- ✔ Coupons
- ✔ Discount offers
- ✔ Special rebates
- ✔ Free gifts

The Freebie Machine (`http://www.webalisciousmall.com/freebiemachine.htm`) has almost all of these things. But, they specialize in the "free gift" department.

See those strings, well — they're attached! In case you haven't heard by now, anything that seems too good to be true, probably is. Before you sign-up for anything, always make sure to read the fine print and make sure that you understand exactly what your obligations are going to be. The classic case is the book or record club that makes it seem like you are getting books for free. In actuality, you are obligated to buy so many more items at a grossly inflated price that you wind up no better off in the long run!

When It's Time to Change, You've Got to Rearrange

Is your boss starting to get on your nerves? Are you looking for more interesting work? Or, is the commute to and from the office starting to get to you? If you answered "Yes" to any or all of these questions, then it may be time to start investigating what other jobs are out there.

One of the best job-search sites out there currently is called Dice.com, which you can visit at

```
http://www.dice.com
```

Although the service seems to focus most heavily on contract workers, you can find plenty of postings for all sorts of interests and scheduling needs.

If you work with computers (and there's a good chance that you do, if you own a broadband Internet connection), then you have even more options out there than the rest of us. One of the top sites specializing in computers-only jobs is ComputerJob.com:

```
http://www.computerjobs.com
```

Using ComputerJobs.com, you can conduct your job search at a national level if you want to see everything that's out there. On the other hand, if you want to stay local, you can restrict searches to your own state or metropolitan region.

More Than Ten Sites You Could Well Do Without

Sometimes, you get curious about exactly what else is out there. So far, we've shown you everything that we believe to be among the best that the Internet has to offer. But, what about the worst?

Thankfully, some people on the Internet have been hard at work on documenting exactly this problem. They have given us their contribution to recognizing truly bad, tasteless, weird, or just plain boring sites on the Web: the Worst of the Web (`http://www.worstoftheweb.com`).

You can use a few different ways to review these selections:

- ✔ The current day's selection
- ✔ Stepping backward, day by day
- ✔ Jumping straight to something from the archives

Just a sample of recent Worst of the Web honorees includes

- ✔ Three Kids Kicking the Crap out of a Chair for No Particular Reason
- ✔ Foster-a-Fish
- ✔ Great Mobile Homes of Missouri
- ✔ The Spam Haiku Archive

Chapter 21

Ten Flashy High-Speed Things You Can Do to Impress Your Friends

*I*f you've got it, flaunt it. What you've got with your new broadband connection is speed — lots and lots of speed! So, in this chapter, we have compiled a list of some of the niftier things that you can do now that you're all hooked up.

You can try the things outlined here all at once or one at a time. Mind you, if you're going to try doing all of these things at the same time, you had better have one heck of a computer to go along with that fancy new Internet connection!

Being a DJ

Once upon a time, the only people who could start their own radio stations were multimillionaires and large corporations. Besides the astronomical costs of equipment, the licensing fees charged by government agencies that regulate public broadcasts are quite beyond the common man's (or woman's) budget. Fortunately, *streaming* Internet audio allows you to overcome all of these barriers easily and affordably.

RealNetworks offers a free product called RealServer Basic that allows you to play audio *and video* over the Internet for others to listen to. You can download the free version from their site at

```
http://www.realnetworks.com
```

This product supports up to 25 simultaneous users. If you need more than 25, you may consider buying the more advanced versions of their product.

Every time a radio station plays a song, it must pay a small fee to whomever owns that song's publishing rights. In the United States, an organization known as ASCAP is charged with collecting and distributing the bulk of these funds. If you plan on playing copyrighted recordings of any kind over the Internet, then you are going to have to pay these fees as well, you might find a whole new meaning to "Jailhouse Rock."

Exploring Strange New Worlds

If you ever get tired of seeing the same old Web pages time and time again, it might be time to sample a little virtual reality on the Web! At many sites on the Internet, it is possible to view and interact with completely simulated, artificial environments known as *worlds*. These worlds may contain scenery, objects, and other people just like your self!

Many of the sites providing virtual reality content on the Internet today make use of a standard known as VRML, which stands for Virtual Reality Modeling Language. Yes, another acronym! Unless you plan on building your own environments for people to visit, it probably isn't necessary for you to know any more about this other than that it is the current standard.

Many of the sites you can visit appear directly within your Internet browser, assuming you have an appropriate plug-in to support VRML. A good source for these plug-ins is at this site:

```
http://www.vrml.org
```

Other virtual reality sites on the Internet operate completely under their own stand-alone software packages. One of coolest of these places is the 3D Videoranch. This site is actually run by Michael Nesmith, former Monkee and video music pioneer. Look for the link to the 3D portion at

```
http://www.videoranch.com
```

Figure 21-1:
Hanging
out at the
Videoranch.

Seeking Out Alien Life

At the start of many science fiction stories, a scientist sitting alone at a radio telescope begins hearing something new in his headphones and is instantly able to recognize it as a signal from an alien civilization. In real life, any signals that we may receive will have to be detected through the very intense efforts of some extremely powerful computers.

Or will they? A recent program begun by SETI (Search for Extra-Terrestrial Intelligence) offloads much of the work involved in sifting through received signals to volunteer computer users in their own homes.

SETI offers free software that allows you to download, process, and report on space transmissions straight from your own computer, so you can help them out. You can download this software at

```
http://setiathome.ssl.Berkeley.edu
```

The whole idea behind SETI@Home is that the work involved in detecting alien transmissions is too much for a single computer to handle effectively. By using this software, you will be shouldering a portion of this load yourself. If you should find your computer acting sluggish or unresponsive, always remember to check to see if SETI@Home is running. When it is active, this software can drain considerable processing power (measured in CPU cycles) away from the rest of your computer's applications.

Kicking Butt in Online Games

It used to be quite difficult to play computer games against other people. First, you had to find someone from among your own personal circle of friends who owned exactly the same game. Then, you had to arrange for one of you to call directly to the other person's house because all play was strictly modem-to-modem. Fortunately, the Internet solves both of these problems for you.

Most modern computer games come with built-in support for Internet game play. This is not the case with slightly older packages, however. Whenever you're considering the purchase of a new computer game, check to make sure that Internet support is clearly mentioned on the outside of the package. In fact, you should try to verify in advance that any new game purchase specifically supports play over TCP/IP networks, because TCP/IP is the protocol on which the Internet operates.

To get started in the world of online gaming, you can check out the following links on the Internet:

- ✔ Club SSI, `http://www.clubssi.com`
- ✔ KALI, `http://www.kali.net`
- ✔ Battle.Net, `http://www.battle.net`
- ✔ Stargate Networks, `http://www.stargatenetworks.com`

Living in a Fish Bowl

As you see in the chapters on video conferencing and Web cams, you can hook a camera directly into your computer and transmit images of whatever you like across the Internet. Now that you have an always-on Internet connection, you may elect to leave one or more such cameras always on as well. Combined with a Web server, you can share constant live video of whatever you like with anyone on the Internet who's curious enough to look.

Talking Among Yourselves

Hosting an area for conversation is one of the best ways to attract visitors to your Internet site because people participating in such a conversation must return to your site multiple times to follow the discussions in which they are interested. Forums that offer expertise are a great way to advertise in your print media to pull in visitors, too.

Currently, Microsoft FrontPage seems to offer the easiest way to add a discussion group to your Web site. Using this package, you can easily add a discussion area directly to your Web pages with just a few clicks of the mouse. Of course, for this setup to work, you must be using Microsoft's Internet Information Server as your Web server!

For more information on these products, browse these Web sites:

```
http://www.microsoft.com/frontpage
```

```
http://www.microsoft.com/iis
```

Showing Off on Video

In the DJ section of this chapter, you see how you could become the head of your own Internet radio station using streaming audio. With only a little more effort, you can upgrade your fledgling radio station into a full-power Internet TV broadcaster!

Right now, true digital video cameras are still exceedingly expensive. If you already own a traditional video camera, however, we know some cheaper options available for getting your video up on the Net. Many vendors sell devices that accept video feeds from your camera or VCR and convert it into a digital format that your computer can understand. The quality is not as good as with a regular digital camera, but it is good enough for most people with nonprofessional requirements.

The quickest, cheapest way to begin sharing video streams over the Internet is by using the same RealServer product described in the section on being a DJ. The URL for this site is

```
http://www.realnetworks.com
```

Playing the Name Game

When you first get your broadband Internet connection, the chances are good that you are only able to address your computer by its IP address. For example, your computer may be known as something like this:

```
183.2.44.6
```

For a relatively minor expense, you may purchase your own Internet domain name for use in identifying all the computers on your network.

You have to put together two pieces to associate an Internet domain name with the computers on your network. The first is registering your domain name. The second is getting that domain name hosted somewhere.

Purchasing the hosting is, by far, the simplest piece of the equation. Simply visit the Web site of any registrar organization (such as `www.register.com`), fill out a form specifying your contact and billing information, as well as your choice of name), and then pay for it (usually by credit card).

In the earliest days of the Internet, computers were known only by their numeric identifiers on the network, known as IP addresses. If this were still true today, instead of being able to enter a simple Web site name, such as `www.eviloscar.com`, you would have to enter a string of digits such as `63.212.1.75`. Fortunately, the modern Domain Name System (DNS) spares you from such chores.

Under the DNS system, domain names such as `eviloscar.com` are able to register humanly readable names, such as `www` for every computer on their network. Today, whenever you request a certain Web site on your computer, your browser is able to find out what the numeric address of that machine is thanks to DNS.

Getting your domain name hosted somewhere is the piece of the equation that actually allows you to start using it. If you know all about this subject already, then you should be able to set up and run a DNS server on your own computer. If this is a mystery to you, you are probably better off purchasing this service from your provider or a local ISP.

Seeing Your Name in Lights

How many times, other than now, have you ever read a book that was just so wonderful that you had to tell the whole world about it? With Amazon, you can satisfy this desire by writing online book reviews for just about anything in print.

The process is simple:

1. **Open Amazon.com in your Web browser.**

2. **Find the book that you would like to review.**

3. **Select "Write a review" from the list of options.**

4. **Fill out the online form with this information:**

   - A certain number of "stars"

   - A brief text description

   - Your name (optional)

   - Your location (optional)

5. **Submit your review.**

In general, your review will be posted on the Web for the whole world to see within 5 to 7 business days. Think how impressed your friends will be to see your thoughts — and your name — up in lights on the World Wide Web!

Grabbing Your Files from Anywhere

If you've ever done much work at home, then you're probably familiar with the experience of leaving something important on one computer when you desperately need it on another. Imagine, for example, that you have stayed up all night working on a big presentation for the president of your company. After you arrive at work in the morning, you discover that the copy of your presentation that you put on a floppy disk is no good for some reason.

With an always-on connection to the Internet, you should be able to reach across the Internet to your computer at home and grab whatever files you need. The mechanism for doing this can either be an FTP server (if you are running on a non-Windows platform) or simple Windows network sharing.

If you share it, they will come! Under Windows, you can share a directory in such a way that everyone has access to read and write files in it. The same holds true for standard FTP under most operating systems. Don't think for a second that just because you don't tell anyone about your shared drives or FTP site that they just won't find out about it. Many hackers now scan the Internet constantly looking for shared drives and FTP sites running on pre-defined ports. For this reason, you should never open shared drives under Windows for access by the group, Everyone. With FTP, you should make sure that anonymous access is denied by default.

To share a directory under Windows NT, you can follow these simple steps:

1. **Locate the directory you would like to share.**

2. **Right-click the directory's icon.**

3. **Choose Properties from the pop-up context menu.**

4. **Select the Sharing tab.**

5. **Make sure the radio button labeled Share This Folder is enabled.**

6. **Type a name to refer to this shared folder.**

7. **Click OK to confirm your changes.**

To access a shared directory from another Windows NT computer, you can follow these simple steps:

1. **Locate the icon for your computer on your desktop.**

2. **Right-click this icon.**

3. **Choose Map Network Drive from the pop-up context menu.**

4. **Choose a drive letter to refer to your shared directory.**

5. **Enter the name of your remote computer (*machine*) followed by the shared directory name (*sharename*) in the following format:**

   `\\machine\sharename`

6. **Click OK to confirm your creation.**

At this point, you should be able to access all of the files in this directory on your remote computer just as if they were located in a disk on your local computer!

Part VI

Appendixes

The 5th Wave   By Rich Tennant

Arthur inadvertently replaces his mouse pad with a Ouija board. For the rest of the day, he receives messages from the spectral world.

In this part . . .

*W*hat would a computer book be without appendixes? In this part, you'll find handy references to
the best way to keep your old Internet accounts (if they're
cheap enough) alongside your new broadband service, so
you don't have to change your e-mail address or send out
those little change-of-address cards to everyone you
know.

Finally, there's a handy glossary you can use as a quick
reference in case you run across a term that's new to you,
or that you've seen before but need a quick reminder.

Appendix A

Keeping Old Accounts

*J*ust because you've installed this spiffy new high-speed Internet account doesn't mean you have to give up your old friends, whether you're talking about old (and often cheaper) e-mail accounts, Web pages, or other services you used over a modem. This chapter describes how to keep your existing services while you're exploring exciting new services.

America "OnBroadband"

Many people start connecting to the Internet using America Online as their Internet Service Provider (ISP). When you sign up for a high-speed Internet account, it usually comes with an ISP of its own, so instead of being YourScreenNameEverybodyKnows@aol.com, you've now become SomeNameNobodyHasEverHeardOf@yournewisp.com.

Fortunately, if you have a little spare cash left over after getting your broadband connection installed, you can keep your AOL account and connect to it at newer, faster speeds than before.

Because ISPs must pay for the Internet access they offer you, most ISPs are thrilled when you use their services (such as an e-mail account) without tying up their phone lines and modems. They're so thrilled, in fact, that they'll often charge you less money if you'll promise never to use their phone lines again. In that spirit, AOL provides a service called *Bring Your Own Access* (BYOA), which lets you continue to use AOL as you always have, but without using AOL's modems and without tying up access that someone paying a higher monthly fee may need. With the BYOA plan, AOL charges a lower monthly fee (currently, $9.95), and you connect over broadband instead of a modem.

Here's how it works: When you launch AOL, you'll see a screen similar to the one in Figure A-1.

Figure A-1:
Signing on
with AOL.

Follow the instructions below for your operating system (Mac OS or Windows) to set up access over the Internet.

Setting up Win AOL for Internet access

To connect to AOL over your broadband connection in AOL for Windows:

1. **Click the Setup button at the bottom of the Sign On screen to reach the Edit screen shown in Figure A-2.**

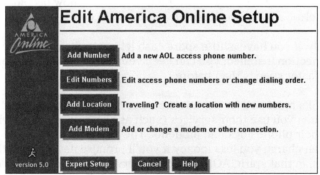

Figure A-2:
The first
AOL Setup
screen.

2. **Click the Add Location button to create a "location" that connects over the Internet as shown in Figure A-3.**

3. **Type a name you'll remember (such as AOL over Internet or Home) in the Name field.**

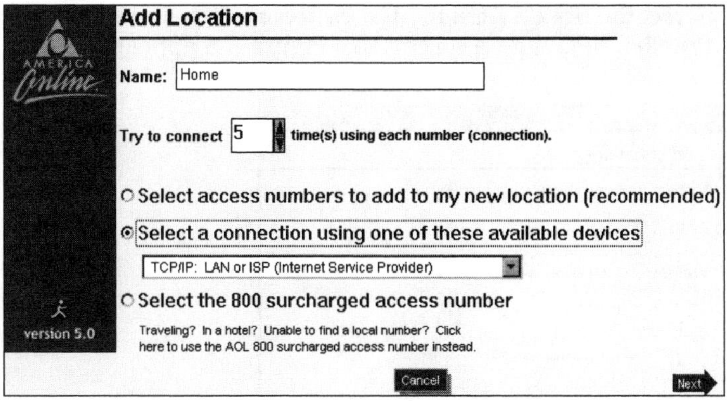

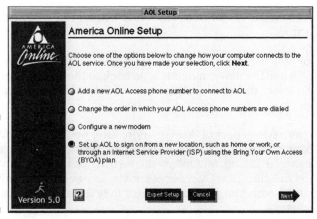

Figure A-3:
Adding
the new
location that
connects
to AOL.

4. **Select the radio button next to Select a Connection using One of These Available Devices.**

5. **Choose TCP/IP: LAN or ISP from the drop-down list and click Next.**

That's it. Your Windows version of AOL now has a new location that connects over the Internet. To use the new connection, go back to the Sign On screen (refer to Figure A-1), select the new location from the Select Location drop-down list, then click Sign On.

Setting up Mac AOL for Internet access

To connect to AOL over your broadband connection in AOL for Mac OS:

1. **Click the Setup button at the bottom of the Sign On screen (refer to Figure A-1), and AOL gives you a screen similar to Figure A-4.**

Figure A-4:
Setting up
the new
location for
signing on.

2. **Select the Set Up AOL to Sign on from a New Location radio but-tonclick Next, and a screen like Figure A-5 appears.**

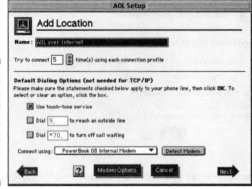

Figure A-5:
Creating
the new
location and
how it
connects
to AOL.

3. **Type a name you'll remember (such as "AOL over Internet") in the Name field, then click Next.**

   You can ignore the other options on the page shown in Figure A-6 for this kind of AOL connection.

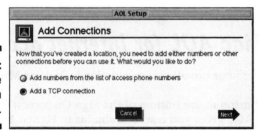

Figure A-6:
Adding the
TCP location
setting.

4. **In the Add Connections window, select "Add a TCP Connection," then click Next.**

That's it. Your Mac version of AOL now has a new location that connects over the Internet. To use the new connection, go back to the Sign On screen (refer to Figure A-1), select the new location from the Select Location pop-up menu and click Sign On.

Don't forget the savings part of this equation. After you've set up AOL to use your broadband connection, try for a lower rate. Next time you sign on to AOL, go to keyword, Billing, and follow the instructions there to change your billing method to Bring Your Own Access. If you use another e-mail account, you should check with that provider to see if they'll charge less if you switch access methods.

Keeping Other E-Mail Accounts

If you have an established e-mail account from your modem-based Internet provider (ISP), you don't have to lose it simply because you're using a different ISP with your broadband account. In fact, if you can keep your old e-mail account active for a lower monthly fee, you may never need to use your broadband e-mail account at all.

You can also keep several e-mail accounts active at the same time, if you want. You might, for example, use your old e-mail account because that's the address all of your friends know, but you would check your broadband account's e-mail in case your ISP sends you mail about your account.

Before you can do that, however, we need to cover a few of the basics about e-mail. After that, we can cover how to set up some of the major e-mail programs to handle multiple accounts.

POP3 goes the weasel

When we use e-mail, two processes are involved: sending and receiving. Unlike some other Internet communication, which uses a single protocol, e-mail uses different protocols for sending (usually SMTP or *Simple Mail Transfer Protocol*) than it does for receiving (POP3, *Post Office Protocol* or IMAP, Internet Message Access Protocol). Your ISP handles the mail it sends to you, but another server handles the mail you send out. The only reason you care about that is to know how to configure your e-mail programs.

Here's the twist for reading mail on old accounts from your new broadband connection: To avoid enabling spammers (the bane of Internet existence), each ISP prevents you from using its SMTP server to send mail unless you're connected to that ISP. For example, you can't log on to CompuServe (or your new broadband connection) and use an EarthLink SMTP server (or the one for your old account) to send your mail.

For this reason, you have to change your old e-mail configuration so that it sends mail differently. Your setup for *receiving* mail stays the same (name, password, and all), but for *sending* mail you have to change from your dialup account's SMTP server to your broadband ISP's SMTP server. If you want to set up multiple accounts (say, your old e-mail account and the new one that came with your broadband connection), each account must use its own POP3 or IMAP server to retrieve mail, and each may have its own user name and password. Whoever provides the e-mail account can provide you with the server name, user name, and password you should be using if you've forgotten it.

Multiple accounts example in Outlook Express

This section provides a quick summary of how to set up more than one e-mail account in Outlook Express for Windows. The same principles apply to Outlook for Windows, Outlook Express for Mac OS, and any other e-mail program that supports multiple accounts. You need to have the basic account information for your e-mail account, including the following:

- ✔ Your broadband ISP's SMTP (sending) server name

  This can be any server name, such as smtp.example.com or mail.example.com, as long as your current ISP indicates it's the server for sending mail.

- ✔ Each e-mail account's ID and password
- ✔ Each e-mail account's POP3 or IMAP server

Armed with this information, launch Outlook Express and begin.

1. **In Outlook Express, choose Tools⇨Accounts.**

2. **In the Internet Accounts window that appears, click the Add button, then click Mail from the pop-up menu that appears.**

   A screen prompting for your display name appears, as shown in Figure A-7.

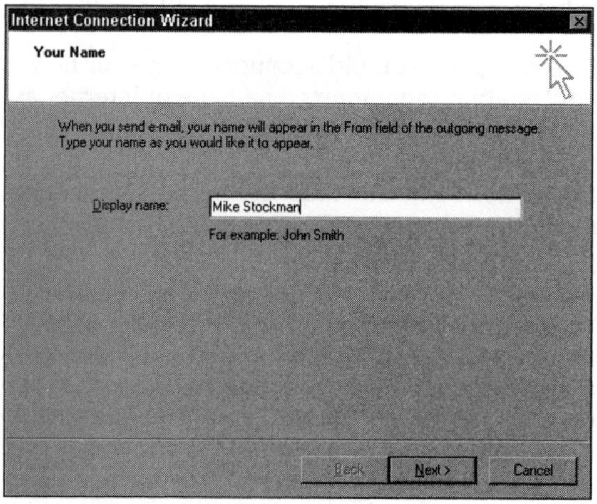

Figure A-7:
Typing your
actual name
to display
on mail
messages.

3. **Type your name as you want it to appear on outgoing e-mail messages, then click the Next button.**

4. **Type your e-mail address as people enter it to send you mail, such as the one I'm using in Figure A-8 or** yourname@example.com**, and then click the Next button.**

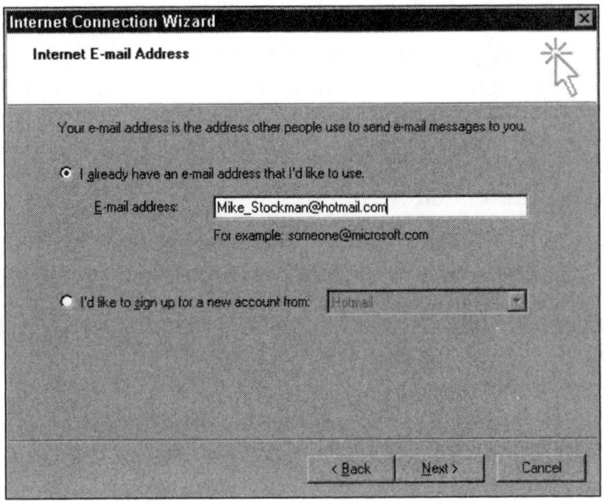

Figure A-8:
Setting up your e-mail address for this account.

5. **Select the kind of mail server you're connecting to from the "My Incoming Mail Server Is a" drop-down list, such as POP3 or IMAP, as shown in Figure A-9.**

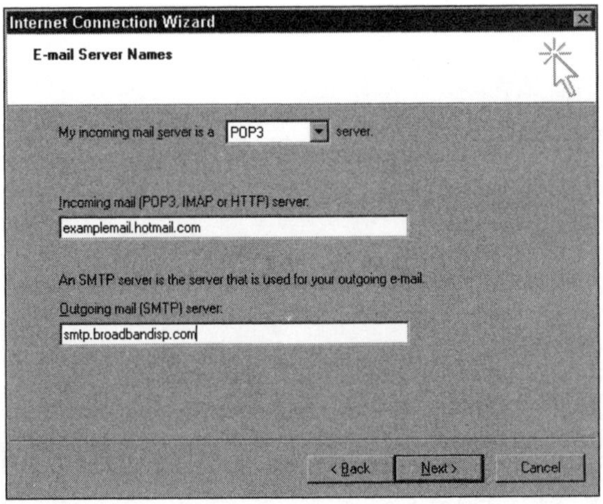

Figure A-9:
Entering your mail server information.

6. **Type the e-mail account's POP3 or IMAP server as provided to you by that account's provider into the Incoming Mail Server field.**

   Remember that the POP3 or IMAP server is the account that sends your e-mail. For example, to receive mail from my example.com e-mail account, I'd type popmail.example.com here.

7. **Type your broadband ISP's outgoing mail server (the SMTP server) into the Outgoing Mail Server field, and then click the Next button.**

   Every e-mail account you set up on this computer will use the same outgoing mail server, regardless of who provides the e-mail account.

8. **On the next screen, simply type your account name in the form of youraccount@example.com (refer to Figure A-8) and password in the fields provided; then click Next.**

   This information is provided by the organization providing you with the e-mail account, and is unique to each account you're setting up.

9. **In the final screen, click the Finish button to complete the new account wizard.**

Appendix B

Glossary

10Base-T: A standard setting up an Ethernet network, transmitting data at 10 Mbps. 10Base-T cables use an RJ-45 plug on each end, which looks like a very wide modular telephone plug. Most broadband connections are slower than 10 Mbps, so this kind of networking is fine for use with broadband.

100Base-T: A standard for setting up an Ethernet network, transmitting data at 100 Mbps (10 times faster than 10Base-T). The cables for 100Base-T look just like the ones for 10Base-T. This kind of speed is overkill for a broadband connection, but is useful for fast connections between the computers in your home or office.

Administration: The act or process of setting up and maintaining software or hardware.

ADSL: Asynchronous Digital Subscriber Line. A kind of dedicated broadband Internet connection with different upstream and downstream connection speeds.

Analog: Any technology that relies upon a continuous flow of electricity to represent data. This is different from digital technologies.

Apache: A popular web server for Unix platforms, free for non-commercial use.

Archie: A software system to automate searching the Internet for specific files.

Attachment: The term for files, such as photos, that are included with e-mails.

Bandwidth: A measure of how much data a given network connection can carry over a certain length of time. The "band" in "broadband" refers to bandwidth, and the "broader" the bandwidth, the faster your connection.

Billing cycle: The amount of time between bills from your service provider, typically a month, a quarter, or a year.

Bit: The smallest amount of data that a digital system may represent. It may store either a 0 (false) or 1 (true).

Bits per second (bps): The speed with which data is transmitted. Usually shown as Kbps (kilobits per second, or one thousand bits per second) or Mbps (megabits per second, or one million bits per second). A fast analog modem can transmit up to 56 Kbps, while an Ethernet network transmits at 10 Mbps. A broadband connection falls somewhere in between.

BMP: Byte Mapped Picture, a native, non-compressed format for storing images under Microsoft Windows.

Byte: A group of 8 bits.

CDR: Compact Disk Recorder. A consumer-oriented system for recording your own CD's! Typically write-once, read-many times.

CDRW: Compact Disk Recorder reWriteable. A consumer-oriented system for recording your own CD's. The added value over CDR's is that you can re-record on CDRW's.

CLEC: Competitive Local Exchange Carrier. A company that competes with your incumbent local exchange carrier (ILEC) — the local telephone company.

CO: Central Office. Where your local telephone company keeps all their equipment.

Coaxial cable: The kind of cable that connects your cable box to the wall.

CPU: Central Processing Unit. The "brain" of your computer.

Dedicated: Equipment used for only one purpose.

Denial of service: A hacking attack that tries to break a computer by overloading it with requests.

Digital: Any technology that represents information as individual, discrete pieces (called "bits") rather than as continuous, analog signals.

DOCSIS: Data Over Cable Service Interface Specification, the dominant standard for Internet access via cable modem in North America.

Domain name: An alias, such as "eviloscar.com," for a given network of computers on the Internet.

DNS: The system supporting domain name aliases on the Internet.

Downstream: The connection *from* the Internet *to* your computer.

Driver: Software responsible for making a given piece of hardware work with your computer and operating system.

DSLAM: The equipment your phone company must install in their CO in order to offer DSL service.

DSS: Direct Satellite Service.

DVB: The dominant standard for Internet access via cable modem in Europe.

DVD: A standard for recording data onto optical disks which can store several times more than previous CD formats.

Dynamic IP: A system of assigning constantly changing IP's to computers.

Ethernet: One of the most established technologies for connecting computers into LAN's.

Firewall: A security device (a computer with firewall software, or a dedicated box that plugs into your network) that sits between your computers and the Internet, preventing unauthorized network data from passing through in either direction. The rules used to decide what's "unauthorized" depend on how you set up the firewall.

FTP: File Transfer Protocol, used for exchanging files over the Internet.

Geosynchronous: A kind of orbit that keeps satellites constantly over the same place on the Earth below.

GIF: Graphics Interchange Format, a way of storing and exchanging images.

G.Lite: an emerging standard for quicker and easier DSL installations.

HTML: Hypertext Markup Language, the language used to describe Web pages for display by web browsers.

IDSL: A dedicated ISDN connection.

IIS: Internet Information Server, Microsoft's web server included with Windows.

ILEC: Incumbent Local Exchange Carrier, your existing local telephone company.

IM: Instant Messaging, software that allows you to immediately transmit and receive small messages over the Internet.

IMAP: Internet Message Access Protocol, a standard for sending and receiving e-mail on the Internet. Using IMAP, your mail generally stays on a central mail server, while you connect to read and send mail using an IMAP-compatible e-mail client.

IP: The computer networking protocol (Internet Protocol), or language, that all computers on the Internet use to communicate with each other.

IP Address: A number that uniquely identifies a given computer on the Internet, such as 192.168.23.5. Also called an "Internet address."

ISDN: A 128 Kbps data connection popular before the advent of broadband.

Java: A programming technology that allows the creation of software that can be used on all of the most popular computing platforms.

JPG: An open standard for the storage and exchange of images.

L2TP: Layer 2 Tunneling Protocol, a standard used to set up virtual private network connections over the Internet.

LAN: Local Area Network, a group of computers connected by a small-scale network.

LERG: Local Exchange Routing Guide, a document used to determine your telephone charges for placing calls.

Linux: A free variant of the Unix operating system created by volunteers on the Internet.

Link exchange: A collaborative effort to increase traffic at member web-sites by creating links amongst all the members' pages.

Logs: Records maintained by web servers' detailing their visitors over time.

MAC address: Also called a hardware address, the MAC (Media Access Control) address you may need to know is the unique identifier assigned to your network card in your computer. Many broadband providers identify your computer by this address, and use it for accepting a connection or setting up your Internet address.

Mbps: Megabits per second, a common unit used in measuring the speed of network connections.

MB per second: Megabytes per second

Megabit: One million bits.

Megabyte: One million bytes.

NAT: Network Address Translation, an Internet standard that, among other tricks, allows several computers on a private network to share one public Internet address. Because the computers on your local network has only a private Internet address, they can connect to sites on the Internet, but nobody on the public Internet can connect to them (without special configurations).

NIC: Network Interface Card, the device in your computer that connects the computer to a network or, in the case of a broadband connection, to the broadband device (cable modem, DSL modem, and so on). If your computer doesn't have a NIC built-in, you can install one to connect to broadband.

Operating system (OS): The software that provides the most basic of services for running your computers' hardware.

Packet: A small piece of computer networking data that travels over the Internet. When you send or receive data over a network, the data is broken up into millions of packets, transmitted, and re-assembled in order on the other end.

Peer-to-peer: An architecture for connecting computers over the Internet, typically used for sharing software and files (such as MP3's).

PGP: Pretty Good Privacy, a popular program for encrypting e-mails and other files for security.

Pixel: One of the many small "dots" on your computer screen that provide you with images.

POP3: Post Office Protocol version 3, a standard for sending and receiving e-mail. IMAP is the other standard currently in wide use. Generally, you download your mail from a POP3 server using a POP3-compatible e-mail client. Once you download the mail, it's usually removed from the POP3 server.

POTS: Plain Old Telephone Service, an actual telephone industry term for your regular analog telephone connection. Broadband doesn't use POTS, instead relying on faster, more accurate digital connections.

PPPoE: PPP over Ethernet, a method by which broadband providers allow you to "connect" to your always-on Internet connection before using it. Generally, you run a PPPoE client on your computer each time you want to use the Internet, closing the PPPoE software when you're done. There is no advantage to this kind of connection for the user, but it makes account management easier for the broadband provider.

PPTP: Point-to-Point Tunneling Protocol, a standard for setting up virtual private network connections made popular by Microsoft Windows. All versions of Windows after Windows 95 support this protocol for VPN connections. Beginning with Windows 2000, Windows supports the IPSec protocol for much more secure VPN connections.

RAM: Random Access Memory, the kind of memory into which you may write your own data, such as programs and documents.

ROM: Read Only Memory, the kind of memory that holds programs important to running your computer.

Router: A device that helps data travel from one point to another on a network, switching and forwarding packets of data based on the information contained in their headers. Data travels from router to router across the network until it reaches its final destination.

SAG: Street Address Guide, the database used by your local telephone company to determine the CO out of which your location is served.

Scalability: The desirable ability for a given computer system to smoothly accommodate increasing and decreasing levels of usage.

SDSL: Symetric Digital Subscriber Line, a kind of DSL with matching upstream and downstream speeds.

SMTP: Simple Mail Transfer Protocol, a protocol used for sending and forwarding e-mail across the Internet. You need to specify which SMTP server to use in your e-mail software before you can send any mail, and generally you can use only your Internet provider's SMTP server for security reasons.

SOHO: Small Office / Home Office, a category of customers typically targeted by broadband Internet access providers.

SSL: Secure Sockets Layer, a means for encrypting traffic as it travels across the Internet.

Static IP: A system for assigning unchanging IP's to computers on a network.

TCP/IP: The language spoken to one another by computers on the Internet.

Text: The most basic format for storing words on your computer.

Traceroute: A program included on Unix and Windows computers for determining the path traveled by information from your computer across the Internet.

Truck roll: Any service provided by your telephone company that requires them to dispatch service people to your location or to the CO.

TWAIN: A standard for image capturing devices, such as scanners and cameras.

UPS: Uninterruptible Power Supply, a piece of equipment that provides battery backup and surge suppression to your computer's electrical input.

Upstream: The connection from your computer to the Internet.

Usenet: A collection of "newsgroups" allowing the posting of messages for public retrieval.

VDSL: Very High Bit-Rate Digital Subscriber Line, an emerging technology for providing even faster broadband connections to the Internet.

VoIP: Voice over IP, a standard for sending voice communications (such as telephone calls) over the Internet instead of standard telephone lines. With a VoIP client installed on your computer, you can make telephone calls over your broadband connection instead of using your telephone.

VPN: Virtual Private Network, a kind of "tunnel" between your computer or network and another computer or network anywhere else on the Internet. By setting up a VPN connection, you can gain access to all of the services on the remote computer or network securely. For example, you might set up a VPN connection to your office network from home, letting you transfer files or use printers in the office from across the Internet.

VRML: Virtual Reality Modeling Language, a language used to describe virtual reality environments in a way that can be displayed by VRML browsers on the Internet.

WAN: Wide Area Network, a network created by connecting multiple smaller networks (LANs) across separate geographic locations, such as building to building, city to city, and so on.

Web cam: A cheaper model of digital camera intended for use strictly in conjunction with your computer.

Web hosting: The process of making web content available for retrieval by other computers on the Internet.

Web ring: An association of web sites aimed at increasing traffic to member sites by linking together all of the member sites in the approximate shape of a circle.

Web server: A piece of software that makes web pages available for viewing by other computers on the Internet.

Winzip: A program that shrinks and joins multiple files into single, smaller "archive" files.

xDSL: A term used to refer to DSL in all its variety of flavors, regardless of speed or specific delivery format.

Index

● Z ●

YOUR ONLINE RESOURCE

WWW.DUMMIES.COM

Discover Dummies Online!

The Dummies Web Site is your fun and friendly online resource for the latest information about *For Dummies* books and your favorite topics. The Web site is the place to communicate with us, exchange ideas with other *For Dummies* readers, chat with authors, and have fun!

Ten Fun and Useful Things You Can Do at www.dummies.com

1. Win free *For Dummies* books and more!
2. Register your book and be entered in a prize drawing.
3. Meet your favorite authors through the IDG Books Worldwide Author Chat Series.
4. Exchange helpful information with other *For Dummies* readers.
5. Discover other great *For Dummies* books you must have!
6. Purchase Dummieswear® exclusively from our Web site.
7. Buy *For Dummies* books online.
8. Talk to us. Make comments, ask questions, get answers!
9. Download free software.
10. Find additional useful resources from authors.

WWW.DUMMIES.COM

For other technology titles from IDG Books Worldwide, go to **www.idgbooks.com**

Link directly to these ten fun and useful things at **http://www.dummies.com/10useful**

Not on the Web yet? It's easy to get started with *Dummies 101*®: *The Internet For Windows® 98* or *The Internet For Dummies®* at local retailers everywhere.

IDG BOOKS WORLDWIDE

Find other *For Dummies* books on these topics:
Business • Career • Databases • Food & Beverage • Games • Gardening • Graphics • Hardware
Health & Fitness • Internet and the World Wide Web • Networking • Office Suites
Operating Systems • Personal Finance • Pets • Programming • Recreation • Sports
Spreadsheets • Teacher Resources • Test Prep • Word Processing